Soundtracks of Asian America

Soundtracks of Asian America

NAVIGATING RACE THROUGH MUSICAL PERFORMANCE

Grace Wang

DUKE UNIVERSITY PRESS   *Durham & London*   2015

Library of Congress Cataloging-in-Publication Data
Wang, Grace
Soundtracks of Asian America :
navigating race through
musical performance / Grace Wang.
pages cm
Includes bibliographical references and index.
ISBN 978-0-8223-5769-8 (cloth : alk. paper)
ISBN 978-0-8223-5784-1 (pbk. : alk. paper)
1. Asian Americans—Music—Social aspects.
2. Asian American musicians. 3. Stereotypes
(Social psychology)—United States. I. Title.
ML3560.A85W36 2014
781.89'95073—dc23
2014020687

ISBN 978-0-8223-7608-8 (e-book)

Cover art: Leehom Wang performing in Langfang,
Hebei Province, China, 2012. Photo courtesy of
Hongsheng Artist Management.

For my family

CONTENTS

[Music] both articulates and offers the immediate *experience* of collective identity. Music regularly soundtracks our search for ourselves and for spaces in which we can feel at home.

—Simon Frith, *Performing Rites*

In Lan Samantha Chang's novella *Hunger* (1998), Tian Sung, a Chinese violinist, flees China for the United States to pursue his musical dreams. Leaving behind home and family, he escapes in the dark of night by swimming out to sea—violin held precariously above water—until a cargo ship takes him aboard en route to Taiwan. From there, Tian earns a visa sponsorship to continue his music training in New York City. He practices diligently, pinning all his hopes on securing a full-time position at a prestigious music conservatory. Still, despite his musical talent and prodigious work ethic, he fails to gain a teaching position. Disillusioned and unwilling to compromise by working at a "lesser" institution, Tian gives up playing the violin. Resigning himself to the unskilled labor of bussing dishes and chopping vegetables at a local Chinatown restaurant, he transfers all of his dreams and ambitions onto his youngest daughter, Ruth. Tian's daughter takes to the violin quickly and shines as a young prodigy. But as a teenager, overwhelmed by her father's relentless pushing and expectations, Ruth rebels and runs away from home. By the end of *Hunger*, Tian is crushed—shattered by the weight of carrying dreams of "such flagrant and extravagant design."[1]

For Tian, being denied a permanent teaching position signaled not just a professional failure, but also a broader rejection from the classical music community and the nation as a whole. He came to the United States buoyed by the faith that hard work and talent would be rewarded equally; he upheld what he perceived as his part of the bargain by giving a brilliant faculty recital performance. But as readers of the novella come to realize, no amount of practice would have gained Tian full entrance into the exclusive culture of Western classical music. While the school cites his limited English proficiency as the official reason for discontinuing his employment, it is clear that language serves as a proxy for a broader lack of fluency in the unwritten social codes and behaviors that guide conservatory culture. Tian's refusal to go out for drinks after concerts, his awkwardness in social situations, and his inability to joke and banter with his colleagues with casualness, comfort, and ease translate into tacit understandings that he does not belong. In the eyes of his colleagues, Tian is, at best, aloof and antisocial. At worst, he is devious and untrustworthy, accused (falsely) through rumor and innuendo of pilfering a colleague's precious tuning fork. Put differently, Tian fails to inhabit fully what Pierre Bourdieu calls the social habitus of a cultural field, unable to speak with "native" fluency and ownership the language of both English and Western high culture. In the landscape of fiction, as in the realm of the everyday, distinguishing which disappointments stem from racial barriers rather than individual shortcomings is inherently imprecise. Through the accumulation of small slights, opportunities passed over, and hushed murmurs of difference, Chang's novella punctures the myth that music represents a shared universal language that transcends social categories while at the same time underscoring its continuing allure for so many.

The author's choice to have Tian work in a Chinese restaurant is fitting for a novella in which music gives expression to the hungers—the aspirational desires sought but infrequently met—that racialized immigrants experience living in the United States. Tightly coiled within the figure of Tian are conflicting layers of hope, anger, ambition, and regret: fierce belief in the promise and ideals of the U.S. nation; a deep sense of loss and alienation associated with the experience of migration; and an ever widening gulf between dreams and lived realities. In Chang's narrative, music translates this inchoate tussle of emotions into moments of breathtaking beauty: the "pure melody of the violin rising over all of it like a great rope of silk, smooth and shimmering, shot through with glints and shades of beautiful light" (61). Music soundtracks the feeling of longing, seduces with the promise of full and unregulated belonging, gives voice to the drama of complex interior lives, and indexes the contradictory dynamic of inclusion and exclusion that marks Asian American racial formation in national and transnational spaces.

I open with *Hunger* to introduce some of the central questions explored in this book. How do Asian Americans use music to construct narratives of self, race, class, and belonging? How do musical and racial discourses converge, simultaneously eliciting feelings of transcendence and limitation, racialization and deracialization, mobility and constraint? And how do Asian Americans mobilize the multiple meanings contained in music to engage with, critique, and, at times, profit from their racial positioning in national and transnational spaces? A constellation of discourses and ideas surrounds different music genres, acquiring new meanings and ideologies as they proliferate in local and global contexts. This book investigates how Asian Americans manage, rework, and accommodate the parameters of their belonging in musical fields often considered distinct—Western classical music, U.S. popular music, and global Mandopop (Mandarin language popular music). Placing particular case studies from classical and popular music in dialogue with each other allows for greater recognition of the resonances and differences in how the racialized imagination works across music genres.

Soundtracks of Asian America interrogates the cultural work of music in the production of contemporary Asian American identities. It considers middle- and upper-middle-class Chinese and Korean immigrant parents whose intense involvement in their children's classical music training registers their race, class, and linguistic anxieties brought about by living in a new nation and speaking a new language. It listens in on Asian and Asian American classical musicians whose visibility and prominence in their chosen profession is both celebrated and turned against them. It follows the path of young Asian American singer-songwriters who capitalize on the democratizing possibilities of YouTube to contest the limitations they face in a racialized U.S. media landscape. And it journeys with Asian American pop stars to East Asia, where their pursuit of recording contracts and fame in their respective "homelands" abroad grants them some freedom from a racially stratified U.S. music industry. Analyzing how racial constructions about Asians and Asian

Americans both facilitate and hinder the terms of their belonging in particular forms of music, each chapter foregrounds a musical space where Asian Americans are visible and investigates how and under what conditions Asian Americans have gained (and been granted) that visibility. More than an examination of specific music genres, however, this book investigates how music maps the circulation of race in national and transnational spaces and how race matters in the practices and institutions of music making. It argues that music making does not just reflect the racial order, but helps create and naturalize it as well.

Soundtracks of Asian America does not offer a comprehensive overview of music making by Asian Americans. Nor does it explore the contours of something we might call "Asian American music." Such a marker, as music scholar Joseph Lam helpfully suggests, holds analytic utility more as a "flexible heuristic device" that enables particular modes of critique than as a musical category that somehow encompasses a heterogeneous pan-ethnic collectivity.[2] Rather, following the model established by ethnomusicologist Deborah Wong in her impressive study *Speak It Louder*, this book investigates how Asian Americans narrate and understand the meanings of music making in their lives. Adopting a capacious sense of what music scholar Christopher Small refers to as "musicking"—the dynamic and interactive modes with which individuals engage in music making practices—this study explores Asian Americans' music making through a diverse range of activities, from uploading music videos to YouTube to driving kids to music lessons.[3] Thinking about music as a social process that exceeds what we might imperfectly call the "music itself" disrupts a fundamental premise of Western classical music and, to a lesser degree, other music genres as well: "the extraordinary illusion—for that is what it is—that there is such a thing as music, rather than simply acts of making and receiving it."[4]

I began this study as a way to make sense of aspects of my own background, one that overlaps with parts of the musical case studies investigated in this book. I started violin lessons at the age of five and enrolled at the Juilliard School's Pre-College Division four years later. And while I was aware that many Chinese, Korean, and, to a smaller extent, Japanese Americans populated the music schools and summer festivals I attended growing up, this was not an aspect of music making to which I gave much thought, even if our collective presence did, at times, feel bundled up in uncomfortable essentialisms about Asianness. I certainly intuited the powerful association of class, refinement, and erudition that my immigrant parents attached to classical music and sensed that my mother clung to these aspirational symbols even more tightly when our economic situation deteriorated after my father passed away. But when I thought about my background in music, it was in personal terms rather than through broader narratives shaped historically by immigration legislation, global economic shifts, and imperial legacies.

Still, this larger context had a way of lodging itself into my own understanding of making music. During the 1990s, when I spent a year living in Taipei playing with Taiwan's National Symphony Orchestra and freelancing around town (jobs that easily came my way on the basis of a few choice words: U.S.-trained, Juilliard, and Dorothy DeLay, a well-known teacher with whom I had studied), it was difficult to ignore the unequal relations of power that structured the global circulation of Western music. This sojourn took place during the height of the Three Tenors marketing bonanza—a moniker bestowed on the opera singers Plácido Domingo, José Carreras, and the late Luciano Pavarotti as they sang their way through sports arenas and concert halls around the world—and the Taiwanese government, presumably in a bid to raise its international profile and signal its parity with other modern states, invested astonishing sums of money to bring two of these tenors to perform (on separate occasions) with the orchestra. Such priorities felt troubling to me then even as I felt uneasily implicated within such processes. "Why fetishize a European art form rather than local or traditional music?" I remember questioning rather simply, observing the frenzied hype and adulation that accompanied the performances by Carreras and Domingo. At the same time, it was not entirely clear to me what constituted the so-called native music of a geopolitically contested island like Taiwan. It certainly did not appear to be the popular music of Taiwan, where boy bands like the L.A. Boyz (a trio of middle-class Taiwanese American teens hailing from Orange County, California) were racing up the music charts with hip hop–tinged tracks that traded on their Americanness and decontextualized citations of blackness to project a different image of modernity, hipness, and cool. I did not realize then that the 1990s marked the beginning of Taiwan's emergence as the geographical and cultural epicenter of Mandopop, the stylized pop music genre that now dominates the listening tastes of an immense global market comprising mainland China, Taiwan, Hong

Kong, Southeast Asia, and the vast Chinese diaspora. The staggering market potential symbolized by Mandopop continues to beckon aspiring Chinese American pop stars, whose dreams of commercial viability and mainstream celebrity often feel unattainable, if not wholly unimaginable, within the racialized landscape of the United States.

While aspects of my own situation led me to consider how music offers a window into a changing Asian American demographic and the affective dimensions of belonging in national and diasporic spaces, I did not intend to write on any of these topics when I shifted my focus away from music performance to academic pursuits. Not only did music making feel like a wholly separate part of my life, but within the interdisciplinary realms of ethnic and cultural studies, investigations into cultural practices marked by middle-class interests, upwardly mobile aspirations, and economic and cultural privilege felt less important than detailing the struggles, intersectional politics, and oppositional strategies of disenfranchised groups. Within Asian American studies more specifically, an ideological framework of resistance had, as a number of scholars observe, structured and limited the scope of particular topics of study. Literary scholar Viet Nguyen, for instance, notes that the privileging of Asian America as a site of "ethnic consensus and resistance to an inherently exploitative or destructive capitalism" exposes the ideological conflict, if not political discomfort, that progressive Asian American scholars feel toward increasingly neoconservative elements of the Asian American population.[5] We can perceive such ambivalences, as literary scholar erin Khuê Ninh asserts, in the focus that Asian American studies scholarship has placed on debunking the model minority discourse as a myth—emphasizing its mobilization of misleading statistics, its elision of the poverty and criminality that exist in Asian America, and its deployment in the service of whiteness and fictions of meritocracy. Such critical refutations, however, fail to consider the affective power (and harm) that the model minority narrative holds for those who subscribe to, if not hunger to embody, its central tenets.[6] Ninh's own elegant examination of fictional accounts of intergenerational conflict within Asian immigrant families, alongside Nhi Lieu's compelling analysis of the bourgeois ideals that Vietnamese refugees and immigrants strive to project through their cultural productions and consumption practices in the United States and Christine So's literary investigation of modes of Asian American visibility through economic exchange, among others, demonstrates the broadening of scholarship already under way within Asian American cultural studies.[7] *Soundtracks of Asian America* draws on ethnographic and oral interview methodologies to analyze how music registers the everyday contradictions of race, desire, and belonging as experienced by middle- and upper-middle-class Asian American subjects. The narratives that the various music makers I interviewed tell, from affirming the hard-working and disciplined nature of Asians to upholding the incidental nature of race in their lives, can have the troubling appearance of replicating hegemonic narratives placed on Asians and Asian Americans. My goal is not to garner further validity to such discourses, nor to parse out what some might call the truth lodged behind stereotypes. Rather, this study analyzes how, in what contexts, and for whose benefits and interests certain narratives gain currency.

Using music as a lens of analysis, *Soundtracks of Asian America* investigates the uneven relationship that Asian Americans have to whiteness, foreignness, and color, particularly in light of the symbolic alignment between racial minority status and socioeconomic class in the United States. Given the economic integration enjoyed by some Asian Americans and their purported overrepresentation in such fields as Western classical music, engineering, science, and technology, the collectivity Asian American is often negatively articulated as "white" and no longer impacted by racism. The perception, as David Palumbo-Liu contends, is that "Asians are no longer 'minorities' in the sense that they are economically disadvantaged, and therefore the sensitivities of the American political economy are excused from laboring to 'include' Asian Americans—we have already made it 'inside.' "[8] And yet, as Asian American studies scholars have aptly shown, the economic diversity within Asian America notwithstanding, being on the "inside" and even achieving success has yet to yield Asian Americans the full benefits of acceptance and belonging.[9] *Soundtracks of Asian America* asks: How and when are Asian Americans configured as minority subjects in the U.S. racial imaginary? How do Asian American musicians assess what counts as racial discrimination within prevailing frameworks that place their pan-ethnic group as somehow exempt from racism and music as an international language that exceeds social boundaries? And how do Asian Americans resolve the racialized perceptions they encounter in their music making against their own, often stated, faith in meritocratic inclusion? This book argues that the rationalizations used to manage and explain Asian Americans' purported overrepresentation in Western classical music and underrepresentation in U.S. popular music illuminate the broader mechanisms that limit the scope of Asian American integration into the United States. The contradictory parameters of Asian American belonging find evidence in, among other fields, classical music. Whereas the wide-ranging accomplishments of Asian American classical musicians are framed and even, at times, pathologized as the product of technical natures, excessive discipline, and rote cognitive styles, the ambivalence that young, enterprising singer-songwriters express about identifying themselves, and being recognized collectively, as Asian American performers on YouTube reflects an understanding of how this ethnic marker locates them on the outskirts of U.S. popular culture.[10]

The first part of *Soundtracks of Asian America* investigates stories that help drive images of Asian American success. It examines how Asian American achievement in fields such as Western classical music can serve as confirmation of the magnanimity and meritocracy of the United States and of the embodied realities of "model minority" racial and immigrant subjects. It assesses stock characters at the uneasy core of model minority narratives—the "pushy" Asian parent, the over-achieving Asian American subject, the skilled Asian American classical musician—and asks: How and when do these figures function as touchstones for a broader range of intersecting racial, musical, and global anxieties? How do Asian immigrant parents and Asian American classical musicians themselves arbitrate, accommodate, and rework the multiple beliefs ascribed to their participation in classical music? And finally, how does music simultaneously provide freedom from and confirmation of racial hierarchies? In offering some answers to these questions, I follow the shifting line that separates praise and threat, tracking how unease about spaces becoming "too Asian" activates "yellow peril" anxieties that domesticate understandings about Asian and Asian American success.[11]

The second part of the book considers how a U.S. racial imaginary loosely informed by normative assumptions of Asian Americans as model minority embodiments and not fully American/Americanized citizens functions to naturalize the dearth of Asian American performers visible in the U.S. popular music landscape. It tracks the path of

Asian American singers searching for and creating spaces and markets that would yield them some reprieve from the limitations of musical and racial inheritances in the United States. It investigates how young Asian Americans have responded to prevailing U.S. racial logics by turning to YouTube and global Asian popular music industries to imagine and promote new meanings about Asian America. These DIY (do-it-yourself) and diasporic spaces have yet to result in an Asian American singer achieving mainstream pop music stardom in the United States. At the same time, these divergent paths suggest that in a fragmented media landscape and a global cultural economy increasingly marked by the growth of Asia-Pacific dominance, "crossing over" into U.S. traditional media may not represent the only—or even the most desirable—path for Asian Americans to make music and pursue celebrity.

As these case studies differently show, newly configured stereotypes, as well as new opportunities and markets, have emerged in the wake of successes attained by Asian American music makers. I emphasize the uncanny resilience of hegemonic racial representations by closing the book with an examination of the term "tiger mother" into U.S. everyday lexicon following the publication of Amy Chua's memoir *Battle Hymn of the Tiger Mother* (2011). Drawing evidence through classical music involvement, Chua's "tiger mother" argument recycles dominant racial paradigms about Asian/Chinese parenting and cultural difference, recasting them in a neoliberal era of global competition.

Race, Universalism, and Color-Blind Intimacy

While soundtracks typically refer to the music accompanying a film and appear as background—as sonic wallpaper that shadows a scene—they also actively move a narrative forward, direct our mood and reactions, modulate pace, and shape how we imagine entering and inhabiting different social worlds. Film studies scholar Claudia Gorbman observes that "film music is like the medium of a dream, forgotten in the waking state; but this medium is itself not neutral. It embodies and disseminates meaning, all the more powerful in not actively being noticed."[12] Like the soundtrack to a film, race filters how we listen to, experience, and rework intersecting social boundaries in music. Race hovers everywhere and yet seemingly nowhere, intuitively understood as infiltrating our understanding of music and yet frequently disavowed as actually mattering. The effort to maintain these bifurcating beliefs can, as Deborah Wong astutely contends, lead Americans "to recognize and to deny (all at once) their understandings of how American music is racialized and ethnicized."[13]

Music represents a particularly trenchant lens through which to explore how race operates in the contemporary U.S. landscape because it is simultaneously grasped as raceless and highly racialized, a contradictory dynamic that reverberates with dominant U.S. frameworks of color blindness and meritocracy. For while music demarcates racial boundaries, reflects and reinforces social hierarchies, and conditions how we hear, feel, and even construct racial difference, it does so less through explicitly racialized claims than through other guises: coded inferences about cultural difference, claims of musical authenticity and innate ownership, intimations about possessing (or lacking) musicality and soul, and/or "neutral" articulations about talent and skill. Understanding how implicitly racialized beliefs about Asians and Asian Americans circulate through music can thus shed critical insight into how ideas about race and discrimination operate in a "post-race" era or what Arif Dirlik incisively calls a "moment of reconfigured racism."[14]

Universalizing beliefs about music represent more than discursive strategies that conveniently circumvent discussions of power and politics. Rather, discourses of transcendence hold powerful resonance because individual responses to music feel spontaneous, immediate, and highly personal. Indeed, while listening to and performing music— especially music that one loves the most—the sound seems to envelop both mind and body unmediated, vibrating directly into the deepest recesses of one's being. Ethnomusicologist Steven Feld elaborates that "the significant feature of musical communication is . . . [that] its generality and multiplicity of possible messages and interpretations brings out a special kind of 'feelingful' activity and engagement on the part of the listener, a form of pleasure that unites the material and mental dimensions of music as a metaphoric process, a special way of experiencing, knowing, and feeling value, identity and coherence."[15] Still, while the " 'feelingful' activity" of music can appear intuitive and individual, it nonetheless depends on particular cultural, social, and ideological discourses. Such correlations emerge clearly, for example, in journalist Ben Fong-Torres's recounting of his devotion to rock and roll as a young Chinese American growing up in Oakland's Chinatown during the 1950s and 1960s. Connecting his ardor for rock and roll—a music form often symbolic of the nation itself—to his yearning to feel (and be recognized) as American, Fong-Torres recalls that "inside the jukebox, there were no racial borders, no segregation. . . . Rock and roll was an equalizer. And for me, it was more than a way to have fun or to feel like part of the crowd. It was a way to feel Americanized."[16] Rock and roll, however romantically, allowed him to imagine inhabiting the United States differently—to glimpse an idealized vision of a nation that granted him full access and to experience, however fleetingly, the *feeling* of belonging to a nation less freighted by racial borders and inequities. Such reflections speak to the affective power of popular music and culture—its unique ability, as George Lipsitz observes, to conjure alternate configurations of race, nation, and power: "to rehearse identities, stances, and social relations not yet permissible in politics."[17] At the same time, the experience of being transported outside of time and space is mediated through socially constructed beliefs about what that sound embodies and the bodies and beliefs attached to those sounds. For transcendence, as Simon Frith suggests, "marks not music's freedom from social forces but its patterning by them."[18]

While heeding the "feelingful" pleasures of music, *Soundtracks of Asian America* emphasizes how discourses of universalism and transcendence obscure the critical role that music plays in constructing and reinforcing boundaries demarcating race, cultural ownership, native understanding, and belonging. As Ronald Radano and Philip Bohlman aptly remind readers, "the longstanding metaphysical properties associated with music enhance the imagination of racial difference: race contributes fundamentally to the issues of belonging and ownership that music articulates."[19] How Asian Americans negotiate the terms of their participation in the U.S. culture of classical music and popular music—genres in which being Asian rarely represents a benefit—indexes, more broadly, the parameters of their belonging in the national terrain.[20] The contrast, for instance, with the meanings accrued to Asian American identity as it is positioned internationally in global pop music industries underscores the localized cultural and geographical contexts that buttress musical and racial claims.

While disavowals about the salience of race find resonance across music genres, they are particularly widespread in Western classical music given that cultural field's historical entrenchment in discourses extolling its universalizing principles—its unifying qualities, shared humanity, and unique capacity to transcend racial and national borders. Alex Ross, music critic for the *New Yorker*, describes the expansive and amorphous contours of Western classical music this way: "It is hard to name because it never really existed to begin with—not in the sense that it stemmed from a single time or place. It has no genealogy, no ethnicity: leading composers of today hail from China, Estonia, Argentina, Queens."[21] He writes, in part, against perceptions of classical music as elitist and enshrined in the past (and a musty collection of dead, male European composers). While these views imbue the music with prestige, they also make it appear ossified, archaic, and culturally irrelevant to many Americans. In contrast, Ross offers an appealing vision of a shared global culture—one free of temporal, geographical, and racial barriers and unyoked from the legacies of imperialism and Western dominance that have historically structured the movement of classical music around the world.

The rhetoric that classical music is an international language that belongs to no single group or place holds powerful allure to racial minorities as well, particularly in light of equally entrenched understandings that the music form represents the unsurpassed embodiment of European essence, achievement, and tradition, even when performed by individuals of non-European descent. The contradictions inherent within this logic allow racialized minorities to gain access to this elite cultural field while also subtly stoking suspicions that they are interlopers trespassing on terrains in which they cannot claim full "native" understanding or ownership. In this sense, although classical music may well represent the music genre most closely associated with Asian Americans in the contemporary period—indeed, playing the violin and/or piano is itself part of the stereotypical embodiment of what it means to be a middle-class Asian American—its cultural capital continues to rest on an investment in whiteness.[22] At the same time, even as Asians and Asian Americans in classical music profit from this association with whiteness, their racial difference also limits their ability to access fully the benefits of its privileges and social returns.[23]

While the overlap between "Asian" values of discipline, diligence, and filial piety and the rigors of classical music training helps facilitate Asian American participation and success in that field, the dominance of such racial narratives also hinders their full inclusion in both classical music and other musical fields. Reporting on the lack of Asian American pop singers in the United States, the *New York Times*, for instance, emphasized the disabling function of normative constructions of Asian Americans: "The image of the studious geek, the perception that someone who looks Asian must be a foreigner—clash with the coolness and born-in-the-U.S.A. authenticity required for American pop stardom."[24] The cognitive dissonance implied by the terms *Asian* and *American pop stardom* operates on both a visual and sonic level. That is, the idea of Asian American pop stardom feels discordant not only because of prevailing perceptions of a foreign and nerdy imprint seemingly implanted in the DNA of this racial group but also because of the position that Asian Americans occupy outside of the authenticating links connecting race and popular music ownership. Although Asian Americans have always participated in U.S. musical cultures, they continue to remain absent from the racial and ethnic shorthand that intuitively exists for different popular music styles. And while the sonic linkages between "music codes and ethnic markers" are shifting and unstable—dependent on particularities of history, geography, context, and individual subjectivity—the persistent trace of authenticating beliefs continues to be patrolled in everyday assumptions that structure how we comprehend race through sound.[25] "Compliments" that Asian American singers receive, for instance, of sounding like a "black girl" while covering R&B songs on YouTube register the extent to which codified beliefs about race and musical genres frame Asian American music making and reception. For the pleasure derived from the asymmetry of sight and sound simultaneously reifies the normative boundaries linking race with musical ownership and expression.

The racialized landscape in which all music making takes place underscores a critical point: There is no pure mode of listening. Music education studies have shown that beliefs about race and music genre influence how listeners—even music experts—evaluate musical performance. Put differently, what we think and see influences *how* we hear. In one such study, investigators asked undergraduate music majors from nine universities across the United States to assess the performance of white and black conductors leading a choral ensemble in two different music genres, Western classical music and spirituals.[26] The videos were synchronized to the same musical performance such that the race of the conductor represented the only changing variable. Music students rated white conductors higher than blacks when conducting classical music and black conductors more favorably than whites when leading the group in spirituals. Results such as these quantify the extent to which preexisting assumptions about race—from the implicit racialization of classical music and spirituals along white/black binaries to presumed correlations between racialized bodies and musical styles—serve as self-fulfilling predictions about the validity of musical perceptions. And while the controlled parameters of such studies may not find precise equivalences in the messier realms of everyday life, they nonetheless highlight the difficulty of extricating visuality from aesthetic response—of separating race and other social categories from the distilled performance of the "music itself." Listeners tune their ears differently, filter sounds through networks of ideology that are then authenticated through purportedly impartial evaluations based on musical performance and skill. How individuals listen to and make musical evaluations is neither natural nor neutral but structured through racial regimes that exist within and beyond the realm of music.

Even in Western classical music, a music field steeped in the language of universalism and transcendence, music professionals concede that possessing knowledge about a performer impacts musical evaluation. Yet, such an acknowledgment, as *New York Times* music critic Anthony Tommasini contends, need not imply a shortcoming. Rather, awareness of a performer's background—knowledge of his or her life story, music training, stage in career, and other biographical details—can enrich a listener's perception and even help the listener hear "better": "Whether a young soprano was trained in Tokyo or Boston, whether she studied singing throughout childhood or discovered her voice in a college choir, whether she is big-bodied or petite, loose-limbed or stiff: all of these factors are crucial to assessing an individual's gifts and needs. In other words, whether you are a master teacher, an opera buff, a concertgoer or a critic, knowing something of the background of the artist you are hearing will inevitably affect your perceptions."[27] Tommasini was, in this instance, defending his colleagues who had fallen for the hoax perpetrated by Joyce Hatto, a British pianist who near the end of her life plagiarized a series of recordings as her own to great critical acclaim.[28] Emphasizing that music takes place in a social context, the critic noted that to dismiss this backdrop as immaterial ignores the human drama and emotional connection that music making, at its most powerful, entails. At the same time, it is worth noting that Tommasini attempts to limit his remarks to the realm of the personal and autobiographical, arguing that we should resist pigeonholing artists, remain receptive to surprise, and eliminate prejudicial assumptions based on race, ethnicity, sex, age, or other social factors. What emerges from his apologia is what I call the fantasy of color-blind intimacy, a liberal humanist proposition that music critics—and listeners more generally—take into account the individual circumstances and backgrounds of performers but refrain from placing them within, or even considering that they are being influenced by, the matrices of power that delimit that subject position. Put differently, color-blind intimacy, and the corresponding faith in the possibility of color-blind listening, preclude an understanding of race as the expression of relations of power and dominance while emphasizing race as part of the incidental, anecdotal, and even pleasurable backdrop provided by a musician's personal narrative.

The belief that such modes of color-blind listening are tenable and desirable comprises part of the critical apparatus that Asian Americans and other racial minorities encounter in attempting to achieve success in musical fields in which a yearning for human connectedness is marked simultaneously by a reluctance to recognize, much less engage with, the less comfortable aspects of race. Color-blind listening confuses hearing and seeing, obscuring the soundtracks of race intimately woven into how individuals experience music making. It proposes that audiences recognize and respect difference as an articulation of humanity that somehow transcends racial (and other) histories. The entwinement of color-blind intimacy with discourses of multiculturalism means that downplaying the existence of racial barriers—at the structural and individual level—takes place alongside oft-repeated rhetoric about celebrating the racial and ethnic diversity of the nation. The powerful sway that color-blind and multicultural frameworks hold in the contemporary U.S. landscape helps explain why Asian American musicians working in both classical and popular music might express pride in their ethnic heritage while downplaying the impact that race and/or racism play in their professional lives or seek to commodify their ethnic identity while disowning the existence of racial barricades. Likewise, some musicians mobilize discourses of racelessness, universalism, and meritocracy even when such narratives do not necessarily align with their own music making experiences.[29] Covering the unpleasant aspects of race and locating racism as an old problem rooted in the past are, as legal scholar Kenji Yoshino puts it, part of the implicit "social contract" that racial minorities broker in exchange for the promise of success.[30] Color-blind intimacy, in this way, allows for the simultaneous entrenchment of racism and its disavowal.

The metaphor of color blindness deems race a visual medium and, in so doing, elides its aural dimensions. Indeed, the invisibility of Asian American performers in the popular U.S. landscape stands in stark contrast to the visibility of orientalist sonic stereotypes proliferating what music scholar Josh Kun trenchantly calls the "American audio-racial imagination."[31] In countless films, television shows, and commercials we see race by hearing it, regardless of whether a racialized body appears on-screen.[32] Asians, for instance, are illusively present in the stereotyped sounds that masquerade as proxies for "Asia" or the "Orient."[33] Such sonic signifiers do not just reinforce racial hierarchies; they also structure how we apprehend race through sound. Beliefs about racial difference (and other social identities) populate the U.S. auditory landscape, from the realm of speech to the purported "accents" audible in a musical performance. Asian immigrants (and racialized immigrants more broadly) encounter language discrimination living in a monolingual nation where "accented" English maps onto broader assumptions of competence and national belonging. Asian and Asian American classical musicians continue to confront the belief that their Asianness can leave a perceptible ethnic trace in their musicianship, despite the fact that practices like "blind" auditions reveal otherwise. As I show in chapter 2, most major symphony orchestras have instituted the practice of blind auditions in which musicians play behind a screen for all (or almost all) rounds of the hiring process.

While music critic Tommasini draws his example from Western classical music, the contradictory dynamic and desire underpinning color-blind intimacy also finds resonance in the realm of popular music. Consider, for example, the public image promoted by the Far East Movement (or FM), the first Asian American group to earn the top spot on the Billboard Hot 100 and iTunes charts with their breakout electro/pop/hip hop hit "Like a G6" in 2010. A pan-ethnic group composed of members with Chinese, Filipino, Japanese, and Korean American backgrounds, the Far East Movement built their base through ethnic networks and hometown fans drawn from Los Angeles's Koreatown but began framing their Asianness as incidental, if not insignificant, as they gained commercial viability. As FM member Prohgress (James Roh) claims: "I don't know if it's cool to be Asian so much as it's just cool not to care."[34] While the group's name directly references their "Far East" heritage—within the context of U.S. multiculturalism, not being proud of who you are is, as fellow FM member Kev Nish (Kevin Nishimura) puts it, "wack"—the musicians also emphasize that they are just as American as any other kid who grew up in Los Angeles: they just happen to be Asian American.[35] We see the contradictions at the core of color-blind and multicultural frameworks in FM's public contentions that it is "cool" both to celebrate who you are and not to care. While the group acknowledges their ethnic background, they refrain from dwelling on or contextualizing race as part of an institutionalized hierarchical system that produces differences in experience. The band members instead articulate and project membership in a millennial generation of technologically savvy youth who see beyond racial barriers and connect virtually through social networks. That is, their attitude, fashion, and lifestyle reflect the increasing irrelevance of race and identity politics in a digitally connected, "free wired" (as one of their album titles suggests) landscape. As Kev Nish asserts: "We live in a new world where you live by your screen name. I might know more about the music you listen to, the sites you go to, before I know your last name or your heritage. We're not out to represent any race, political thought, any religion. It's just about making music and having fun doing it."[36]

Kev Nish is, on the one hand, replicating familiar beliefs about the radical possibilities for fluidity, mobility, and choice heralded by the Internet, a narrative of "post-identity" he may well feel synchronizes with his life experiences. On the other hand, we might also interpret his statement as reflecting an aspiration rather than a description—a deflection of race based on an understanding of how Asianness limits his commercial prospects in the U.S. mainstream and an indication of how he would like FM to be perceived and received. Either way, Kev Nish's claim invites further consideration of the ways in which, in a neoliberal economic and cultural environment, consumption and commercial technology can serve—if even just rhetorically—as sources of identity. Sarah Banet-Weiser details, for instance, how digital lives mediated through commercial social media sites like YouTube are intimately linked to a broader culture of branding, where users "reference brands not simply as commodities but as the context for everyday living."[37] This context helps explain why some young Asian Americans describe their burgeoning visibility on YouTube as a social movement—an "Asian American movement" that represents an unprecedented and empowering moment of self-definition/self-branding. At the same time, as I show in chapter 3, Asian American singers also recognize how racial presumptions filter perceptions about their music making and their position within niche markets on YouTube. In this sense, rather than representing freedom from racial regimes, the pervasiveness of the digital may well signal new and contradictory spaces for the deployment, surveillance, and reinforcement of race. These technologies are shifting, as Lisa Nakamura and Peter Chow-White put it, "our understandings of what race is as well as nurturing new types of inequality along racial lines."[38] Through its investigation of new media and digital technologies, this book seeks to uncover how ideas about race and music find expression in the interactive space of YouTube, particularly in the lives of Asian American youth.

As an Asian American group seeking commercial viability in a U.S. popular landscape marked by their absence, it may be that the Far East Movement successfully capitalizes on discourses of Asian technical prowess and roboticism, reconfiguring ethnic stereotypes by recasting negative perceptions of technicality into futuristic visions of Asian techno and cool. In so doing, they begin muddling dominant fictions about what "Asianness" brings to musical production. Still, while it would be difficult to identify FM's music sonically or lyrically as "Asian," it nonetheless remains racialized in black cultural referents valorizing braggadocio, materialism, and excess. Aligning Asianness with the commercialized cool of blackness, "Like a G6" is specific in its aspiration for a high-flying lifestyle marked by luxury and revelry. The superficial veneer of their lyrics suggests the extent to which the grounds of a postracial landscape rest on an investment in a capitalist structure built upon a racial logic. As Jodi Melamed astutely observes, the "nonracialized language" of capitalist accumulation and market-driven individualism functions to rationalize racial inequalities such that "race remains a procedure that justifies the nongeneralizability of capitalist wealth."[39] The chart-topping success achieved by the Far East Movement validates the capitalist project upon which the commercialized music industry depends while also eliding the racialized terms of the group's belonging.

At the same time, a constellation of changing dynamics, including small shifts in traditional media marked by the success of groups like FM; openings facilitated by technological transformations, social media, and DIY artistic productions; and the emergence of global cities in Asia as spaces of cosmopolitan lifestyles and stylized modernity, represent part of a global cultural landscape that is reconfiguring the significations accrued to Asianness in national and transnational contexts. The advent of global media platforms such as YouTube, as well as the commercial growth of Asian popular music industries such as K-pop (Korean popular music) and Mandopop, have established alternate paths for young Asian Americans to pursue their musical aspirations. And while social networking platforms such as YouTube, like global pop music industries, are embedded in corporate structures, commercial interests, and U.S. racial histories, they also provide Asian American performers with opportunities that extend beyond a racially stratified U.S. music industry.

Global Circuits of Asian America

The global reach of music and the transnational travel of people, musical practices, and cultural ideas underscore the multiple affiliations and identifications that post-1965 Asian American communities hold in the contemporary period. Drawing on Michael Omi and Howard Winant's now-classic understanding of racial formation as the "sociohistorical process by which racial categories are created, inhabited, transformed, and destroyed," *Soundtracks of Asian America* charts the competing political, economic, and cultural demands placed on the category "Asian American" as it travels in local and global contexts.[40] A pan-ethnic collectivity that emerged through social movements during the late 1960s and 1970s, "Asian American" coalesced different Asian ethnicities under a single category to contest shared racisms encountered in the United States, to claim cultural and political citizenship, and to create a viable alternative to the existing racial category "Oriental." And yet, as an organizing principle, a coalition identity, an imagined collectivity, an emerging market segment, a transnational formation, and a census term, the conceptual coherence of the term *Asian American* continually fractures under the weight of its heterogeneity.

New patterns of immigration have shifted the composition of Asian America to an increasingly foreign-born population and produced a socioeconomic demographic of upwardly mobile immigrants (and off-spring) who may not identify with the histories of struggle, labor exploitation, and racial oppression that in the past powerfully connected Asian Americans with other communities of color.[41] For the professional and managerial class of Asian immigrants whose economic and cultural capital is linked to the ascendency of modernizing Asian nations and changes in U.S. immigration policy, the paths they take to identity formation interrupt earlier, more familiar immigrant narratives about "becoming American."[42] For example, the middle- and upper-middle-class Chinese and Korean immigrants who enroll their children in classical music training view their involvement in this "high" cultural field less as a route toward inclusion into mainstream America (which they correlate with whiteness and mass American culture) and more as a means of aligning themselves and their children with a field of culture recognized internationally as the embodiment of universal achievement and cultural prestige. On the other hand, for 1.5/second-generation Asian Americans, racial barriers in the U.S. popular music industry may lead them to reconstruct ethnic homeland as a "land of opportunity"—a space where dreams of pop music stardom can (and for a select few have) come true. *Soundtracks of Asian America* tracks how changing demographics, patterns of migration, and global relations produce new understandings and affiliations. It analyzes how the term *Asian American* can signify a form of symbolic capital that holds commercial appeal when transplanted to popular music industries abroad.

In a global cultural landscape mediated by ethnoscapes, mediascapes, technoscapes, financescapes, and ideoscapes, to cite Arjun Appadurai's influential formulation of the globalizing scapes that structure the modern world, the "U.S. is no longer the puppeteer of a world system of images but is only one node of a complex transnational construction of imaginary landscapes."[43] Transnational music industries like Mandopop, which is dominated by a Taiwanese music industry powerhouse and a mainland Chinese market powerhouse, make visible processes of globalization anchored less through so-called East–West polarities (and a hegemonic U.S. center) than through the multidirectional traffic of cultural, popular, and market influences in Asia.[44] As Koichi Iwabuchi keenly observes, the transnational flow of popular culture in Asia necessitates "recentering globalization" to encompass consumer markets and cultural brokers that, while influenced by U.S. popular culture, are situated outside the West and/or the United States.[45]

At the same time, the migratory behavior of young Asian Americans to media platforms and cultural representations they find relevant, empowering, and relatable make manifest the imbrication of local and global markets.[46] For Asian American youth, K-pop singers and bands, alongside YouTube stars and U.S. chart toppers, may all be equally familiar household names. The overlap between seemingly distinct markets also materializes in collaborations forged between Asian Americans pursuing careers in different geographical and media contexts. Korean American K-pop star Jay Park, for instance, has appeared in music videos and skits with popular Asian American YouTube performers such as singer Clara C. (Clara Chung), rapper Dumbfoundead (Jonathan Park), and comedian Ryan Higa.[47]

As media platforms like YouTube allow Asian Americans to connect more easily and intimately with each other, and as Asian American music makers turn to Asian popular markets as alternate landscapes of sonic belonging, hegemonic attributions placed on Asianness in the U.S. racial order take on new resonances. For instance, model minority ascriptions, rerouted through global pathways, become extolled for embodying neoliberal principles promoted in East and South Asian narratives of modernization and progress.[48] Harnessed to neoliberal discourses of modernity, flexibility, and globalization, the model Chinese American/Asian American subject becomes celebrated, for instance, in Mandopop, a global pop music industry dependent on both corporate support and state approval.[49] For the model minority trope, as Helen Jun keenly observes, locates Asian Americans as the "ideal subject of neoliberal ideologies under global capitalism."[50] Characteristics such as diligence, discipline, and sacrifice are lauded as flexible traits that transfer efficiently in globalized economies rather than "Asian" traits used to discipline the shortcomings of other groups and to accentuate the perpetual foreignness of Asian Americans.[51]

Soundtracks of Asian America investigates moments when Asianness, untethered from U.S. contexts and ascriptions, becomes an embodied marker that allows potential entry into powerful and even empowering diasporic formations. Highlighting the allure that global diasporas can symbolize to disenfranchised communities in their country of residence, Ien Ang attests that "diasporic identity holds the promise of being part of a world-historical political/cultural formation, such as 'China,' 'Asia' or 'Africa,' which may be able to turn the tables on the West, at least in the imagination. It is undeniable, then, that the idea of diaspora is an occasion for positive identification for many, providing a sense of grandiose transnational belonging and connection with dispersed others of similar historical origins."[52] The potential to transform conditions of minority exclusion into occasions of majority inclusion— particularly in the context of narratives that script Asia and China, in particular, as "on the rise"—can hold powerful appeal to Asian Americans. Still, while identifying diasporically allows Asian Americans to affiliate on the basis of strength, it also reinforces long-standing U.S. racial discourses that disenfranchise this group as racially and culturally distinct. Moreover, when Asian American music makers seek professional opportunities in Asia, they can quickly find themselves aligned with populations, languages, and cultural practices about which they may neither possess knowledge nor feel identification. The parameters of Asian American belonging in global Asian pop music industries are equally tenuous, contingent on continual practice and labor. Building on the work of such scholars as Ien Ang, Shu-Mei Shih, Andrea Louie, and Sau-ling Wong, who critically interrogate beliefs about Chineseness in narratives of diaspora, this study follows the "unnatural" trajectory of Chinese American singers into global Mandopop.[53] At the same time, I attend to the presumed naturalness attached to such journeys through diasporic discourses of roots, return, and homecoming and U.S. racial discourses that construct Asian Americans as cultural outsiders with allegiances to "homelands" abroad. I forward an understanding of Chinese American diasporic subjectivity as embodying a particular combination of what I call lack and privilege—lack of native fluency in Chinese language and culture, which are at the presumed core of Chinese identity, alongside the privileged possession of U.S. academic credentials, intimate knowledge of American popular culture, and unaccented (that is, American-accented) English.

Far from stable, natural, or freely chosen, diaspora identities emerge, as Stuart Hall critically reminds, in dialogue with and against powerful metaphors of essence, purity, and ancestral return: "Diaspora identities are those which are constantly producing and reproducing themselves anew, through transformation and difference."[54] Hall's model of identities in flux—"a matter of 'becoming' as well as of 'being'"—provides a useful framework to consider the complex cultural and geopolitical terrain of the Chinese diaspora.[55] If the marketing of various ethnic Chinese singers in Mandopop depends on commodifying and essentializing linkages between discrepant forms of Chineseness, these transnational celebrities also make visible its ruptures: the imperfect translations across linguistic and national communities; the ongoing cross-straits tensions between China and Taiwan; the uneven power relations between China, Taiwan, Hong Kong, the United States, and within the Chinese diaspora; and the hegemonic presence of China in the diasporic imagination, even for those who may claim a different homeland. As anthropologist Lok Siu has shown, Chinese diasporic identities are forged at the triangulated intersection of the imagined homeland, the nation of residence, and the larger diaspora; they are then maintained through the continual labor of practicing "cultural and social belonging amid shifting geopolitical circumstances and webs of transnational relations."[56] Siu's understanding of diaspora informs my investigation of how Chinese Americans rehearse and profit from performances of Chineseness forged at the intersection of multiple geographical and political terrains; commercial and state demands; U.S. and Chinese discourses; and competing narratives of music and race. Analyzing how Asian American music makers understand and navigate the various meanings placed upon identities that we might call Chinese, Asian, diasporic, and Asian American, *Soundtracks of Asian America* emphasizes the increasingly critical role that Asia plays in the making and remaking of Asian America.

Sonic Belongings

While Chang's novella *Hunger* depicts a fictional landscape about a Chinese violinist who migrates to the United States, it resonates historically with a perceptible shift in the demographics of Western classical music training over the past few decades. By the mid-1960s and 1970s, a growing number of East Asian international students began traveling to the United States to pursue classical music training. The first wave of musicians came from Japan, followed in the ensuing decades by South Korea, Taiwan, and finally China, where the increasing popularity of Western classical music functions, in part, as material evidence of the economic growth of East Asia and a rapidly growing middle class able to support these cultural practices. At the same time, passage of the 1965 immigration reforms produced a sizable growth in the Asian American community, many of whom began arriving in the United States under occupational preferences for professional and skilled labor implemented by the legislation. This particular cohort of immigrants began enrolling their children in classical music training, and these second-generation Asian Americans began to gain visibility in music schools and youth orchestras. By the late 1970s and 1980s, U.S. media reports auguring an Asian "takeover" in Western classical music (given the breathless pace of construction of symphony orchestras, concert halls, and music schools in such cities as Tokyo and Seoul) converged with media dispatches about second-generation Asian American "whiz kids," which folded their prodigious achievements in classical music into broader model minority narratives.[57] As this confluence of Asian and Asian American classical musicians gained international prominence as solo performers, secured seats in major symphony orchestras, and crowded the practice rooms and recital stages of music schools, a wide range of stereotypes emerged to explain and ameliorate their burgeoning presence. Not only does being an Asian/Asian American classical musician itself embody a stereotype, but the very qualities used to rationalize successes attained in that field—their work ethic, impressive discipline, and overbearing parents—have also come to mark their limits.

The first part of this book examines how Asian immigrant parents and Asian American classical musicians differently draw from existing narratives about race and music to rework the boundaries of their participation in Western classical music. Comprising textual analysis of media sources, oral interviews with Asian immigrant parents at Juilliard Pre-College and Asian and Asian American classical musicians, attendance at a range of events (including parent meetings, master classes, and performances), a research trip accompanying a small group of music faculty and administrators on a recruiting trip to China, and countless informal conversations with students, performers, parents, and teachers, the first part of the book interrogates how ideas about race circulate in the global culture of classical music.

While model minority narratives simultaneously facilitate and constrain Asian and Asian American success in Western classical music, they also impact the parameters of their participation and belonging in other musical fields. The second part of the book examines the divergent routes undertaken by young Asian American singers in response to U.S. racism, technological transformations, and shifting media and global cultural landscapes. This section similarly draws on a wide range of materials and sources: oral interviews with Asian American YouTube singers; attendance at performances featuring YouTube stars, U.S. and Chinese media sources; surveys with Asian American fans; North American and Chinese fan websites; and the vast archive of videos, music, images, and writing uploaded by, and posted about, the various singers I investigate on social networks, blogs, artist websites, and online media.

Soundtracks of Asian America follows a narrative arc that begins with Asian immigrant parents and Asian and Asian American classical musicians before turning to the complex reimagining of Asian American subjectivities by 1.5/second generation youth through popular music, new media, and diaspora. Having laid out the broad thematic connections between chapters, I now turn to chapter summaries. The first chapter begins by historicizing the dissemination of Western classical music in Asia and providing an overview of racial and musical discourses embedded in this field of culture and their expression and reinforcement through U.S. media representations. From there, I turn to an investigation of how middle- and upper-middle-class Chinese and Korean parents at Juilliard Pre-College narrate the reasons for their intense family investment in Western classical music. I argue that through their involvement in classical music Asian immigrant parents seek to demonstrate their educated status and sophisticated tastes and, at the same time, teach their children to appreciate the benefits accrued from discipline, diligence, and persistence. And while many of the Asian parents I interviewed recognized how music professionals, broader parent communities, and even their own children might interpret their behaviors as zealous and hypercompetitive, they continued to articulate faith in the notion that the accumulation of cultural prestige would minimize, if not for them, for their children, the race, class, and cultural exclusions encountered in the United States.

The second chapter shows how these parents' aspirations have, in many ways, already become a reality. Asians and Asian Americans now constitute a normative, if not sought after and praised, demographic in the global culture of Western classical music. The Asian American classical musicians I interviewed repeatedly upheld democratizing beliefs about the meritocracy of this music field. At the same time, their observations simultaneously underscored the provisional nature of their acceptance. Perceptions that Asians and Asian Americans are overrepresented and undifferentiable in classical music—the embodiment of a stereotype rather than an individual—strip them of their distinctiveness and originality, the very traits prized in a musician. I argue that the contradictory responses that my interviewees articulated about the role that race plays in their music making highlight the difficulty in disentangling the coded mechanisms of race in classical music specifically and U.S. culture more broadly.

The third chapter shifts focus to young Asian American singersongwriters who have gained popularity through YouTube, exploring how Asian Americans have creatively mobilized that social media platform to build an audience and a visible network of talent, friendship, and support. I show how the limitations placed on these YouTube singers' music making drive their desire to be perceived as universal *and* to frame their collective visibility as an unprecedented racial moment for Asian Americans. This chapter charts a broad story about how a fragmented media landscape is transforming the nature of fandom, celebrity, and music making and a specific story about how young Asian American performers narrate the meanings and impact of their fame on YouTube.

In contrast to the niche celebrity achieved by Asian American YouTube musicians, the fourth chapter investigates the pursuit of global fame through diaspora, using the massive pop stardom enjoyed by Chinese American singer Leehom Wang as its case study. Through an examination of the new significations accrued to Chinese American/Asian American identity in Mandopop, this chapter analyzes how the singer theorizes, markets, and commodifies a structure of diasporic closeness through his music and image. It shows how gaining commercial appeal in Chinese markets required the singer to gain not only linguistic fluency in Mandarin but also cultural fluency in a field of popular music often derided as "cheesy" and "corny" in the U.S. context.

There is a moment near the end of the novella *Hunger* when readers realize with a start that the story is being narrated by a ghost—Tian's late wife, a spectral presence lingering in the shadows of her former home, suffusing the air and transferring her desires onto those of her older daughter Anna, who eventually takes up residence there. The image evokes a sense of how race haunts our understandings of music, infiltrating how we hear and erecting walls both durable and unseen. The image also recalls the powerful assertion with which Radano and Bohlman open their edited collection *Music and the Racial Imagination*: "A specter lurks in the house of music, and it goes by the name of race."[58] In bringing this apparition to the foreground, I seek to illuminate not only the racial soundtracks that powerfully shape narratives about music but also the ineffable yearnings—for beauty, freedom, self-definition, and community—that music simultaneously thwarts, fulfills, and inspires in racialized subjects. From the Asian immigrant parents who compel their children to practice classical music instruments to the "tiger mother" who caricatures their impulses and desires, *Soundtracks of Asian America* uncovers the multiple ways that Asian Americans narrate, contest, and resolve the contradictory intrusions of race into their musical lives. In tracing how, as Simon Frith puts it, "music regularly soundtracks our search for ourselves and for spaces in which we can feel at home," this book follows the wide-ranging national and transnational terrains that Asian American music makers traverse to envision, create, and experience belonging.[59]

ONE

Interlopers in the Realm of High Culture

"Music Moms" and the Performance of Asian Difference

In 2002, as part of a series of articles about summer camps, the *New York Times* reported on the Perlman Music Program—a prestigious six-week instructional program led by the renowned violinist Itzhak Perlman. Tellingly, the article focused less on the teenagers who attend the camp and more on the efforts and ambitions of their parents, the "music moms" who enroll their children in advanced programs of music study. As the reporters note, "'Music moms' seasons are far longer than those of soccer moms. Their financial payoffs are far smaller and more elusive than those of tennis moms. But they are every bit as competitive, protective, ambitious and self-sacrificing." The ethos of self-sacrifice emerges clearly in a comment offered by one of the article's featured mothers, Mrs. Kim, who bluntly states: "First priority is Yoon-jee."[1] For this mother, such prioritization has meant living apart from her husband, a South Korean diplomat whose work required him to return to Seoul, so that her daughter, Yoon-jee, could continue her piano studies at the Juilliard School's Pre-College Division. As the *New York Times* article makes clear, from the initial decision to enroll their children in music lessons to the continued labor of driving back and forth to music lessons, rehearsals, and performances, "music moms" like Mrs. Kim play an integral role in the realm of classical musical training.

To understand the broad context of Western classical music making, an examination of the "music moms" who facilitate, organize, and support their children's musical pursuits is critical. Variations of the "stage mom" exist in many different realms, from competitive sports to beauty pageants. Yet, while such figures as the "soccer mom" typically bring to mind the image of a white, middle-class, suburban parent, this chapter reveals how the traits of sacrifice, pushiness, and determination embodied in the "music mom" have increasingly become associated with being Asian.[2] This chapter asks: What new meanings and significations have emerged alongside the racialization of this character? How has classical music training come to emblematize particular race and class notions about "Asian" parenting in the U.S. public imagination? And how do Asian parents themselves mobilize the multiple meanings contained in music to engage with and challenge their racial construction in the United States?[3]

The contemporary racialization of the "music mom" is, at first glance, not necessarily surprising in light of the increasingly visible presence of Asians and Asian Americans in classical music since the 1960s and 1970s. In the following decades, Asians and Asian Americans constituted anywhere from 30 to 40 percent of the student population at leading U.S. music schools and departments, with numbers often higher at the pre-college level. Indeed, by the 2000s, Asians and Asian Americans made up more than half of the student body at highly regarded music programs, such as Juilliard Pre-College; the two largest groups represented are students of Chinese and Korean descent studying the violin or piano.[4] We can trace the growing participation of Asian and Asian Americans in classical music over the past few decades to multiple, overlapping contexts: the historical deployment of Western classical music in East Asia; the economic ascension of East Asian nations; and the wave of educated and professional Asian immigrants who have arrived in the wake of changes in U.S. immigration policies in 1965.[5]

Still, socioeconomic and demographic shifts tell only part of the story. To contextualize the narratives placed on and mobilized by Asians and Asian Americans involved in classical music, this chapter draws from a range of sources—U.S. media representations, oral interviews conducted with Asian parents (primarily Chinese and Korean immigrant mothers) at Juilliard Pre-College, attendance at meetings held for Juilliard parents, and countless informal conversations with parents and musicians.[6] Within the confluence emerging from these accounts, racialized discourses about Asians and Asian Americans—as disciplined, hard-working, family-oriented, imitative, and zealous embracers of

Western culture—map unevenly onto beliefs that classical music connotes an "international" or "universal" language, a site of transcendent beauty, the unique cultural property of the West, and a cultural system through which the power of the West is enacted and authorized. As the media accounts I analyze in this chapter underscore, this complex and sometimes contradictory set of racial and musical discourses arises out of the colonial contexts through which classical music was institutionalized in East Asia and the imbalanced relations of power that have historically framed U.S. understandings of Asian and Asian American participation in this field of high culture.

Given these power dynamics, when Chinese and Korean immigrant parents enter conversations about their involvement in and affinity for Western classical music, they do so on unequal footing—in a new country, a new language, and through a cultural framework established and reworked through long-standing claims of Western superiority. Many of my interviewees articulated feeling that their actions are often misunderstood, hesitated to acknowledge the racism they encountered in their everyday lives, and expressed ambivalence at times about what it means to parent well in the U.S. context. They generalized broadly about characteristics that distinguished "Asians" from "Americans" and the ways in which these traits translated well into achievement in classical music and beyond. Still, while the emphasis my interviewees placed on possessing such characteristics as diligence, pushiness, and discipline can appear, on the surface, to reproduce stereotypical beliefs about their racial difference, this chapter suggests a more complex relationship between cultural practices and narratives. In what follows, I demonstrate how Asian parents choose from and reformulate available cultural narratives to claim alternate ascriptions of their race and class positioning in the United States.

To better understand the alignment between race, class, and cultural hierarchies, this chapter draws on Pierre Bourdieu's articulation of culture as a multidimensional field wherein groups and individuals compete to gain various forms of capital and extends his analysis to consider the transnational circulation of cultural capital.[7] Participating in a global cultural economy historically structured by Western dominance, Asian parents understand Western cultural norms and capital as yielding the highest forms of recognition on an international stage. At the same time, the decline in popular attention paid to classical music in the contemporary U.S. context allows these parents to narrate their place within a field of culture that is marginal and prestigious as setting themselves apart from—and indeed above—mainstream American norms and values. Underpinning Asian parents' involvement in classical music is a desire to be arbiters of high cultural knowledge and to inhabit class and cultural identities of their own choosing rather than those imposed upon them as racialized immigrants in the United States.

Historicizing Western Classical Music in East Asia

Classical music was part of the mandatory education. . . . Everything was based on classical music. They just started making Japanese traditional music mandatory as well. So classical music is part of the culture. The fact that I grew up and didn't know anything about Japanese traditional music is more of a surprise to many non-Japanese people. —Midori, violinist

When violinist Midori noted in our interview that Western classical music—rather than Japanese traditional or art music—formed the basis of her music education in Japan, her observation highlighted the degree to which she views Western music as part of her own background and contemporary Japanese culture more broadly. Her characterization of Japanese traditional music as unfamiliar and classical music as unmarked (i.e., assumed to be Western classical music) blurs the boundaries of race and nation typically placed on ideas of musical ownership. Indeed, over the past few decades, the strong educational structure and government support for Western classical music in Japan, Korea, and China have made East Asia a key site for the global circulation of Western music. U.S. media reports have even begun pointing to East Asian performers and composers as the best hope for preserving and revitalizing Western classical music in the contemporary period.[8]

To better understand the intensity of interest in Western classical music in East Asia, and to contextualize more fully the value and meanings that Asian American families ascribe to this music form, it is useful to historicize briefly the dissemination of Western classical music in Japan, China, and Korea. In all three nations Western classical music first arrived by way of Christian missionaries and missionary schools but spread through government interventions that linked modernization to the adoption of Western music principles.[9] Recognizing the pragmatic use of Western music for social and political purposes in East Asia helps debunk, at the outset, beliefs that the transcendent or universalizing properties of Western classical music propelled its global circulation. Rather, the specific ways that Japan, China, and Korea adopted Western classical music emphasize how definitions of culture figure critically into global struggles over political, economic, and national power.

In Japan, classical music did not grow in popularity until the Meiji government (1868–1912) incorporated it into its military and educational system as part of a broader "national goal of catching up with the West."[10] Driven less by aesthetic reasons than by social and political concerns, the Meiji government sought to refashion the cultural and musical landscape of Japan in an effort to win respect within a Western-dominated world order. While Japan was not subject to literal colonial rule, unequal power relations shaped by Western imperialism set the terms and context for the spread of Western music in that country. Historian E. Taylor Atkins observes that "the Meiji government's motivation for adopting Western music as the standard for the nation's military and educational system was part of the larger program of importing Western culture and technology in order to achieve parity with Western nations and renegotiate unequal treaties."[11] In this way, the Meiji government deployed Western classical music in the service of political and economic goals.

In China, state-directed reforms also facilitated the spread of Western music. Inspired by the successes of the Meiji government, Chinese nationalists introduced educational reforms based on Western principles as part of a broader project of nation building. Andrew Jones notes that by the late nineteenth century, "musicians, cultural critics, and educators promoted music as a means of national mobilization, resisting Western imperialism, and fighting Japanese aggression. Musical modernization, moreover, was conducted not under the auspices of the bourgeoisie, but of the nationalist state."[12] The social and political meanings attributed to Western classical music shifted during the Cultural Revolution (1966–1976), when the performance and study of European composers were banned owing to their association with foreign and bourgeois influences. However, because music played a central role in nation-building processes during the Cultural Revolution, large numbers of musicians were trained in Western instruments and traditional Chinese music and performed the model operas and revolutionary songs that proliferated during that decade. This musical training unintentionally helped provide the basis for the renewed public embrace of Western music following the Cultural Revolution.[13]

During the Japanese colonization of Korea (1910–1945), the Japanese government limited music education to the teaching of Japanese and Western songs. While the Korean government reintroduced traditional Korean music into the formal educational curriculum following liberation from Japan at the end of World War II, Western music training continued to flourish as colleges and universities established music departments. By the 1990s, ninety-four universities had music schools offering majors in Western classical music performance. The first music conservatory—modeled after schools such as the Juilliard School in New York City and the National Conservatory of Music and Dance in Paris—was established in Seoul in 1993.[14]

In Japan, China, and South Korea, the aesthetic appeal of Western classical music continues to be imbricated with the extramusical meanings of cultural prestige and modernity ascribed to it.[15] Yayoi Everett attests: "From a sociological vantage point, modernizing East Asian nations legitimized and embraced Western art music as a marker of status, along with their commodification of the Western lifestyle."[16] The lavishly constructed concert halls and the proliferation of professional symphony orchestras in the major cities of Japan, China, and South Korea function as visible symbols of the economic growth and modernity of the region and the emergence of a rapidly growing middle class able to patronize these performances.[17]

The rising status of and interest in Western classical music in East Asia helps account for the increasing numbers of both Asian musicians traveling to the United States to continue their musical training *and* Asian immigrants enrolling their children in classical music training. After the removal of national-origins quotas and the implementation of occupational and investor preference categories in 1965, the wave of professional and educated Asian immigrants who arrived to the United States brought with them an understanding of classical music as the embodiment of high cultural status and transnational cultural capital. Understanding the history of Western classical music in East Asia thus allows us to see how Asian parents are participating in a long tradition of using music to pursue particular cultural, political, and pragmatic goals.[18] ⚘ ⚘ ⚘

Racializing Musical Encounters

While the universalizing discourses associated with Western classical music naturalize the performance rituals, audience etiquette, and veneration of musical text and (the usually dead European) composer as seemingly timeless practices, it is useful to recall the historical construction of such beliefs in the United States. As cultural historian Lawrence Levine elucidates, the "sacralization" of high culture in the late nineteenth century mobilized artificial distinctions between "highbrow" and "lowbrow" culture as a mode of rationalizing and reinforcing social, class, and racial hierarchies.[19] The codification of behaviors meant to express proper appreciation and understanding of classical music (i.e., silent and attentive listening designed to inspire contemplative reverence for the composer and musical text) linked the elevated status of this revered high art form to its European origins. In this way, the implementation of cultural hierarchy in the United States and the nation's emergence as a center for the performance of classical music—that is, as a site with the cultural and institutional infrastructure to support it (from opera houses to professional symphony orchestras and training centers)—map the nation's twentieth-century rise as a global power. The disciplining mechanisms and racial ideologies embedded in the culture of classical music became institutionalized along with the "music itself" as it traveled to other regions and populations around the world, allowing for the further legitimation of U.S. dominance. The same procedures used to regulate the "improper" behavior and responses of American audiences and musicians at the turn of the past century were applied to East Asians, whose purported inability to appreciate and understand Western classical music reflected their racial and cultural differences.

While unequal power relations structured the dissemination of Western classical music across East Asia during the twentieth century, music professionals tended not to consider such "extramusical" concerns, framing the institutionalization of Western classical music in East Asia less as the further entrenchment of Eurocentric imperial power and more as an (albeit unidirectional) form of "cultural sharing" marked by openness, generosity, and patronage. As Richard Kraus asserts in his study of Western music and politics in China, the metaphor of music as an "international language" proved "comforting to both conquerors and subjects alike. The West's musicians, if they thought much about empire, preferred to imagine their art opening new opportunities for shared pleasure and enlightenment, rather than imagining its use as a secondary aspect of an increasingly global web of social control."[20] Crafting Western classical music as the universal embodiment of human achievement—as transcendent expressions of grace, splendor, and sublime beauty—effectively circumvented discussions of politics and power, allowing the more powerful partner in the relationship to dictate the terms and narratives attached to its circulation. Musicians from the United States, as the *Los Angeles Times* reported in 1956, had a duty to spread the gift of their rich musical knowledge and, in the process, to broker cultural understandings with those in the East.[21]

In these transcultural exchanges, orientalist beliefs about "East" and "West," coupled with racialized assumptions about the distinct European inheritance of Western classical music, yielded doubts that East Asians held the capacity to comprehend and appreciate fully this complex music form.[22] Such an uncertainty is best summarized in the following question, posed by conductor Rolf Jacoby following a stint guest conducting the Seoul Symphony Orchestra in 1949: "Do Koreans really enjoy Occidental music?" In Jacoby's view, the lack of proper concert hall etiquette displayed by raucous Korean audiences, alongside their incessant clamoring "for their favorites again and again," betrayed a lack of maturity in musical understanding and, by extension, personhood as well.[23]

Even after Western classical music became institutionalized in countries like Japan, reservations about the depth of musical appreciation lingered. As the *New York Times* reported in 1973, the overriding popularity of the "3 B's" (Bach, Beethoven, and Brahms) in Japan's musical landscape revealed the deep insecurity that Japanese musicians and audiences possessed about their musical tastes and their cultural propensity to imitate rather than develop true understanding.[24] The eerie stillness and silence of Japanese audiences at music concerts provided further evidence of the Japanese inclination to ape (in excess) U.S./European practices. And thus, despite possessing a "work ethic that would startle American Calvinists," Japanese musicians continue to struggle "with the question of 'understanding'" and "need guidance in the Western literature from the best Western musicians."[25]

At the same time, "guidance" can only go so far. The internal difficulties that Japanese musicians particularly and Asian musicians generally feel in their attempts to grasp the emotional depth in Western music may be entangled also in bodily questions of roots and blood. Reporting again on the Japanese zeal for the "3 B's," the *New York Times* quoted a Japanese musician as musing: "We Japanese are one blood. Foreign influence to us is both a contrast and a problem. The skills and discipline of course we have. But the art?"[26] By using native Japanese voices as proxies to legitimate beliefs about their own limitations, "the question of 'understanding'" becomes framed as an internal debate among the Japanese, obscuring the extent to which they are working within a racial logic that assumes Europeans and white Americans to be the proper inheritors of this musical tradition. Such beliefs accrue legitimacy through the discourse of musical authenticity—the belief that different types of music originate from, and therefore belong to, a certain group or place. The idea that some things cannot be taught—passion, expressiveness, individuality, and musicality—weds musical expression with authenticity.[27] Hence, while certain mechanics of technique can be borrowed, imitated, and practiced, the ineluctable essence of the music— its heart, soul, and spirit—is felt most palpably through blood and the "flow of generations."[28]

When European and American music professionals traveled to Asia, they, too, spread and reproduced long-standing orientalist beliefs about fundamental divergences separating "East" and "West" and the inherent difficulties that East Asian musicians face—due to geography, cultural familiarity, heritage, and/or blood—comprehending the emotional subtleties of the Western concert tradition. Such a view emerged, quite famously, in the film *From Mao to Mozart* (1980), the Academy Award– winning documentary that chronicled violinist Isaac Stern's travels in Beijing and Shanghai shortly after the end of the Cultural Revolution. While his trip held tremendous symbolic import for highlighting the role that the arts can play in brokering international relations, the rhetoric of musical diplomacy and friendly exchange repeated throughout the film neglected the uneven dynamics of power that guided interactions between Stern and the Chinese musicians he encountered.[29] Concretizing a framework of racial difference that would impact perceptions of

Chinese musicianship for decades to come, Stern observed that despite a fervent work ethic and desire to improve, Chinese musicians had yet to learn how to express the true meaning of classical music—its heart, feeling, and emotion: "The Chinese are not accustomed to playing with passion and color. . . . They have not had the experience of living with Western music, as we have, for hundreds of years." While such a comment is not, in itself, particularly surprising, it is significant given Stern's role as one of the most important interlocutors for subsequent generations of Chinese musicians. His observations highlight the perspective and cultural influence that even well-meaning music professionals reproduced through their musical tours in Asia.[30]

I gesture to these media examples to contextualize the social and cultural landscape in which Asian and Asian American musicians began attending music schools and conservatories in the United States, a milieu replete with lingering questions about their musical inauthenticity, racial difference, emotive capacities, and ability to belong.[31] The intransigent yet pliable nature of these narratives emerges out of their embeddedness in long-standing racial discourses that script Asians and Asian Americans as conformist, emotionless, and hard-working to a zealous, almost "subhuman" extreme. One can think back to discourses about Chinese immigrant labor in the 1800s, or to narratives about Japanese kamikaze pilots during World War II, or to accounts of the North Vietnamese during the Vietnam War.[32] In the more recent past, racial tropes about the technical but unfeeling Asian (in music and beyond) have become incorporated into heightened U.S. anxieties about the economic emergence of East Asia, most notably Japan in the 1980s and China in the decades that followed.

During the 1980s, a decade marked by U.S. unease over the ascendancy of Japan, racialized discourses about the imitative and conformist nature of the Japanese helped domesticate the nature of their success. As David Palumbo-Liu aptly observes: "Critics responding to the success of Japan in the world economy had to particularize both the Japanese and Americans in order to construct two types of 'success' and thereby downplay Asian success and rehabilitate America."[33] Aligning Japan's high-tech advancements with a culture of robot-like efficiency, discipline, and control allowed the threat of the country's economic growth to be contained and managed through a framework that David Morley and Kevin Robins term "techno-orientalism."[34] Within such anxiety-ridden narratives, Japanese (and Asians more broadly) become the implied foil for normative white Americans, whose balanced pursuit of work and innovation would, in the long run, prove more successful.

A 1983 *Time* magazine article about Western classical music in Japan reveals how the framework of techno-orientalism functioned to ameliorate U.S. concerns about growing Japanese dominance in a wide range of industries. Highlighting the thriving classical music scene in Japan—an astonishing nine professional symphony orchestras and fifteen concert venues in Tokyo alone—journalist Michael Walsh nonetheless cautioned against the deceptiveness of such appearances, querying: "The classics flourish in Japan, but how deep are the roots?"[35] To answer his own (rhetorical) question, Walsh draws an analogy between Japan's music making and its meticulous production of electronic goods.

> Down the long corridors of the Tokyo University of Arts and in the crowded classrooms of the Toho Gakuen School, the technicians are at work, taking the measure of one of Japan's hottest imports. They pore over its structure as carefully as they would over a new automobile design; they grasp it as firmly as they do a microchip on a reflex-camera lens, anticipating the day when their country will be as formidable in this field as it is in so many others. It is not the Three Cs—cameras, computers and cars—that fire their imagination so, but the Three Bs: Bach, Beethoven and Brahms.

By intimating that these "technicians" are poring over microchips rather than canonized composers of the classical music tradition, the reporter exposes the supposedly inherent flaws in Japanese reasoning. For while the efficiency of assembly-line practices might produce high-quality electronic goods, they cannot produce truly accomplished musicians. The photo of a group of students fiddling in unison—replete with the caption "very young violinists perform in Tokyo zealously imitating the teachers' style"—visually harmonizes the article's message that Japanese accomplishments in music and, indeed, other realms are ultimately limited. For a culture of imitation can never overtake a culture of innovation; the technician can reach only a certain level of success.

Despite my glib reproduction and critique of these discourses, the fact that cultural distinctions exist between countries such as Japan and the United States is not under dispute. Differences in education systems, music pedagogy, and cultural resources can produce divergent musical approaches and interpretations. What is under contention, however, are the ways that perceptions of difference pivot on ideas about race and power, producing essentializing, hierarchical pronouncements about the inherent shortcomings of certain groups. These racialized scripts impact how one hears the performance of musicians of East Asian descent and how one perceives their motivations for consuming and participating in Western classical music.

By the 1990s, media coverage about China's emergence as an economic and musical superpower updated the framework of racial difference and techno-orientalism circulating earlier about Japan, pronouncing China as the new "future" of classical music (a future still deferred, it would seem, for Japan).[36] Yet, similar to those about Japan, media narratives about China positioned the nation as marred by a persistent temporal lag in its pursuit of Western modernity.[37] Such a narrative emerges, for instance, in a three-part series that the *New York Times* published in 2007 about the spectacular growth of Western classical music in China.[38] As with most accounts about China, the sheer numbers reported were staggering: thirty million piano students, ten million violin students, and the construction of concert halls at an astounding pace. Thus, while classical music appears to be on a path of steady decline in prestige and market share in the United States, in China it seems to be on the opposite trajectory, a path underwritten heavily by a government that perceives Western classical music to be a critical part of its broader mandate to become an "advanced culture."[39]

At the same time, despite the astonishing embrace of Western classical music in China and the large number of solo performers who have found acclaim on the international stage, the *New York Times* reported that China still lacks the necessary infrastructure to support this musical growth: "It has yet to develop a deep, sustainable culture in Western music."[40] Chinese music professionals themselves complain that classical music is too often treated like a commodity: as a "technology that can be mastered with the right combination of capital, labor, and quality control," invariably leading to performances that sound "wooden and shaped by a cookie cutter."[41] For this reason, the relationship between the United States and China continues to be scripted as mutually beneficial. As a center for classical music training, the United States possesses the resources that allow Chinese musicians to overcome their limitations: it is still where top Chinese musicians clamor to study, where the best schools and teachers are located, where "careers are made."[42] China, in turn, represents a solution for some of the difficulties facing the U.S. classical music industry—it is a place to tour, to market and sell products, and to recruit from a seemingly unlimited supply of talented students. Since the early 2000s, most major music conservatories in the United States have actively recruited students from China to fill their schools.[43]

While reports on China's ascent as an emerging economic and musical power elicit a familiar set of questions about rightful ownership and belonging in the Western classical music tradition, they also demonstrate the flexible deployment of long-standing racial discourses to contain anxieties about its growing strength. The presence and accomplishments of East Asians in Western classical music uphold the notion that racism does not exist in this field of high culture, even while implicit beliefs about their foreignness, cultural preponderance toward imitation, and dependency on the United States/West essentialize the limits of their full integration and belonging. Such characterizations resonate strongly with discourses used to depict Asian American classical musicians—an unsurprising fact given the frequent elision between Asians and Asian Americans and the perpetually "foreign" status that Asian Americans hold in the U.S. racial imaginary. Moreover, placed within the U.S. context, these descriptions become filtered through model minority discourse, perhaps *the* prevailing racialized script placed on Asian Americans in the contemporary period.

Since the mid-1960s, journalists and scholars have pointed to Asian Americans as model minority subjects whose impressive work ethic, compliant temperament, and self-sufficient nature account for their relative success.[44] Much has been written about the ideological function that model minority discourses serve to discipline other racial minority groups for their purported cultural inferiorities while also buttressing white superiority and upholding fictions of U.S. meritocracy.[45] More recently, literary critic Min Song suggested the appearance of an updated version of Asian Americans as the "super minority" in U.S. popular media: "Asian Americans become less of a model whose successes specifically berate blacks and other racial minorities and more a kind of, for lack of a better term, super minority whose successes berate *everyone* who fails somehow to succeed."[46] Situating the model minority myth within the context of global capitalism, literary critic Helen Jun observes how its central tenets—self-reliance, competitiveness, and hard work—dovetail with the mandates of neoliberal economic principles.[47] As a disciplining mechanism and a neoliberal racial formation, the model minority myth capitalizes on beliefs about the cultural difference of Asian Americans, rationalizing their success through a focus on their supposedly unwavering adherence to strong "Asian" values. Such a slippage between cultural and racial difference correlates historically with broader shifts in the post–civil rights era, where allegations about culture increasingly function as proxies for race. As Claire Jean Kim notes, with the emergence of color blindness as the prevailing racial ideology in post–civil rights America, cultural explanations have increasingly replaced overtly racialized statements: "Talk about a group's culture serves to disguise what are fundamentally racial claims. . . . Culture becomes code for the unspeakable in the contemporary era."[48]

In the realm of Western classical music, model minority discourses are particularly salient given the degree to which "Asian" values of obedience, filial piety, and diligence correspond with the view that classical music requires long hours of practice, often from an early age. The demands of classical music training overlap nicely with cultural attributes "naturally" embodied by Asian Americans. Take, for instance, the description offered by the *Los Angeles Times* about the shared Asian (or "Confucian") values that have driven the perceptible "shift in composition" in classical music training: "These people of Japanese, Korean and Chinese backgrounds come from families that share the Confucian values of discipline, honoring parents and teachers, pride in family achievement and respect for culture. Nearly all of them have strong and supportive parents who encourage, or force, their offspring to do the countless hours of childhood practice without which few musicians, and certainly no instrumentalists, can achieve excellence later on."[49] Here the article draws squarely on well-known tropes to account for the increasing number of Asian Americans involved in classical music rather than highlight other qualities commonly associated with musical involvement—for example, creativity, artistry, or love of music.[50] The high participation of Asians and Asian Americans in classical music becomes folded into broader social evidence demarcating this racial group as exemplary filial subjects. Indeed, playing the violin or piano has itself become a key component of what it means to be a model minority—part of the larger stereotypical image of the overachieving Asian American subject. Still, while the accomplishments achieved by Asian Americans in classical music provide evidence of the distinct cultural values prioritized by this group, model minority narratives also domesticate and limit their potential. For despite the many impressive achievements in music by Asian Americans, the perception that they are excessively respectful, driven, and narrow-minded in their pursuit of excellence thwart them from reaching the highest echelons of their profession, where imagination and originality also are necessary. As should be clear, the tentacles of the model minority construction extend far beyond classical music; this racial logic positions Asian Americans as model subjects for managerial and technical positions within global capitalism and is structured by internal limitations meant to prevent Asian Americans from upsetting the existing racial order.

I include this overview of the multiple narratives attached to Asian and Asian American participation in classical music as they structure key racial, cultural, and class hierarchies embedded in a field of culture that often shrouds these politics through the language of universalism, racelessness, and transcendence. While beliefs circulating in classical music about Asian difference help mark the boundaries of rightful ownership and belonging, they also assuage ongoing anxieties about the global and domestic competition posed by the intrusion of Asians and Asian Americans in a variety of fields. At the same time, as my interviews with Asian parents (and, in the following chapter, with Asian American musicians) demonstrate, many Asian American subjects themselves mobilize rhetoric that appears to replicate beliefs about their foreignness, their enthusiastic work ethic, and their cultural difference from normative (white) Americans. The point, then, is not to ascertain the so-called truths contained in stereotypes but, rather, to investigate how and in what contexts certain discourses gain traction. Asian parents cull from existing racial and musical narratives in order to understand and make legible their experiences in a U.S. context. Yet, more than merely corroborating dominant discourses, Asian parents also redeploy them to register the intersecting race, class, and linguistic anxieties they confront as racialized immigrants living in the United States.

Saturdays at Juilliard Pre-College

I always avoided Juilliard on Saturdays. All those moms . . . it's scary.
—Jason, Juilliard College graduate

Flanked by the Metropolitan Opera and Avery Fisher Hall in the performing arts complex at Lincoln Center, the Juilliard School stands as a cultural institution with a long and distinguished history of education in the performing arts. The reputation of Juilliard as a premier site for music training led some families to consider the school quite early in their child's musical career. Commenting on the global stature of the school, Henry, a Chinese immigrant, reflected: "Juilliard is so famous. We heard of it in Shanghai already, but we never expect my son will be a student here." His decision to pursue a business degree and a professional career in the United States was influenced by a concomitant desire to "give his son a chance to develop musically."

In *Nothing but the Best*, Judith Kogan devotes a chapter to Juilliard's pre-college program, describing what she terms the "Juilliard mother":

> The Juilliard mother knows the obstacles but is determined. Her child will be the best. . . . She sacrifices her time and money, her energy and friends. Nothing worth having comes easy. . . . She is actually not a bona fide Juilliard mother unless she accompanies him for the lessons and classes that consume most of Saturday. She does not sit at the wheel of the station wagon waiting for him to emerge. She, like him, works on his career. He works in the classrooms and practice rooms; she works in the lounge and lobby. . . . The Juilliard mother studies the competition. She knows the recitals to check out, the teachers that are hot, and the competitions to go after.[51]

While hardly characteristic of all Juilliard mothers, Kogan's account captures the conspicuous presence of parents milling about the school on Saturdays and the backstage labor they undertake on behalf of their child. And although many of the parents I interviewed might object to appearing so outwardly competitive and ambitious in their child's musical pursuits, they viewed themselves as active participants—if not partners—in their child's music making activities.

Juilliard Pre-College shares much in common with other advanced, pre-college music programs and thus provides a glimpse into the particular subculture of classical music training. Like other high-level preparatory music schools, Juilliard Pre-College provides a comprehensive course of instruction for "students of elementary through high school who exhibit the talent, potential, and accomplishment to pursue a career in music."[52] Students meet on Saturdays to take courses in the core curriculum of Western classical and concert music traditions, including performance training, theory, solfège (ear training), and ensemble experience. Prospective students are admitted on the basis of a performance audition.

While some students travel on their own to Juilliard Pre-College, for others, the weekly commute represents a significant trip that involves at least one parent. Many of the parents I interviewed pointed to the long distances they traveled as a measure of their willingness to make the sacrifices necessary for their children to reach their musical goals. Moreover, similar to the mother, Mrs. Kim, cited at the outset of this chapter, for some parents, studying at Juilliard was enmeshed in the experience of transcontinental family separation and travel. For example, a Korean mother, Sookhyun, continued living in New Jersey with her daughter after her husband's work required him to move back to Korea. Conversely, a Taiwanese mother, Wang Wei, maintained her residence in Taiwan but traveled monthly to visit her teenage daughter who lived with friends in Manhattan. Parents narrated these transnational family configurations as material evidence of the priority they placed on their children's interests, even at their own expense and happiness.

The professional and personal sacrifices undertaken by families typically fell on the shoulders of mothers. Wang Wei, for instance, noted that prior to quitting her job she had less time to help her daughter pursue her musical ambitions. She described herself as a "not so good mother" given the focus she placed on her own professional career. And while she did not view the constant travel and family separation as ideal, she felt that her maternal duties required such sacrifices.

> You have to help them, like it or not, so they never come back and say, "Mom, you should have let me do that." . . . I sacrifice myself and even my career. I'm a business person in Taiwan. I run a company. But now, after two years, my daughter's here. I quit my company. . . . It's not because she is talent or not. It's just because she wants to get into some goal or something, and I just want her to try. Otherwise,

I think maybe she will feel sorry if she didn't try. . . . Because you know in Taiwan, maybe I shouldn't say that, but she's already the best. Some violinist who taught her before said I shouldn't limit her, how to say, don't let her stop here. That's what I'm thinking. Before that, I'm not so good a mother, because I'm really a business person.

Here, Wang Wei draws on gendered and racialized discourses, scripting her actions in the context of being a "good mother" who sacrifices for the sake of the next generation, rather than within a narrative that focuses on her own dreams of the success her daughter might attain as a famed soloist. She frames her time and even her own career as worth sacrificing in order for her daughter to remain competitive in the global culture of classical music. Like other mothers I interviewed, Wang Wei strove not to appear too boastful or personally driven in her actions.

Few of the mothers I interviewed worked full-time outside of the home, a situation some considered a significant sacrifice.[53] Most families were two-parent households that followed traditional gendered divisions of labor in which fathers represented the primary wage earners.[54] While many parents noted the financial strains that music training placed on the family, it is worth emphasizing that they were nonetheless part of middle- and upper-middle-class households that could afford for the mother to limit the amount of professional employment she pursued outside the home. For instance, Katherine, a Chinese immigrant from Vietnam, placed her medical practice on hold so that she could devote more time to helping her daughter pursue her piano studies. While she deemed this decision to be "worthwhile," it still presented some internal conflicts.

I find myself a little bit cranky. Because I ask myself, what am I doing? I mean I ask *myself*, I can go back to being a doctor, but why do I hold back my career, tell my kid to make it? Because it's that hard. I trade a profession for a profession.

So you've made a lot of sacrifices?

I have. I've been doing it for a few years. So [*pause*] but it's worthwhile. . . . I'm a medical doctor. But now I hold my clinical career. . . . It's not because we don't understand that this is a sort of craziness. Some people say, "Look at you guys, you're crazy! You guys are too ambitious." Say whatever you want, but that is not true. When you have a child, they want to approach a goal, they have an ideal. If parents don't help, I don't know who will.

Like Wang Wei, Katherine explained her actions through the rhetoric of parental duty—the idea that "if parents don't help, I don't know who will." While downplaying her own ambitions and desires and affirming that her daughter could stop playing music at any time, she also clearly believed that her daughter possessed unique musical gifts that demanded development. As Katherine elaborated: "The part inside [my daughter], the musical part inside her, that's something. But a teacher did express it in a very fancy way. It's one out of how many million have it. We don't know what it is, but it doesn't matter because she has it."

This "one out of how many million" quality that Katherine's daughter is said to possess echoes what musicologist Henry Kingsbury describes as "talent"—an elusive trait that holds tremendous import in classical musical training. As Kingsbury details it, "The fact is that while being 'talented' may be positively valued, it nevertheless entails definite moral obligations of musical development. A young person's talent is an attribution that demands development for the benefit of others as well as for oneself."[55] Many parents I interviewed noted the "moral obligation" they felt toward their talented children, whom they described as possessing rare and innate gifts for music. Thus, while talent is located in the individual—it is what makes the child singular and exceptional—it is a collective resource for which the family must willingly make sacrifices. In this sense, though none of the parents I interviewed began music lessons with the expectation of becoming seriously involved, they felt slowly drawn in by pronouncements and external validations of their children's talent. This accounts for the sense of powerlessness that some parents described in relation to their children's music training. As one mother contended: "When you get into music you cannot get off . . . so you know when I struggle, but I don't know why I cannot get out; I must be drugged [*laughs*]." The gendered pressure to be a "good mother," coupled with the moral obligation that encircles the idea of musical talent, led my interviewees to depict helping their children develop their musical potential as a maternal duty. They narrated their own stories through the more accepted tropes of good mothering and generational sacrifice rather than other reasons, such as a personal ambition to see their children become international solo performers.

At the same time, many of these same parents expressed ambivalence about the ways in which their sacrifices—or more often than not, the actions of parents even "pushier" than themselves—might place undue burdens or expectations on the child. Speaking specifically about Korean families, Jean Hee, who, at the time of our interview, was interim president of the Korean Parents Association, commented: "I think most Asian parents want [their children] to be performers, solo performers . . . and it's too much pressure, too competitive." She was one of the few parents I interviewed who explicitly discouraged her son and daughter from becoming musicians given the difficulty of the profession and what she termed the "bohemian" lifestyle of musicians (described as waking up late in the day and having an irregular schedule). Jean Hee pointedly criticized the transnational family arrangement of Korean families, particularly when it created geographic separations not only between spouses, but also other children. As she elaborated,

> I think the parents don't like me. Do you know why? I always, some parents who come from families separate, husband and wife, I always [say], "You better go back to Korea!" I always say that. . . . Because it's not worth it. Because families, it's really a short time to live together. If they bring all the children that's fine. But when some children are staying with grandparents or father, and separate, I think it's not good. . . . So I say, "Why are you here? You better go back to Korea. Don't your other children need Mommy too? Wake up! [*laughs*] Since Sarah Chang, how many Sarah Chang is here?"⁵⁶ . . . You know, some parents divorce over this; families break up. I think sometimes maybe the relationship is not that good, or maybe mother-in-law or some family problems, so they just get away from that. That I don't know. That might count.

Jean Hee was not the only parent who expressed concern over the unintended consequences of placing overly high expectations on her children. Indeed, other parents similarly worried about the demands placed on their children, particularly in relation to the scope of the family's sacrifice. At the same time, Jean Hee's observations also imply that there may be other reasons—unarticulated perhaps because they do not conform to the more accepted narratives of being a good parent or sacrificing for the next generation—that a mother might come to the United States without her husband. She intimated that, for some, a move to the United States might be partially inspired by a marital relationship that had already soured or that was strained by mother-in-law issues. Although the topic of marital or family strife prior to (or exacerbated by) geographical separation and travel did not explicitly arise in my interviews, such possibilities should not be discounted.[57] These potentially unspoken reasons complicate too-easy categorizations about the obsessive or overbearing nature of Asian parents.

Socializing among Parents

While their children attend class, parents congregate in the lobby and cafeteria, listen in on lessons or rehearsals, hang out by the practice rooms, or gather for outings to Chinatown or Koreatown. The group atmosphere among parents on Saturdays is fostered through their socialization at the school and a sense of shared understanding about the role they play in their children's musical lives. Some parents, especially newer immigrants, expressed enjoyment at finding a community of like-minded parents with whom they could socialize at Juilliard. As one Korean mother mused, "When I came here to the U.S., I lost a lot of friends. It was so lonely. But for me, when I came to Juilliard, I enjoy it." At the same time, Chinese, Korean, and white parents tended to socialize separately at the school. Language barriers, particularly for recent immigrants to the United States, no doubt played a role in determining social groupings based on racial and ethnic lines. As Christine, a Chinese immigrant from Hong Kong, commented: "Sometimes I think maybe it's the language barrier. Just like to have to communicate in Chinese is hard, we don't know how to speak in Korean. It's a big problem for us in order to talk to [Koreans]." Interestingly, Christine, a native Cantonese speaker, noted that she honed her Mandarin speaking skills, in part, through her interactions with other Chinese parents at Juilliard Pre-College.[58]

While Christine primarily socialized with other Chinese parents at the school, she nonetheless expressed a desire to have more interactions with other parents. As she elaborated: "For me, I like to be united, everybody in one group. I don't want to have separate, your own group, my own group, like gang. I don't like that. But because there's a lot of Korean students here, so there's a lot of parents here, it's a big group. We all speak [some] English, but somehow it depends. It still depends." While she acknowledged that language limitations, especially for newer

immigrants to the United States, most likely intensified group sepa
rations, Christine also intimated that "Korean parents"—with their
"parents club only for the Koreans"—encouraged exclusivity and self-
segregation. In so doing, she downplayed the extent to which Chinese
parents informally engage in socializing practices that could appear
equally alienating to outsiders of that group.

While language barriers no doubt play a role in determining patterns
of socialization, so do perceptions of racial and ethnic difference. While
Asian parents commented at length on the purported distinctions between "Americans" and "Asians," they also detailed differences between
Chinese and Koreans. These divergences were often framed as a matter
of excess and degree.[59] For instance, one Korean mother observed that
"the Chinese is much more competitive than [the] Korean." Another
similarly contended: "Chinese is stronger than our Korean culture . . . they
really work for it, they fight for it . . . they're more disciplined." Conversely,
a Chinese mother suggested that Koreans were merely interested in
increasing their cultural status and producing "the next Sarah Chang."
As a different Chinese mother observed: "Some Korean families . . . they
don't have a TV, they don't have a play time, they practice piano seven
to eight hours a day. . . . And we [Chinese] are just, 'How do you get so
many time?'" While it is likely that my Chinese American status limited
what Korean parents in particular felt comfortably articulating, both
Korean and Chinese parents narrated possessing a parenting style more
"balanced" and defensible than other, more extreme forms of parenting.[60]
While my interviewees were careful not to appear overly ambitious or
status-driven for themselves, they were more comfortable projecting
those traits onto other groups.

At the same time, Asian parents de-emphasized distinctions between
Chinese and Koreans when they discussed how "Asians" differed from
"Americans." In all of my interviews, "American" correlated with white,
an affiliation that underscores the intimate relationship between whiteness and normative Americanness in both the U.S. social landscape and
their Asian countries of origin.[61] Conversely, these immigrant parents'
self-identification as "Asian" can be viewed primarily as a U.S. construction—a means to gain legibility in the United States and a response to
the homogenization of Asian ethnic groups within the American racial
imaginary.[62] In the process, these parents accept or at the very least
recognize their exclusion from the category "American."

Both Chinese and Korean parents narrated their distinction from "Americans" as reflecting broader ideological differences about family and child-rearing practices. Jean Hee, for instance, felt that Americans are less willing to make the sacrifices demanded of the family by classical music.

> I think it's different, American parents and Asian parents. Asian parents [want] what is good for children. They like to provide as much as they can for their children, even if they sacrifice a little. But American parents, if they too hard have to sacrifice, they don't do it. They don't like it, they're kind of children themselves a little bit, so individualized. We always, children is our first choice, right? So how can I say, we always count first our children. Whatever is good for them, we like to provide for them as much as we can even if we waste a lot of time, a lot of driving. American parents, they think Asian parents are crazy.

Here, Jean Hee draws on discourses of American individualism and Asian lack of concern for one's self. Yet she also uses this binary formulation to align individualism with childishness and selfishness. In a reversal of orientalist discourses that infantilize Asians and cast them as needing rescue, Jean Hee interpreted "Americans" as behaving a bit like "children" who lack maturity and foresight. She posited the ability of Asian parents to sacrifice and look beyond their own personal interests and desires as marking their difference from Americans.

While Jean Hee coded traits such as sacrifice as "Asian," one did not necessarily have to be Asian to embody such characteristics. Joan, a white mother, recalled how her daughter once called her an "Asian parent."

> One day, my daughter said, "Mom, it seems like you're an Asian parent." [laughs] I just said, "Well, I guess you know if that's what it takes then yeah, maybe that's what I am." Because I've always been pushing education and for Asians, education is very important, generally speaking. And [pause] I think she said that because I always have extra work for her to do and I push. [My daughter] equates Asian moms with pushiness. Not pushy as a person necessarily, but pushing for what they think is important. And I think it seems to work. My daughter knows my thoughts on it.

For Joan, being "pushy" did not suggest a negative characteristic; it was, instead, necessary to help her child attain success in music and education. Being an "Asian parent," in this instance, represented a set of characteristics rather than a racialized embodiment. Thus, despite having few *actual* interactions with Asian parents at Juilliard, Joan was nonetheless pleased to be at a music school with so many like-minded "Asian moms."

Associating "Asianness" with competitiveness and achievement, Joan sought to align herself symbolically with this racial group through their shared parenting practices and beliefs. This was particularly true given the link she perceived between Asian backgrounds and high musical achievement. For this reason, Joan felt reassured participating in music environments in which there were large enrollments of Asians.

> When [my daughter] went to competitions in Queens, it was overwhelmingly Asian. I mean, there's a lot of Asians in Queens, but at that level, when you start to compete, it was more Asian. . . . And then I noticed that when we went to Mannes [School of Music] it was the same. Well, except for the exception of her other [music] school, and I hate to say it, it sounds biased either one way or the other, and I don't mean to. I always emulate the Asian way; they seem to know what's going on. . . . And I was thinking when she was at that other school, "Why are there no Asians here?" There was just one Japanese girl who was excellent, but other than that there were no others. It just made me wonder, you know, I thought, "Hmm . . . that's something." That for me said something about the caliber, too, along with some other things I encountered there.

About the quality of the school?

Yeah. I mean it seems like wherever you go, the higher you go, the more Asian backgrounds you see.

Given the positive attributions she bestowed on Asianness, Joan found their absence unsettling—a potential statement about a music school's low quality of students and overall lack of competitiveness. It is worth noting that in attempting to not appear "biased," she instead valorized Asians, peppering her statements with verbal asides like "I always emulate the Asian way" and "[Asians] really seem to know what's going on and what needs to be done." At the same time, her equation of Asian backgrounds with high-level music making suggests how, within this subculture of advanced music training, the "Asian" parent represents a particular model for thriving in an era of global competition. As Joan noted, both she and her daughter long dreamed of attending Juilliard and viewed acceptance to the school as evidence that they could compete with the best.

While Joan linked the pushiness of "Asian" parenting to the visibility of Asians and Asian Americans in music, Henry, a recent immigrant from Shanghai, deployed the same rhetoric as a way to claim space and ownership in a cultural field not necessarily viewed as his own. He used the polarities of "East" and "West" to defend against the view that Asians are the paradoxical inheritors of Western classical music. As Henry queried: "If the instrument and music belongs to the West, why [are there] so many Asian kids here at the Pre-College?" He then proceeded to answer his question this way:

> I think this is related to the style of family. I think that West's country, the West's people, West's family, the parents always stop before the line at forcing the child to do something, like instrument, because their culture, I don't know how to say, the relationship between the parents and children . . . they can't force them, right? . . . If the children are not willing to do like that, the West's country, the parents just give up. They say, "It's your thing . . . if you don't want to, it's okay, we don't care." But East's people, East's parents, they always put their dreams on their children. What they want to do, it's correct. We ask you to do something, you have to follow.

Even though Henry acknowledged that the music and instruments are generally recognized to be the cultural property of the West, he coded the *activity* of learning classical music—the sacrifice, determination, and enforcement it required of parents and children—as an "Asian" cultural trait. Put differently, pursuing classical music training became an implicit way of preserving an "Asian" identity in the face of mainstream "American" society. Thus, while the product might be Western, the characteristics necessary to pursue classical music at a high level (including pushing children to follow the wishes of their parents) were scripted as Asian. Aligning success at Western classical music with maintaining "Asian" cultural and family practices allowed Henry to articulate a space for himself and other Asian families in this cultural field.

While many Asian parents readily identified such qualities as focus, hard work, and self-sacrifice as "Asian," these traits were not perceived to be a natural part of one's identity but rather a principle that parents hoped to instill in their children *through* classical music training. Many of my interviewees cited learning discipline, diligence, and persistence—qualities viewed as translating, not coincidentally, into high academic achievement and a competitive edge regardless of the specific chosen endeavor—as a critical factor in enrolling their children in music lessons.[63] Again, Henry's remarks are illustrative.

> I think you will find that most of the children, if they learn an instrument, they don't have any big problems when they are learning science, mathematics, and something. It's easy, easy for them! . . . Because if you have this kind of discipline, the concentration to overcome obstacle, do something over and over again, then you will know, "Oh! If I put in every kind of effort, then I will win." . . . Then, even in the future, if you don't become a pianist, it doesn't matter because you have that kind of training. . . . I can't think of another way to train children at such a young age to understand that kind of principle. By playing the piano, they can feel like "Oh, this music is very beautiful" and in the meantime get this good training and art for the future.

Discipline and concentration were not perceived as attributes that Asians inherently possess, or traits conferred through an inherited cultural apparatus, but qualities to be learned and repeatedly practiced. In this sense, participating in classical music allows children to accrue particular gains: the cultural capital of finely honed aesthetic tastes (including the ability to appreciate and enjoy playing this "very beautiful" music) and the flexible skills of discipline and diligence that translate into achievement not only in music but also in academic fields of study.

While parents like Henry cited learning and practicing such qualities as discipline and sacrifice as key reasons for enrolling their children in music training, this explanation does little to illuminate *why* classical music in particular represented such an appealing vehicle for transmitting those values. The next section examines this central question by investigating how ideas about class and cultural capital influence the decisions that these parents make. To do so is not to align the study of classical music automatically with elitism or class privilege, despite the high cost of classical music training acknowledged by many families. As musicologist Martin Stokes aptly cautions: "The relationships between classes, ethnicities and their music are more complicated than a simplistic model equating class with musical style would allow."[64] Still, paying attention to relationships between ideas of social class and Western classical music enables a more specific analysis of the intersection of cultural capital, cultural taste, and so-called high culture.[65]

"A Very Prestige Kind of Thing"

The transnational travel of Western understandings of culture, along with the historical enmeshment of music, politics, and power in their countries of origins, impacted Asian parents' perception of classical music as elite and prestigious. Many parents viewed amassing the cultural capital of classical music as a yardstick to measure socioeconomic gains on both individual and collective levels, broadly linking the growing popularity of classical music among Chinese and Koreans with the economic ascension of East Asian nations. Such a connection emerged clearly in my interview with Sookhyun, a recent Korean immigrant at the time of our interview. While she had studied some piano during her youth, she noted that this was uncommon for those of her generation, since "my country was not rich enough to educate everyone in piano" at the time. As she elaborated, those who had access to classical music training were "mostly more educated people . . . and more money. You have to have instruments. And at that time, most families could not afford that."[66] However, with the improved Korean economy, she noticed that piano playing had become more commonplace, almost a prerequisite activity for children of middle- and upper-middle-class families: "Piano is very popular. Most of persons, they are not good pianists. But they know how to play a little bit."

While she did not listen to much classical music during her childhood, Sookhyun recalled frequenting places specifically devoted to that activity while in college: "At that time, our age, classical music was very special, a very prestige kind of thing. I mean somebody who is very special can do it. We thought like that. It's not like regular people cannot enjoy or have, but our generation, we really liked to hear the classical music; we had some kind of place [*laughs*] we can actually sit and listen to music. You know, like tearooms or something? But it's just for listener.

Classical listeners. We pay, and then we go in there and listen to music." The tearooms described here provided distinct places for Sookhyun and her friends to distinguish themselves from "regular people" by consuming this "very special" music. While she laughed recollecting the aura of exclusivity attached to classical music during her youth, her perception of the music as a "very prestige kind of thing" continued to influence her sense of class and cultural identity living in the United States. This remained the case even if (or perhaps because) the music does not hold quite the same significations in the United States.

Parents who did not grow up listening to classical music described gaining an appreciation for the music through their involvement in their child's musical activities. By articulating a link between Western classical music and education, Asian parents sought to provide evidence of their sophistication and edification, precisely those traits that, as racialized immigrants, they are viewed as not possessing. Many parents emphasized the seeming erudition required to comprehend classical music. For example, Christine observed that she had little exposure to classical music growing up in Hong Kong and mainly listened to Chinese popular music; as she put it, "Most of the time classical music is hard to understand. It takes education. It's not like pop music that has an easy 1-2-3 beat. You really have to have a lot of knowledge about classical music to appreciate it." This changed, however, over the course of her child's musical development.

> I learn it from my kid. . . . I don't like classical music in Hong Kong. It's not, I don't like; [it's that] I don't have any exposure to it. So yeah. I like the [Chinese popular music]. [*laughs*] . . . But now I know a little bit about the technique, and the color, and when I listen to classical music I can understand better. You know, I don't know *how* to understand classical music before. That's why I have no idea what is classical music. Even though I listen, I don't feel anything. But now I can usually listen [and think] beautiful sound, play very well, or technique, those kinds of things. So for me, I feel advantage I can understand better.

Reinforcing a cultural hierarchy that places popular music below classical music, Christine now felt herself capable of distinguishing subtle differences in musical techniques and styles and to "feel" something when she listened to the music. She articulated her deeper understanding of classical music as an "advantage"—an unexpected cultural benefit accrued through her child. Christine, as well as her child, accumulated cultural capital through her family's intense investment in musical training.[67]

Interestingly, declining interest in and value paid to elite cultural forms in the contemporary U.S. context served to fortify a sense of distinction for Asian parents. Indeed, the belief that most Americans do not appreciate classical music allowed Asian parents to interpret their own interest in this elite yet marginalized cultural field as setting themselves apart from—if not above—mainstream American norms and values. For instance, Mrs. Lai articulated a hierarchical distinction between herself and Americans, contending that "Americans normally like fast food, fast-paced society; people don't want to spend the effort, take the time to love classical music. They love something instant. . . . I don't know, maybe it's the Taiwanese standard, like we are more scholar type of family, or more pay attention to culture; we like to keep a higher society." Mrs. Lai viewed her interest in scholarly and "cultured" pursuits such as classical music as distinguishing her from the massified culture of instant gratification she perceived most Americans as normally inhabiting. She held little interest in assimilating into the "fast food" culture of America, aiming instead to affiliate with what she believed to be universalizing modes of elite culture. Mrs. Lai selectively mobilized ideas around what it means to be Asian/Taiwanese and American to consolidate and aspire toward a class and racial identity associated with putatively higher cultural and intellectual tastes.[68]

The perception that Americans enjoy instant gratification and that Asians prefer a higher society surfaced repeatedly in my interviews with Asian parents. One can discern, for instance, a sense of superiority emerging in Nami's articulation of the differences that exist between Asians and Americans through her comparison of band versus orchestra.

> Not just here [at Juilliard], but also in orchestra, even public school, so many members in orchestra are Asian kids because American kids, they do not have the discipline. They have parties, they have play dates, they have soccer games, outside activities, lots of activities outside. But for music you have to sacrifice. American families cannot do it. . . . So there is orchestra group and band group. Band you don't have to practice a lot, but it's easy to play. . . . You see more American kids in band group. But Asian kids more statistically, you see in orchestra, because they have discipline so well.

Nami's hierarchical understanding of band as easy and orchestra as rigorous facilitated a process of socialization into the United States through a perceived sense of cultural distinction. Her characterization of these differences contextualize the relatively low representation of Asian Americans in fields beyond classical music. Thus, while "American" families might regard play dates and soccer games as necessary to create "well-rounded" children, in the eyes of Asian families these activities neither held cultural capital nor encouraged children to appreciate the importance of sacrifice and discipline. Nami seemed content to yield to American families the multitude of "activities outside" that, in her view, did not place value in hard work.

These remarks about the professed superiority of Asian parents' work ethic and cultural sophistication should not be interpreted as mere elaborations of racial or ethnic conceit. Rather, they are expressions of class, race, and linguistic anxieties on the part of racialized immigrants confronting economic barriers and cultural exclusion. Living in a nation where downward mobility, racism, and language discrimination represent a constant reality, Asian parents viewed their investment in classical music as evidence of their intellect and edification—attributes that, as racialized immigrants who do not necessarily speak English fluently, they are not always perceived as holding. While white and Asian parents alike perceived their intense involvement in classical music to be distinct from the interests of the American mainstream, Asian parents faced additional racial barriers to converting their cultural capital into other forms of social or economic capital.[69]

While the Asian parents I interviewed maintained a familiar rhetoric about the democratic promise of the United States and refused to linger on the difficulties they encountered, references to the obstacles they faced as racialized immigrants nonetheless surfaced in our interviews. As Nami acknowledged, "It's a lot of silence. But even kids, Asian kids born here, my daughter say silent but there's racism. But even racism, it's in our own country [Korea]. So we have to survive. This is America, best country all over the world." Her observation suggests an astute understanding of the unspoken and often unacknowledged racism that structures the experiences of racialized immigrants and even their offspring "born here." And while her choice of the word "survive" hints at these adversities, she also rhetorically silences them, emphasizing that racism is not unique to the United States. Reverting to the more celebratory narrative of America as the "best country all over the world," Nami tailors her remarks to the image of a model immigrant subject who does not excessively complain or appear ungrateful for the opportunities provided by the host nation. In this sense, she conforms to what sociologist Lisa Park aptly describes as the "adaptation strategy of the 'good immigrant,'" which places pressure on racialized immigrants to continually prove themselves as being worthy of inclusion, cultural citizenship, and equal rights in the United States.[70]

While my interviewees affirmed dominant narratives of meritocracy, fairness, and hard work, they also referenced the downward mobility experienced by skilled and educated Asians immigrating to the United States. Pointing to language shortcomings as the most significant obstacle confronting Asians immigrants in the United States, Jean Hee noted: "The parents are more educated, the Asian parents. They are here, but they're not doing the—how can I say?—they are kind of middle class here, or lower middle class. But when they are in their own country they belong to the high class, more educated. The only thing is that language is a problem here." While Jean Hee only mentions linguistic factors as an obstacle, we can contextualize the experiences she describes within a broader understanding of race and language discrimination in U.S. settings. Residing in a monolingual nation that correlates English fluency (and American-accented English) with national belonging, racialized immigrants' language deficits map onto broader beliefs about intelligence, competency, and race.[71] Investing in musical practices aligned with elite cultural distinction allowed "more educated" Asian parents to project social identities that affirmed what they felt to be their (and their children's) rightful place on the American social landscape. They sought to distinguish themselves from their working-class counterparts by demonstrating their "high class" tastes. At the same time, Jean Hee's comments reflect an anxiety that no amount of cultural capital accumulated by upwardly mobile Asian immigrants will prevent a demotion in social and economic status in the United States.

Despite maintaining an association between classical music and cultural prestige, many parents recognized that their involvement in music did not necessarily translate into perceptions of high cultural status in the United States. Nami, for instance, acknowledged that "Americans" tended to perceive her actions less as an interest in the aesthetic value of music and more as evidence of an overzealous drive to push her kids to achieve success. She recognized that her view of what constituted "good" parenting and success did not necessarily align with mainstream "white" standards (or even those of her children).[72] Nami, too, worried about the unintended consequences that could result from placing overly demanding expectations on her children. Nonetheless, she was unwilling and, in her estimation, unable to change her ways.

> You know, the teacher is American. He does not want to involve parents. Said to me, "[Your daughter] goes to college; are you going to college too? Why are you coming [to the lesson]?" So I just let him say. But, especially music, parents have to be involved. . . . When I look at it, I'm a Korean even if I'm here twenty-six years and my children are born here, educated in American school culture. I am a Korean, so somehow I'm too pushy and demanding. I cannot ignore that. It's much more weak than [more recent Chinese or Korean immigrants] but, still, same feel. So sometimes, teenager age, [my daughter] is very against it actually. So then I realize something; if I got to push to my kid more than that, it's going to be a lot of damage, a lot of damage over the lifetime. I don't want to push too hard. So American family they push, but they can't. They have such a limit. But Asian kids, even here, second, third generation, they do so well. Especially in music.

Despite expressing ambivalence about how her parental style might create conflicts and undue burdens on the child with damages unfurling over a lifetime, Nami continued to affirm what she perceived to be its positive results. At the same time, the internal conflicts she articulated about the costs of her parenting strategy on her child (and on their relationship) speak to the ongoing anxieties she feels about proper modes of parenting.

The fame achieved by such musicians as Kyung-wha Chung, Midori, Lang Lang, and Yo-Yo Ma creates the perception that classical music is a site where Asians and Asian Americans can achieve success and recognition on an international scale. For this reason, Asian parents perceive classical music to be a field wherein their children face fewer barriers and where talent can potentially be fully rewarded. Classical music, in this sense, becomes a small but potentially viable avenue through which to achieve exceptional distinction and fame. Such a sentiment emerges in Sookhyun's comments.

> I think maybe in Korea, there's not many people who are famous worldwide. But a few classical musicians, they are very famous worldwide. And they think, that kind of person is very special . . . [we think] they succeed. So if somebody wants to be real famous worldwide, there's not many chances in other fields, but in music they see some few people and they think maybe they can be like that. And they all dream like that, I think. And they think that their children has so much talent, and if they put much effort, then maybe they can be like them.

> *Do you dream like that too?*

> I think so, I think so. [*laughs*] Yeah, and also they have so many difficulties living in America. Being minorities, they have to be somebody. They have to have their profession, or have to be somebody, so everybody cannot ignore them and they can have their right treatment from somebody.

Here, we can read Sookhyun's remarks as giving expression to the aspirational desires sought but not always met by racialized immigrants living in the United States. While she demarcates classical music as one of the few professions in which Koreans have achieved success globally, she locates her remarks within a specific understanding of the difficulties that Korean immigrants and minorities more broadly encounter living in the United States. Sookhyun's assertion that one has to "be somebody" to garner respect and "right treatment" reveals an astute awareness of racial hierarchies operating in the United States, including the fact that racialized minorities continue to "have so many difficulties" living in the United States. In this sense, we can interpret Asian parents' intense striving to accumulate economic and cultural capital as a relentless attempt to compensate for invisibility: "So everybody cannot ignore them." Sookhyun linked the efforts of Asian parents pushing their children to attain musical success with the desire for recognition in an elite cultural field that circulates within and beyond the United States. To gain visibility in the global culture of classical music—a cultural field guided by the standards of the West—would, according to this logic, elevate the racial position of Asians in the United States and "worldwide." In so doing, Sookhyun demonstrates the ways in which Asian parents mobilize the potentials of Western classical music in their efforts to negotiate the racialized terrain of the United States.

Conclusion

When Mrs. Kim, cited at the outset of this chapter, states that her "first priority is Yoon Jee," it is worth noting that her daughter cringed in response. Yoon Jee's discomfort suggests the extent to which her mother's narrative does not necessarily match her own and the degree to which Mrs. Kim's bluntly stated comments evoke disquieting stereotypes about racial difference. As the next chapter shows, Asian American classical musicians possess a very different relationship to music making, one that often runs counter to the stated desires of their parents. The motivations articulated by the parents in this chapter are not necessarily perceived, understood, or narrated in quite the same ways by their children.

This chapter demonstrated how Asian parents reinforce sweeping generalizations about the sacrifice and discipline of "Asians" and the individualism and laziness of "Americans" to rationalize the success that Asians and Asian Americans have achieved in classical music. However, these articulations of racial difference do not represent a mere reproduction of dominant ideologies or empty claims of "Asian" superiority. Rather, they should also be understood as an engagement with, and reformulation of, a range of racialized beliefs placed upon Asians—as model minorities, as "yellow peril" masses overtaking fields in which they implicitly do not belong, and as racialized immigrants unable to speak the language of English and Western high culture with fluency, ease, and ownership. Asian parents selectively draw on these discourses to position themselves, their cultural tastes, and their parenting styles as superior to their American counterparts. In the process, they reframe learning classical music—a Western cultural system long imbricated in global struggles over power, modernization, and imperialism—as an "Asian" cultural practice. They recast Asians and Asian Americans as the rightful inheritors of this field of high culture and resignify the pursuit of classical music as an implicit means of preserving an "Asian" identity in the face of mass American culture.

Assimilation and incorporation into the "fast food" culture of the United States does not appear to be the ultimate goal of the middle- and upper-class parents I interviewed. Rather, they seek to insert themselves and their children into a universalizing field of culture that they believe will generate the greatest degree of cultural capital for their investment. Race and class anxieties, and an awareness of their status as racialized subjects in a nation structured by nativism and racism, underpin the choices they make and the rationale they use to explain their decisions. Asian parents seek to levy the cultural capital they gain through classical music against the racist structures that make class demotion and invisibility a constant reality they experience as racialized immigrants living in the United States.

Ironically, it might be the increasing marginality of classical music in the United States that has allowed Asians and Asian Americans greater access to, and visibility within, this field of high culture over the past few decades. As the next chapter shows, many musicians I interviewed noted the shrinking and graying audiences for classical music and the diminished cultural value and relevance the music holds for most contemporary Americans. In this light, it is worth questioning whether Asian parents' lack of cultural fluency and their outsider status in the United States lead them to misapprehend the amount of cultural capital that can be accrued through classical music training. It may be that the increasing participation of Asian Americans in classical music has merely re-entrenched prevailing stereotypes about Asian parents as excessively pushy, competitive, status-driven, and overbearing and Asian Americans as model minority subjects who are culturally distinct from their normative and allegedly more balanced American counterparts. Rather than provide evidence of their sophisticated tastes, cultured lifestyle, and cerebral pursuits, Asian American achievement in classical music becomes further testimony of their disciplined and diligent nature. The conundrum of race and white privilege may be that as Asian Americans gain cultural fluency in Western classical music—that is, as classical music training becomes racialized (and increasingly stereotyped) as an "Asian" practice—the cultural capital yielded by that form of culture is devalued.

The multiple narratives generated by and about "music moms" expose the complex routes through which race, class, and cultural hierarchy circulate in classical music specifically and the broader U.S. landscape generally. If, on the surface, Asian and Asian American participation in classical music threatens to reinforce stereotypical perceptions about essentialized racial differences, further examination reveals the ways in which the participants themselves actively mobilize these notions in their own struggles over power, transcultural exchange, class mobility, and identity. Refusing their status as interlopers, "music moms" assert their own cultural and personal agency in the face of racialized discourses imposed upon them and, in the process, reformulate the boundaries of Western high culture and their place within that sphere.

TWO

"This Is No Monkey Show"

Racializing Musical Performance

When Keng-yuen was eighteen, he put aside his violin for six months. The child of a violin teacher, he left Taiwan for New York at the age of thirteen to live with a host family and pursue his musical studies. While he practiced diligently and excelled on the instrument, music did not necessarily feel like his own chosen path. As the violinist recalled:

> After a concert, a couple of old ladies said, "You know that young boy plays very well, but I don't remember a thing that he played. It's very technical but there's not a lot of feeling or music at all." And that hit me like a ton of bricks. And I immediately realized, "If there's no music, why the hell are you playing the violin? This is no monkey show." So I stopped playing for six months to see if I still wanted to play after that. I still did, and six months later I looked at music entirely different. And that's when my music came.

Keng-yuen's account of how his "music came" repeats a familiar narrative that musicians tell about finding their own passion for music outside of the external expectations placed on them. His statement "this is no monkey show" locates music making as the antithesis of imitation and technical wizardry. By taking a short break from his instrument, he gained an "entirely different" perspective on music, including an understanding of musical performance as the personal expression of self.

Keng-yuen's use of the phrase "monkey show" is telling, for it implies a performance aimed at pleasing others. A trained monkey executes a repertoire of tricks through learned behaviors and reinforcement. While the performance is amusing and entertaining, lurking beneath the appearance of domestication is the threat of danger— a wild and unpredictable nature that can potentially veer out of control. In this way, the term *monkey show* evokes an image that approximates the function of racialized constructions placed upon Asians and Asian Americans in classical music specifically and in the U.S. racial imaginary generally. They are, according to stereotype, superb technicians whose impressive arsenal of skills cannot fully compensate for the lack of an original mind. These stock narratives persist even as they are constantly undone, contradicted, and upended by the nuanced musicality and creativity of the many "exceptional" Asian and Asian American performers populating the classical music world.

While the heightened visibility of Asians and Asian Americans in classical music has made their presence normative and extolled, it has also re-entrenched particular racial ideologies, especially those intersecting model minority and "yellow peril" mythologies. Armed with the "unfair" advantage of a compulsive work ethic and overbearing parents, Asians and Asian Americans threaten to overtake their competitors in a field of culture that is not even implicitly their own. At the same time, charges of overrepresentation notwithstanding, Asian and Asian American musicians continue to be courted and desired, particularly by U.S. music schools, which depend on their talent and tuition dollars to fill their student rosters. As such, classical music represents an apt space in which to understand how success morphs into threat— how anxieties about overrepresentation trigger "yellow peril" anxieties that, in turn, contain Asian and Asian American achievement.

I begin this chapter with Keng-yuen's description of his musical development to highlight how his music making goals differ from those articulated by Asian parents. The previous chapter analyzed the disciplining mechanisms, racial ideologies, and colonial legacies embedded in the U.S. culture of classical music and their manifestations in the racial and musical discourses that structure U.S. media accounts about Asians and Asian Americans in this field. These racialized scripts rely on a broader cultural logic of Asian difference that Asian "music parents" themselves use to signal their distinction from normative "Americans." More than expressions of arrogance, however, the narratives of Asian parents should be placed within the context of exclusions they encounter as racialized immigrants living in the United States.

While the "Asian parent" is a familial figure that places particular demands and expectations on the second generation, it is also a stock figure flexibly mobilized to embody "Asian" values of hard work, discipline, and filial respect at the core of model minority narratives. In this sense, the "Asian parent" represents both a real and symbolic entity that provokes feelings of ambivalence among Asian American classical musicians. Moreover, while the investment that Asian parents make in classical music depends on an understanding of this cultural field as elite and prestigious, such an emphasis can be the source of further unease in their children. For not only do such associations reify views of classical music as archaic, dull, and culturally irrelevant to most Americans, but they also emphasize status rather than the passion and desire for self-expression that Asian American musicians narrate as their primary reason for pursuing music professionally (often against their parents' expressed wishes).

This chapter examines how Asian American practitioners of classical music navigate a cultural, musical, and national landscape replete with racialized perceptions about their musicianship, personality, family background, and presence. I analyze how Asian American classical musicians manage, accommodate, and, at times, capitalize upon divergent racial beliefs placed on them by music professionals, audiences, and the professionalization apparatus often referred to as the business side of music. Although many musicians I interviewed claimed that race does not enter into assessments of playing, they all acknowledged the manifold ways that race and other social factors intrude upon the business of music, particularly given the limited specialized knowledge that many audience members bring to classical music performances.[1]

On the one hand, the visible presence of and success achieved by Asians and Asian Americans in classical music can make claims of racial discrimination and minority status in this field seem counterintuitive, if not unwarranted, a stance that emerged frequently in my interviews. My interviewees consistently affirmed democratizing views that talent and musical skill are rewarded equally, that competition represents an equalizing force, and that the emotions and values reflected in classical music are universal. They cited the international prominence of musicians such as cellist Yo Yo Ma, pianist Lang Lang, and violinist Midori as evidence that racial barriers do not exist in classical music. On the other hand, such disavowals of racism should not suggest that Asian Americans do not experience classical music to be a highly racialized field of culture. Evading questions of identity and refusing to wage complaints of racism may well represent effective strategies that Asian Americans use to secure success and legitimacy within the inherited parameters of this musical field. By downplaying the significance of their Asianness, Asian and Asian American musicians distance themselves from the negative characterizations associated with "Asian" playing while also assimilating to the view that race does not matter in this cultural field. And yet unease about a wide range of tacit assumptions about belonging, inheritance, and cultural difference regularly emerged in my interviews. My interviewees articulated further discomfort with perceptions that Asians and Asian Americans are overrepresented and undifferentiable, particularly since such presumptions stripped them of their individuality—a quality prized in classical music performance—and framed them instead as the embodiment of a stereotype. Although the field has changed in the wake of demographic shifts, what we see rather than an emergent color-blind inclusion are newly refigured racial metaphors and tropes structuring the U.S. culture of classical music.

Through an analysis of the narratives that Asian and Asian American musicians tell about the nature of their success and belonging in classical music, this chapter investigates how ideas about musical talent and labor are racialized in a cultural field that paradoxically insists that race does not matter. Investigating how race circulates in a field of culture guided by discourses of color blindness, universalism, and meritocracy allows for a broader understanding of the maintenance of racial hierarchies in a U.S. cultural landscape where claims about the decreasing significance of race abound.[2] As I show, within the field of classical music, racialized beliefs are embedded in the discursive frameworks used to discuss, interpret, and evaluate musical texts and performances. How individuals hear and make musical judgments are shaped by grids of ideology that exist within and beyond the realm of classical music. Contextualizing the negative associations attached to sounding or playing like an "Asian," this chapter reveals the conundrum that Asian and Asian American musicians confront in their pursuit of a "universal" sound. Their Asianness, while for the most part visually inescapable, must remain sonically invisible. And yet, playing at the "universal" level can also make Asian American classical musicians suspect, subject to such backhanded compliments as, despite their Asian background, their music making sounds innate.

While stereotypes in classical music typically refer to the "Asian" musician, with little distinction made between different Asian ethnic groups, my interviewees acknowledged their wide-ranging application to Asian Americans. As one violinist put it, "People don't really differentiate. We all look the same, especially onstage." Within the U.S. culture of classical music, the *idea* of Asian American foreignness is heightened by the large international presence of East Asians pursuing music training and professional careers in the United States. While the paths and backgrounds of Asian and Asian American musicians often differ, they converge in the United States in the racialized assumptions placed on them. At the same time, the practicality of fixing precise boundaries between "Asian" and "Asian American" can be tricky, particularly when discussing the experiences of foreign-born musicians who, despite being long-term residents of the United States or possessing U.S. citizenship, do not identify as "Asian American" but rather as their specific Asian ethnicity. While I shift between the terms *Asian* and *Asian American* in this chapter, I am mindful of how the conceptual overlap merging these terms is shaped by a longer legacy of racism that frames Asian Americans as not quite American, within and beyond the realm of music.[3]

Performing Western Classical Music

To understand more fully how racial ideas circulate in classical music, it is helpful first to outline the context in which most classical music making takes place in the United States. Within the established norms of the Western concert tradition, the composer occupies the highest realm of musical genius and creativity. As such, the performer's primary role is to reproduce faithful interpretations of the original musical text. They are not supposed to improvise on or deviate from the written notes and musical markings on the composer's original text. Individuality and expressiveness—qualities used to evaluate musical caliber and feeling— are bound within a strict framework of what constitutes a purportedly correct interpretation based on the musical style, historical period, and cultural context in which the composition first emerged.[4] As one of my interviewees noted, "It can be constraining. There are a lot of rules. You have to think, 'Oh there's a dot over that note' or 'What does that dynamic marking mean?' A lot of [musical interpretation] is about trying to figure out what the composer had in mind." Within these boundaries, however, performers often describe the search to understand the inner workings of a composer's mind as a process that can encompass an entire lifetime of creative and rewarding study. According to the logic of high culture, the great (usually dead, male, European) composers who make up the core canon of the Western concert tradition possess the continued capacity to surprise and transport us—both listeners and performers alike—to new realms and revelations about the human spirit.

To deepen their understanding of a particular work, musicians frequently search for clues from the composer and the broader context of the composition. For instance, violinist Nai-yuan remarked that his interest in playing a particular work by Bach developed only after he learned more about the composer's motivation for the piece. As he elaborated:

> For the longest time, I didn't know what I wanted to do with it. . . . Only until four years ago, I found some materials that somebody was saying about Bach's Chaconne being written as a memorial to his first wife who passed away, and it struck me [because] the standard approach of playing it with open strings was something I was never convinced about.[5] It was loud and didn't seem right for the style of the period. So I was never convinced of that . . . and not until three or four years ago did I find this way to approach this music, this very personal way, and only now do I have an interest to play Bach.

Acquiring this new insight allowed the violinist to feel closer to the musical work and to find a "very personal way" to express himself. This communication of self was, as he put it, the very definition of being a musician: "To play music you have to think of what you want, what you believe in. . . . *That's* a musician."

Violinist Midori similarly reflected on the musical inspiration derived from the social and cultural contexts in which the composer lived. She explained that studying words and phrases in the composer's native tongue, for example, provided insight into the parallels between spoken and musical language: "For instance, Bartok. His music is closely related to Hungarian diction and all that. Sometimes I do think about it. . . . I always learn by the words, and sometimes I think it's by the way the language sounds, the diction, the breathing, or the nasalness of that language, that I try to incorporate in my music making when I play it on the violin. So in a way it's so closely related to language." Midori's meditation on the overlapping realms of words, diction, and music highlights both the critical role that the composer plays as the primary source of inspiration as well as the assumed links between the musical text and the soundscapes of nation and language. Knowledge about the composer's motivations and influences, along with a mastery of the notes, allowed the violinist to craft a musical interpretation that was faithful to the original work while also carrying her unique musical imprint.

The musicians I interviewed frequently referenced the lengthy process of practice, reflection, and learning that informed their music making while also voicing the view that many subtleties of musicianship are lost on the majority of the listening public. Not only is the U.S. classical music market small, but my interviewees felt that even within this limited group many did not care for or appreciate the music beyond the trappings of elite cultural value. This, not coincidentally, was also a critique that some of my interviewees waged against their parents, whom they viewed as motivated less by a love for the music than a combination, as one cellist put it, of the "status thing" and the belief that "classical music shows you're erudite or more intelligent than others."

All of the musicians I interviewed spoke passionately about the professional difficulties that classical musicians encounter in the United States given the shrinking and graying of audiences, the decline in radio stations devoted to classical music programming, and the steady decrease in arts education funding in public schools.[6] They further lamented the perception that the "general public" has of classical music as elitist, old-fashioned, and uptight—as a "white man's game" that lacked any cultural relevance to people's everyday lives. My interviews were punctuated with descriptions such as the following: "Most people think what we do is museum stuff and that the composers, what they write is very esoteric or very difficult for listening. . . . In America it's like, 'Classical music? What's that?' They don't respect it."[7] Such an observation reveals an understanding of how the exclusivity attached to classical music imbues it with prestige and aesthetic value while simultaneously making it appear ossified and archaic. Much has been written about the extent of and reasons for the declining market for classical music in the United States.[8] These ongoing debates form a critical backdrop within the musical lives of all of my interviewees, even while they remained uncertain about how best to counter such concerns.

Wen, a violinist with the Metropolitan Opera Orchestra, felt that given the incommensurability between codified performance practices and the quickened pace of contemporary life, wholesale changes were necessary to halt the dwindling public interest in classical music. "Now, it's a very different environment," she reflected. "You have Internet. TV with two hundred channels. Fast-actioned movies going on. So why would you rather see a concert that sometimes the musicians are not even into? You think, 'What are you going to get out of it?' It's like go there. Take a nap. And spend $200." Rather than yielding cerebral and contemplative reflection, Wen suggested that the ritual of behaviors regulating "proper" consumption and appreciation of classical music creates environments so sluggish as to encourage napping. Moreover, she intimated that musicians themselves, bored with the repetition of performing the same core repertoire and/or the anonymity that defines orchestral labor, sometimes communicate disinterest to audiences. During our interview she recollected reading early in her career a *New York Times* article that placed the job satisfaction and happiness of New York Philharmonic orchestra members on par with prison employees.[9] While asserting that such dissatisfaction was "pathetic"—particularly compared to the racialized labor she engaged in briefly as a dishwasher and delivery person for a Chinese restaurant when she first arrived in the United States from China—Wen nonetheless understood how the priority placed on individuality and self-expression in classical music can lead to discontent over the collective nature of orchestra work.[10]

In contrast to the contemporary moment, many of my interviewees idealized the early part of the twentieth century as the "golden period"—a time when commerce and art seemed less intertwined and classical music performances were regarded, as Keng-yuen put it, as "the greatest thing that people could hear or see." His characterization of this period as an era when cultural distinctions were fixed and sanctified, classical music embodied the deepest and most sublime expression of humanity, and the nation's social and intellectual elite shared an interest in appreciating and upholding the value of high culture, corresponds historically with the institutionalization of cultural hierarchies in the United States.[11] While Keng-yuen was likely articulating nostalgia for a romanticized version of the past, he was not alone in voicing frustration over the pressure that musicians now face to "sell" classical music to an increasingly disinterested public.[12] Violinist Nai-yuan similarly affirmed that "for me, the golden age will always be the first part of the twentieth century, the days before television, when people really learned how to listen carefully. . . . Now, individually it's hard to differentiate one's self musically as different, so [musicians] tend to do other things to compete, from their publicity photo or other things to attract people." His observation suggests that the struggle that musicians encounter attempting to differentiate themselves on the basis of music alone stems from the lack of a cultivated and knowledgeable audience able to discern individuality as expressed through musicianship alone. The limited market and relevance of classical music represented a source of "huge frustration" for musicians, many of whom began to learn their craft at a very young age. Ming, a violinist with the Metropolitan Opera Orchestra, lamented: "You look at pop music and you just can't compare. Nobody's buying [classical music] records, and considering the amount of effort we put into it from so young. It starts to make you sick if you think about it. [*laughs*] Ridiculous." He was not the only musician to express cynicism for having devoted a lifetime of practice and training to work in such a highly segmented market.

Like other high cultural fields in the United States, the classical music industry is grappling with the challenges of continuing to appeal to a core audience while also democratizing its consumer base, adopting new marketing strategies, and developing alternate methods and technologies to distribute and perform music. Understanding the context in which classical music making takes place in the United States allows for a greater understanding of how such social categories as race accrue meaning in this field of culture. Place, composer, and musical interpretation are closely entwined, a factor that impacts implicit beliefs about native understanding and belonging. At the same time, anxieties about a dwindling marketplace and the commodification of musicians introduce race and other social factors as elements through which performances/performers are marketed and sold.

Race, Talent, and Skill

While Asian and Asian American musicians have found tremendous success in classical music, it continues to remain a site that reaffirms ideas about racial/cultural difference. The assertions made by the musicians I interviewed exemplify the contradictory logic contained in their beliefs that music is a meritocratic culture wherein race does not matter *and* that race is a feature which differentiates one's playing and position in this field of culture. While the musicians I interviewed frequently drew on discourses about the universality of music to buttress beliefs about the irrelevance of race, they also pointed to material practices such as blind auditions to corroborate claims that classical musicians are judged solely on skill. In blind auditions—a practice instituted by most major symphony orchestras beginning in the 1970s and 1980s—musicians play behind a screen (with shoes taken off or a carpet laid out to remove the detection of a "gendered" gait) that conceals their identity completely. While such practices are themselves premised on the existence of politics, they have since helped to blunt claims of racism, sexism, and/or favoritism in the hiring process. Studies have shown that the advent of blind auditions has helped "orchestrate impartiality" in the hiring process, increasing by 50 percent the probability that a woman candidate will advance to the next round and by severalfold that a woman will win the job in the final round.[13] Beyond these quantifiable effects, blind auditions engender beliefs that a level playing field should (and does) exist as the desired default position while also countering assumptions that race and/or other social categories leave audible traces in one's musicianship. As the late violin teacher Dorothy DeLay once stated: "If you have musicians play behind a screen, I would defy anyone to pick Asians out."[14] Still, while blind auditions have been praised for creating an "equal playing field" for musicians, it is worth emphasizing that they do little to confront the barriers that racial minorities (particularly African Americans and Latinos) face in access and opportunity prior to the audition process.[15]

However, most music making does not occur behind a screen. While asserting the absence of explicit discrimination, all of my interviewees could easily rattle off stereotypes that circulate about Asian musicians, suggesting that the racialized terrain has become accepted as part of the context in which they make music. My interviews were laced with observations such as the following: "[Asians] are always in the practice room working to get things right, but they don't have an emotional connection to the music" and "Some people want to assign Asian Americans with an assembly-line mentality, even toward music." As such views, along with the media representations analyzed in the previous chapter, underscore, the hours of focused practice that classical music training requires lend themselves to reproducing a range of racialized beliefs about Asians and Asian Americans.

These stereotypical characterizations extend beyond the realm of musicianship to encompass a broader set of assumptions about the background, and personality traits, of different groups. Take, for instance, the following informal taxonomy of music students offered by Mary Gray, the admissions director of Juilliard's college and graduate divisions:

> If one is asked to generalize, it may be said that there are three major categories of music students (and several minor categories!). First the Eastern European student, who has tremendous confidence and flair, and often comes from a really difficult situation where musical training has been something that they achieved at great personal cost and little financial backing. These are kids who approach the process with great intensity to get what they want; they know what they want.
>
> Second are American students brought up through the system. Usually they have tremendous amount of family or community support, a lot more confidence, a more integrated approach. They've been to good schools and many come through performing arts schools, have been in a youth symphony or community system, and have traveled to pre-college programs on weekends.
>
> Third is the Asian student, whose family was single-minded from birth about instrumental education. They tend not to be as well rounded; in some cases, the academics may fall by the wayside. The arts have been chosen as the road to success, and this is what you're going to do and this is what you're going to focus on. It's more the Asian-American student who might consider going to Harvard, as an undergraduate and Juilliard as graduate. To those from Asia, Juilliard has been a goal since third grade. It takes a little while to sort out for those kids whether it's their own idea, or whether it's parental pressure.[16]

Gray's admittedly generalizing remarks reveal the type of stock characterizations and banter around race and ethnicity that circulates in classical music. Such perceptions, falling along racial and geographical divides, make up part of the spoken (and unspoken) climate of conservatory culture, impacting the narratives available to understand differences that emerge among students. Gray herself selects from and reinforces familiar racial and national/geographic discourses to categorize students. Eastern European students possess "confidence and flair" and an intense personal drive that stems from overcoming adversity. American students (an unmarked category that implies whiteness) are nurtured through a more balanced and "integrated approach." And finally, Asian students tend to be narrowly focused, burdened by family pressures that muddle individual and parental ambitions. Only the "Asian student" emphasizes line of descent from birth. Gray's imprecise positioning of Asian Americans—excluded from the category "American" but grouped with (and also in contrast to) Asian students—encapsulates the ambiguous racial positioning of Asian Americans in the U.S. racial imaginary. Here, as elsewhere, Asian Americans are identified racially first and nationally second—categories that often seem incompatible in subtle, implicit ways.

The perceptions about Asians and Asian Americans in the U.S. culture of classical music cannot be separated from growing anxieties over the specter of increasing Asian dominance and unease about their seeming overrepresentation in a range of fields over the past few decades. In 1989, Michael Ishii and Emma Moon, two Asian American students enrolled at Juilliard at the time, wrote an editorial for the *Juilliard Journal* exposing what they described as a climate of racial resentment against Asians and Asian Americans.

> At Juilliard, some students feel that Asians are over represented in the school, and so they do not consider Asians or especially Asian Americans to be a minority group. But to belong to a racial minority group is not just a matter of numbers. It is a matter of perceptions and treatment. For instance, many people think that Asians are fashioned to fit the stereotype of the prodigious, "conscientious and diligent." . . . Often, white Americans view Asians as exotic people who all look alike and can't speak English correctly. If you see Asians speaking their own language, don't accuse them of being exclusive,

foreign, inaccessible; don't say they came to America to overtake it, culturally and economically; and don't say they don't belong, because they do belong. Racism like this occurs so frequently that it may not seem like racism. But it is.[17]

In their outspoken and public remarks, Ishii and Moon contend that seemingly insignificant remarks referring to Asians and Asian Americans as foreigners, model subjects, and invasive masses have become so entrenched and accepted that they seem like articulations of shared understanding rather than racism. Their observations surface a central contention about what constitutes racism and minority status and compel readers to reconsider whether Asians and Asian Americans can claim an experience akin to racism in a field of culture in which they enjoy success and are abundantly "over represented." The perception that racism entails explicit barriers to access and opportunities and that minority status correlates with lack of privilege and disenfranchisement led my musician interviewees to make contradictory statements about the relevance of race in their music making. Yet, if racism includes more than overt acts of discrimination but also tacit assumptions about proprietary ownership and belonging, it is clear that the classical music community is marred by racism.

Here it is worth investigating how the discursive framework of overrepresentation itself suggests that Asians and Asian Americans have somehow exceeded their rightful place—a presence no longer signaling pleasing racial diversity but rather an unsettling capacity to outperform their white counterparts. As Ghassan Hage deftly observes, debates about overrepresentation embody contestations over the proper management of space: "Concepts such as 'too many' are meaningless unless they assume the existence of a specific territorial space against which the evaluation 'too many' is arrived."[18] While Hage's discussion centers around the white backlash against migrant settlement (specifically Asian and Muslim) in Australia, his observations resonate within the U.S. culture of classical music, where allegations of "too many" similarly imply that an ideal configuration exists with whiteness at its implicit core. Put differently, those who are most authentically qualified to dominate the field—those who have, to paraphrase the violinist Isaac Stern, lived and breathed Western music for hundreds of years—ought to retain the right to admit and include "others" at their behest.[19] The

encroachment of "foreign" bodies at the ranks of students, practitioners, and performers —an "Asian invasion" more threatening in perception than in numbers—is magnified by a concomitant feeling of loss,
an impression of dwindling control and authority.[20] The discourse of
white disenfranchisement extends beyond classical music to other sites
where nonwhites are perceived as having claimed (or desired) too much
and, through their presence, altered the values and belief systems of
that space.[21]

We see how the descriptor "too Asian" has been similarly mobilized
to register and contain racial anxieties in other realms.[22] For instance,
media coverage of the "new white flight"—white families who leave
high-achieving suburban school districts that have become heavily populated with Asian American families—depict Asian American students
as having transformed public schools into excessively competitive environments. In such scenarios, Asian Americans are said to place their
white counterparts at an unfair disadvantage given their cultural disposition for discipline and their pushy immigrant parents who spare no
expense when it comes to extracurricular academic activities for their
children.[23] At the same time, areas in which Asian Americans have the
highest representation—math, science, classical music, and so forth—
become constructed as fields that *merely* require relentless practice and
diligence rather than creativity, passion, or even inventiveness. For example, in college admission applications, being an "Asian student who
wants to major in math and science and who plays the violin" can provide further evidence of the student's Asianness—that is, their supposed lack of originality and balance.[24]

Despite its contradictory nature, the "too Asian" rhetoric nonetheless continues to hold affective impact, translating into feelings of
being "one of many." While Melissa, a violinist who attended the University of Southern California for her bachelor's degree, contended
that she sometimes enjoyed the anonymity of blending into the "mass
of Asian girl violinists" at the music school, most of my interviewees
were hard pressed to articulate the beneficial aspects of being perceived
as undifferentiable—a stereotype earned simply by being a violinist.
As Ayako put it, "The 'Asian violinist' is such a stereotype. People just
think, 'Oh, she's just another Asian violinist who started playing when
she was three years old.' [*laughs*] I like to think that I'm more interesting than that. But there's so many good Asian violinists so it's hard to

distinguish yourself." Here, it is worth emphasizing that the racialization of Asians as indistinguishable represents a fundamental hurdle for musicians working in a field of culture that prizes the creative expression of self—that defines musicianship, as Nai-yuan put it earlier, as expressing yourself in a "very personal way." For this reason, it is not surprising that my interviewees produced such conflicted responses to the role that race plays in their music making, as dominant beliefs about Asianness strip them of their distinctiveness, the very trait esteemed in a musician.

For musicians like Eric, a second-generation Korean American cellist who grew up in a predominantly white, upper-middle-class suburb in southern California, personal attitudes toward the visibility of Asians and Asian Americans in classical music shifted with advanced studies. He recollected how, as a teenager, the opportunity to socialize with other Asian Americans made classical music a particularly enjoyable activity. "The main reason [my brother and I] enjoyed going to Colburn was that there were a lot of Korean people that we saw.[25] Especially at that point in high school when you're trying to find your identity, it made it more enjoyable. It was like, hey, there are a lot of Korean girls. We could hang out with them, and we also got to see a more diverse group there, compared to where we were. I think that was part of the intrigue." During high school, a period marked by questions about identity and belonging, the potential to fraternize with a "more diverse group" that included Koreans of the opposite sex represented part of the pleasure and "intrigue" of classical music for Eric and his brother. The visibility of Asian Americans at his music school contrasted with his local neighborhood, yielding what he viewed to be a pleasing diversity. His ambivalence grew, however, as he advanced in his studies and became increasingly aware of the negative racial ascriptions placed on Asians and, by extension, himself. At Juilliard, where he obtained a master's degree, he described the subtle and yet steady undercurrent of resentment this way: "There's a lot of negativity towards Asians. . . . I felt like, okay, you know, there's another Korean kid, there's another Japanese kid, and then I felt like some of the professors felt that too and just assigned basically numbers to us. It wasn't anything necessarily personal. And by having so many Asians around, too, walking down the hallway, you're just another one, you know, and there's not really a way to distinguish yourself from other people unless you're given the opportunity to perform." Given the limited opportunities he had to distinguish himself through performance, Eric felt hypervisible as one of the many interchangeable Asian students roaming the hallways of the school while at the same time, given the lack of individual recognition granted to him due to his race, invisible. The very impulse that drove many of my interviewees to pursue music as a professional career—a desire to express themselves—conflicted with the disconcerting feeling of being a number, a homogenization bolstered by the stereotype that Asians all "look the same."

Although they were critical of the racial presumptions placed on them, musicians I interviewed nonetheless struggled to find sufficient distance. As Katherine commented: "There are all these unspoken assumptions in classical music about race. It's hard to put your finger on all of them. For Asian Americans the whole model minority thing definitely gets played out through music. And there's not a lot you can do about it. You can try and differentiate yourself with your playing, but it's hard because so much of the audience doesn't really know anything about the music. So, it's just this image of another Asian female violinist—and it's hard to feel like you're anything different." Katherine's remarks reveal an astute awareness of how, visually and ideologically, Asian American bodies are endowed with meanings beyond their control. She felt like an unwilling accomplice in fueling the many "unspoken assumptions" circulating about Asian American classical musicians by the mere fact of her chosen profession. And yet, given the lack of specialized knowledge that many audience members bring to their assessment of musical performance, Katherine was skeptical that musicians could differentiate themselves, let alone contest prevailing stereotypes, on the basis of playing alone.

Despite acknowledging the racialized landscape in which they make music, my interviewees continued to preserve musical performance as a space of meritocracy. Such a stance emerges in Eric's contention that "a lot of the stuff about race is away from the instrument, in everyday things. But when you're in the music, it's all about the music. . . . It has nothing to do with your race, but whether you're a good player." This belief speaks to the affective power of music—the feeling of transcendence produced by a powerful performance and the corresponding faith it engenders in the potential for color-blind listening. Beyond finding evidence in affect, Eric's claim finds substantiation in the large number of Asian American performers who have achieved tremendous acclaim for their solo performances on the international stage and for whom race, presumably, does not represent an impenetrable obstacle.

Moreover, while my interviewees critiqued the racial essentialisms embedded in stereotypes about the Asian player, they were also complicit in accommodating, internalizing, and authenticating the partial truths contained in such beliefs. Observing that "the majority of non-Asians believe" these stereotypes, Eric added, "I tend to believe them too. . . . But I think it's not a fault of their own; it's a fault of their training." On the one hand, he disassociates himself from the foreignness of Asians as a way to cope with the racism inherent in the stereotype, a strategy that tellingly leaves the racial logic of these stereotypes intact. On the other hand, Eric rearticulates them less as inherited traits than as matters of pedagogy. As Vivek, a South Asian American violist, similarly attested: "If you happen to see more Koreans with a fast vibrato, it might have to do with what they're told to do over there. It's not something inherent that causes them to vibrate faster." He recasts the source of divergences one might hear in sounds and techniques to the particularities of a teacher and school.

At the same time, given my interviewees' own assessment of the necessity for musicians to find inspiration from the composer, the cultural context of the composition, and soundscapes of nation and language, it is not surprising that beliefs about geography, nation, and culture/race enter performance pedagogy. The negative attribution placed on perceptions of "Asian" musicianship in classical music should be contextualized alongside other ethnic/national backgrounds of playing praised as embodying the height of musical expression—German, Russian, French, and so forth—the same background, not coincidentally, of composers who make up the core canon of Western concert tradition. Given the centrality of the composer and musical text in classical music performance, this overlap sheds light on the entrenched links between musical interpretation and racial inheritance naturalized within this field of culture.

The positive affiliations ascribed to European ethnicities and nationalities in classical music performance create a quandary for Asian and Asian American musicians. For if sounding "Asian" is perceived negatively, then Asian and Asian American musicians need to produce performances that somehow transcend their racialized bodies; their Asianness should not leave a sonic trace on their musical performance Such a racial logic is presented in the three-part *New York Times* series about the rise of classical music in China (discussed in chapter 1), in which the reporters quote a Chinese violinist as hoping he can "play so well that musical experts would not be able to tell his nationality unless they looked at his face."[26] As the young violinist elaborates: "Much of what people talk about as being identifiable as the Chinese accent in music is really just not measuring up to the international standard. . . . That's what I want to overcome." This "Chinese accent" in music is, as the journalists report, a musical inflection that lacks that elusive combination of "technique, culture, and creativity" needed to produce multifaceted and emotionally rich performances. Yet, if the "Chinese accent" implies a "wooden" and "cookie cutter" sound produced by a rigid Chinese music education system and culture, then the so-called international standard should also be understood as culturally specific and emerging out of a long Western/U.S. tradition of normalizing and valorizing the standards and techniques of Europeans and white Americans as universal, authentic, and raceless. Differently put, the racial and national descriptions embedded in the language used to describe masterful playing betray the extent to which the "international standard" privileges European ethnicities. It may be, as political scientist Richard Kraus suggests in his study of Western classical music in China, that "the allegedly international language of music speaks only with a European accent."[27]

To disassociate themselves from the "foreign" accents and telltale traces of Asianness in their music making, some musicians have chosen to claim musical and racial inheritances outside of their perceived home countries. Take, for instance, Chinese-born pianist Lang Lang's description of Russia as his metaphorical homeland: "the country that mothered me." As the pianist recounts in his memoir: "Early on, I was told that I have a Russian soul. Somehow I feel that Russian music is in my blood." The cultural ties between China and Russia (acknowledged by the pianist) notwithstanding, Lang Lang turns to the language of origins—blood, heritage, and soul—to claim closeness with celebrated Russian performers and emotional intimacy with the "cherished repertoire" of great Russian composers (i.e., Rachmaninoff or Tchaikovsky). Maintaining Russia to be his second motherland, Lang Lang transcends his Chineseness and becomes, if not Russian then, as he puts it, a "citizen of the world."[28]

To have something resembling a Russian soul is a compliment in classical music, a descriptor that contrasts sharply with assessments mapped onto "sounding Asian." And while many of my interviewees lamented how the contemporary period has homogenized playing—leading to a loss of distinctive national performance styles—they continue to be influenced by the hierarchical categorizations used to label, interpret, and even hear certain sounds and techniques. Violinist Midori makes this point directly, reflecting: "When we hear someone play, we might say, 'Oh, that sounds so German,' and inherently we hear that as very positive . . . even when the person is playing French music. . . . When you hear 'He or she sounds so Asian,' it's completely negative, but [hearing] 'He or she sounds so Germanic,' it's positive. Regardless of the type of music that you're playing." When I asked for clarification on what it means to "sound Asian," the violinist equivocated, noting that it is implied by an ineffable feeling rather than defined by a precise set of traits: "It's very, I don't know, but even I hear it sometimes when I'm teaching or in master classes. . . . We hear differences, and I don't know why, but sometimes I hear it like 'Oh, wow, that sounds so much like an Asian.'" Midori's unwillingness to delineate what might sound like racial stereotypes is understandable given the sensitivities that surround candid discussions of race in the United States and her own identification as Asian American. She did elaborate, however, that "sounding German" implies playing that is "masculine" and "robust," venerated qualities which bolster gendered beliefs that "women can't play certain types of music as well as men."[29] Moreover, as Midori clarifies, such descriptors are not linked to actual bodies. One need not be German to sound Germanic or Russian to possess a Russian soul—even if such correspondences are helpful. Rather, these represent styles of playing to which classical music performers might aspire, particularly given their positive attributions in the field.

To "sound Asian," however, is a negative description that appears uniquely limited to musicians of Asian ancestry. As violinist Cara mused, "You won't ever hear a person with a non-Asian background being described as sounding Asian. Actually, it would never even occur to me. But to sound German, especially for an Asian, now that's a big compliment." That is, to "sound Asian" is understood to be a negative assessment—a failure to transcend the limits of one's racialized body. And if the height of musical expression is to communicate emotion and soul, then to be labeled technical and cookie cutter—a style of playing linked, in many instances, with being Asian—represents a fundamental critique.

The observations my interviewees make about race and other social categories elucidate a critical point: race impacts musical judgment. The ways in which we hear and interpret particular sounds and performances are embedded in racialized regimes of difference. These social relationships remain obscured not just through discourses of universalism and meritocracy but also through beliefs that musical feeling emerges from the depth of a musician's inner self. As musicologist Henry Kingsbury observes in his ethnography of conservatory culture: "While playing with feeling is at the core of the meaning of musical performance, it must be emphasized that this is so only as this feeling mediates the social power relations that exist in musical performance situations. The free play of fantasy and imagination, of playing with feeling, are never 'free' in musical performance. Musical feeling mediates social relationships, including the elements of power in those relationships, which constitute the situations of musical performance."[30] In this sense, "playing with feeling"—indeed, identifying and assessing how feelingful playing sounds—is neither natural or given, but structured through social hierarchies within and beyond the realm of classical music. While the precise degree to which evaluations of musical performance can sometimes serve as self-fulfilling prophecies of dominant ideologies is difficult to measure precisely, it is clear that intersecting assumptions about race and gender impact the subjective nature of musical assessment.[31] Put differently, existing beliefs about how a particular musician should or will sound influence how listeners interpret what they hear.

Violinist Cara supports this observation, noting how such musical attributes as technicality are coded differently depending on a musician's racial and ethnic background. She recollected that, while studying in Austria, "I'd hear a lot of things like 'Oh, the Americans are all athletic players.' I'm not saying that's good. It's still a criticism about only being technical, but being seen as athletic is different than how Asian violinists get stereotyped as being technical in a robotic kind of way." Cara's insights illustrate how listeners' preconceived assumptions can influence how they interpret the same type of music making. Presented with (an implicitly) white American musician, listeners might ascribe athleticism to a performer. The characterization of being athletic stands in sharp contrast with the stereotypical tendency to strip Asian and Asian American musicians of character and distinction, even if the speaker is conveying a similar assessment of the music—a belief that the playing sounds technical. It may be that being perceived as hardworking and possessing technical skills is an asset only if one is not Asian.

Regardless of what the interviewed musicians believe about their own musical abilities, they were cognizant of the way that stereotypical assumptions influenced their reception, even if not applied directly to them. For instance, Nai-yuan recalled that when he won the grand prize at a prestigious international competition held in Europe he felt his musical authenticity implicitly questioned by the press and audience members through remarks presented as compliments.

> Definitely there are stereotypes about Asians. Especially, like when I won [the competition], of the twelve finalists, seven were Asian. My background is from Taiwan, another from mainland China, three Korean, one from Japan. The local press was wondering what happened to all the European players. I think a compliment from a European after a concert is if somebody will come backstage and say "Bravo, Bravo. We really enjoyed your concert. You play really beautifully. You don't play like a typical Asian competition winner." And the compliment of course makes me think right away that, in a way, they came to my concert with a preconceived idea.

Assimilating to the purportedly international standard implies distance from being/playing like an Asian or, worse yet, like a "typical" Asian competition winner. The praise he received for performing "really beautifully" exempted him from those stereotypes while nonetheless leaving intact the racial logic that gives credibility to such beliefs.

Music professionals have long leveled a number of critiques against international music competitions—for instance, the standardization of performance (which rewards clean and flawless playing) required to pass through the various rounds, bias and cronyism among judges, and the ethics of having so many competitions given the decreasing viability of solo performance careers.[32] Nonetheless, it is telling that as Asians and Asian Americans began outperforming their white counterparts on the standard criteria established in these rigorous international events, the value placed on winning competitions has not only become proportionally diminished, but also generative of new stereotypes (for instance, the "typical" Asian competition winner) that function to diminish their accomplishments. Still, for Asian and Asian American musicians, who lack the inherited ethnic (and often cultural) capital of their white American and European colleagues, international competitions continue to symbolize a meritocratic route for inserting themselves into the global culture of classical music and potentially launching solo performance careers.[33] While the fact that Asians and Asian Americans have begun to dominate the top spots in international contests speaks unequivocally to the recognition given to their talents and skills, their success also bolsters perceptions that Asians are, as one violinist put it, "really competitive but not in a healthy or artistic way"—obsessed with collecting accolades, accruing global status, and capturing the top prize.

In the United States, the obfuscation of racialized beliefs through praise, unspoken assumptions, and veiled language has created a musical environment in which race is simultaneously visible and underground. In Midori's view, this stands in contrast to other geographical locations.

> I think we hear comments that somehow are based on background in Europe and in Asia, more than in this country. I don't know; in my case it was never used in a negative way; it was always mentioned in a very positive light—"Why does it sound so innate?" or "Why does it sound so natural to her when her background is not where the music was originating from?" It was never, "Oh, she won't be able to play." But there were speculations as such. . . . You hear less of that here in the U.S.

Why do you think that is?

> Well, we're so sensitive to discriminatory comments, and maybe those are things that we just automatically don't say out loud, even though we feel something or think something.

Such observations highlight how public discourse in the United States is, as political scientist Robin Hayes puts it, bound by a code of "racial etiquette" which suggests that proper codes of speech are sufficient to achieve anti-racist action.[34] Propelled by multiculturalism and color blindness, "racial etiquette" intimates that explicitly discriminatory comments and attendant complaints of racism remain unspoken. And yet, such inactions do little to contest the lingering question "Why does it sound so innate?" which continues to materialize as feelings and thoughts that are not necessarily spoken out loud.

This should not suggest that explicitly nationalist, racialized, and gendered ideas do not also circulate in classical music performance. Given the long European tradition of Western classical music, and the extent to which the primary goal of performers is to realize the composer's intentions and render interpretations faithful to the culture in which the composition first appeared, Asian/Asian American musicians can find themselves historically constructed as other and encouraged to find inspiration from this framework.[35] Cara explained it this way:

> Because we play German music, French music, you'll hear teachers or conductors say stuff like, "You have to play this in the German character." . . . And then, anything sounding Asian it's like, "Oh what a wonderful imagination these composers have; you have to imagine you're in China—can't you just hear all those millions of Chinese riding their bikes, 'ding, ding, ding' with their bike horns?" I mean the composers are trying to bring out cultural differences in their music, but a lot of how it's talked about and taught is simplistic. It's sexist, traditionalist, and nationalistic.

Cara's remarks punctuate the broad assumptions reproduced in the language and imagery music professionals use to talk about music. In this instance, musicians are doing cultural and political work that extends beyond the focused practice of making music. Cara's critique reveals not just how music professionals unwittingly promote stereotypical notions of difference through performance pedagogy, but also the ways in which the composers—revered as the original sources of inspiration—embed gender, racial, and national hierarchies within their musical works.

To draw attention to racial ideologies circulating in classical music performance should not suggest that Asians and Asian Americans have not gained enormous international acclaim for their music making. There is far too much evidence to the contrary. Such accomplishments can, in part, make claims of racism seem like gratuitous complaints on the part of Asian Americans, who enjoy privilege, are well represented, and have already achieved so much. Still, as my interviews also reveal, success does not necessarily imply full inclusion. As practitioners in a field of culture historically defined and legitimated by white privilege, these racialized structures of power and hierarchy persist, even as the demographics of the participants change. Being a good player depends on one's ability to negotiate racialized meanings attached to certain social categories and ascribed to certain styles of playing.

Moreover, as the next section shows, discourses of transcendence and abstraction notwithstanding, classical music is a commercial industry that markets and commodifies performers, performances, and personalities. While an assemblage of institutions ranging from universities to private foundations and grantmaking agencies continue to legitimate the prestige of high culture by helping insulate the arts from the demands of the marketplace, my interviewees recognized how commerce intersected with music and the business of making a living.[36] Given the limited amount of specialized knowledge that many audiences have of classical music, my interviewees contended that "extramusical" narratives play a critical role in "selling" classical music to audiences in the United States.

Marketing Music, Modulating Race

All of the musicians I interviewed engaged simultaneously in multiple forms of musical labor: orchestral work, chamber music and solo performance, freelance gigs, and teaching either privately or as faculty members at music schools and/or universities. Acknowledging the contradictions between the ideals and reality of music making, Nai-yuan conceded: "You spend a lifetime learning your art, and then you find there's a whole different side to things, the business element." Like the other musicians I interviewed, he experienced these two aspects of music making—"learning your art" and "the business element"—as incongruous. The business aspect of music was, as one pianist put it, "slimy," a critique arising from her own process of recruiting students (as a professor) to her dealings with management and observations of the commodification of performers. She was not the only musician who lamented the degree to which personality, visual aspects like publicity photos and dress, and other extramusical factors play a large role in making music. For instance, Cara summarized her views this way:

The big part is how you present yourself and how you socialize. The orchestra audition is probably the most straightforward, but for everything else—gigging, teaching, any solo career—it's most important to know how the business operates and to be good at that. It's sad. The knowledge of the public is so low that it doesn't make that much of a difference anymore how you play, in America at least. Musicians are the only ones who really have an opinion about each other, and for musicians who are too opinionated, it can either work to their advantage or disadvantage.

Significantly, Cara places "how you present yourself and how you socialize"—issues of representation clearly inseparable from social categories of identity—at the center of a classical musician's professional career. She came to this assessment of the role that race and gender plays in assessing musical appeal through the accrual of incidents, such as the following:

> I had a manager tell me that the main concern he had was having [more than one] young, attractive, Asian, female violinist on the roster. I basically know that if there's already an Asian female violinist on their roster, it's a long shot that I'll get signed. It's incredibly frustrating that people think this is acceptable to tell you. . . . I mean at least say it's about your playing or something musical about yourself. It makes you realize how much about music is not about your playing at all, and it's like *this* is what I've been working all these years for?

In this instance, Cara's sense that traits having little to do with musical talent played a significant role in her career was not merely a matter of perception. For musicians who spend years honing their craft, such comments from managers provide a bitter reminder of the material impact of purportedly insignificant categories in classical music performance, such as race, age, gender, and physical appearance. In this sense, the prevailing belief that Asians and Asian Americans are undifferentiable and, at the same time, racially different constrains their marketing potential as distinctive performers. And in this particular instance, the manager articulated aloud a feeling held by Asian American musicians that the business side of things informally restricts how many racialized performers can reach the highest rank of solo performers so as to preserve, as best as possible, that select space from becoming "too Asian." As Jason, a Japanese American violinist, reflected: "If you look at soloists these days, there's only room for one Korean at a certain age level, another Korean at another age level, even though there's many that play as well, if not better." He expressed cynicism that the situation would change, blaming the business aspect of music for enforcing such restrictions.

Working in a highly circumscribed marketplace, classical musicians (regardless of race) confront broad and pressing questions about how best to generate new interest and audiences for classical music. Popular strategies for commodifying performers include the promotion of child prodigies and the overt sexualization of female musicians. Asian and Asian American musicians have often been successful in capturing the prodigy market, a fact we might attribute to its harmonization with model minority perceptions; touted as whiz kids and praised for their prodigious technical facility, these young prodigies are often cast aside when they grow older.[37] Violinist Midori, who herself successfully transitioned from child prodigy to established performing artist and teacher, felt that the trend toward promoting the technical wizardry of children was not good for classical music as an industry or for the young performers themselves: "They're starting at an age where they shouldn't be starting at. The culture seeks sensationalism. They want the shock element in their life. The younger the better. Not all the kids see a happy end to what happens in their career." Other musicians critiqued how female artists attempt to capitalize on a "sex sells" route toward marketing their performances. As Katherine said, rather bluntly, "A lot of females I've seen really take the dive towards the skanky [laughs]." She was even more critical of attempts that Asian and Asian American women make to exoticize their image by putting chopsticks in their hair for their publicity photos. The "weirdness" Katherine expressed feeling about such examples can be attributed to a discomfort with being implicated in representations that commodify female sexuality in overtly racialized ways. At the same time, Katherine pragmatically acknowledged that given the success popular music industries enjoy profiting from the sexualization of women and girls, "I think that classical music is trying to use what works in other music and make it work for it."

Within the U.S. culture of classical music, multiple strategies have been implemented to expand the concertgoing experience beyond the codified rituals described earlier in this chapter as providing ideal environments for audience members to take a quick nap. A number of these attempts aim to counter elitist perceptions of exclusivity and irrelevance by challenging the boundaries that consecrate the high status of classical music and diversifying the range of repertoire and concert setting. For example, nightclub spaces like Le Poisson Rouge in New York City have emerged as hip alternative venues for classical music concerts and events.[38] The Metropolitan Opera began streaming live broadcasts of its performances to movie theaters and venues like Times Square in 2006.[39] Within the framework of promoting diversity and multiculturalism, concert programmers have placed the performance of Western classical music within broader explorations of racial and ethnic difference.[40] Solo performers like Korean-born violinist Hahn-Bin (who now performs under the name Amadeus Leopold) have garnered wide media attention for combining an arresting visual image, a theatrical flair, and, in his case, a queer, pop culture sensibility, to performances of traditional violin repertoire.[41] And finally, high-profile ventures like the YouTube Symphony have attempted to use the democratizing aspects of new media technologies to counter some of the gatekeeping mechanisms of classical music.[42]

Few musicians have been as skilled at widening the parameters of classical music making as cellist Yo-Yo Ma, who successfully markets himself as a cosmopolitan populist who embraces and celebrates multiple musical traditions and media platforms. His musical adventures beyond the core canon of the Western classical tradition include experimentations in Appalachian, Brazilian, and Argentinean tango music, collaborations with Bobby McFerrin and the Mark Morris Dance Group, and an exploration of European, Middle Eastern, and Asian musical traditions that developed along the historic Silk Road trade route. The cellist's diverse body of work reveals his skillful management of multiculturalism to market himself to concert programmers and audiences. Considering Ma's omnivorous musical interests, it would be an oversimplification to interpret the Silk Road project as a mere reclamation of his cultural heritage or a "return to roots."[43]

Nonetheless, given the appeal that exploring one's ethnic heritage holds within U.S. frameworks of multiculturalism, a "return to roots" represents a familiar discursive trope that Asian American musicians, including Yo-Yo Ma, have drawn on to differentiate themselves and to promote specific performance programs and recordings.[44] While such programs depend on essentialized understandings of musical interpretation, they also represent attempts to convert Asianness into a form of ethnic capital in classical music. Take, for instance, the Ying Quartet, a string quartet comprising (mostly) Chinese American siblings, who programmed a "musical dim sum" featuring selections by contemporary Chinese composers (including Tan Dun, Bright Sheng, Chou Wen-chung, and Chen Yi).[45] While such a performance is in keeping with the Ying Quartet's well-established mission of broadening both the traditional concert repertoire and the performance settings of classical music (the quartet first gained public attention during the early 1990s through NEA-funded residencies that brought classical music to underserved U.S. rural communities), the program of Chinese composers marked the group's first attempt to make ethnicity an explicit part of their public narrative.[46] The idea behind a musical dim sum, according to the group, was to celebrate their cultural heritage and to present a sampling that musically duplicates the experience of eating dim sum: "What we've done is instead of playing complete works and having one whole quartet by a Chinese American composer, we have provided a sort of sampling. The whole idea is that it's fun to eat little dumplings and all these different little dishes, so we thought we would do the same thing musically."[47] Here, the Ying Quartet uses recognizable ethnic markers to connect the consumption of Chinese food with the more "foreign" experience of listening to contemporary Chinese/Chinese American compositions. In the process, they position themselves as ideal interlocutors to mediate a process of ethnicized listening.

While Asian American musicians may feel a special connection to music composed by Asians or Asian Americans, they also recognize the particular appeal that the script of "exploring one's heritage" holds for audiences. Cara, for instance, observed that when she included works by Chinese composers in recital programs, her audiences (which she described as a mostly older and white demographic) expressed particular enjoyment: "I've started programming the Chinese fisherman's song in my recitals. It's a short piece. And it's gimmicky. But the audience loves it. They always tell me it was their favorite piece." Cara's use of the word "gimmicky" is telling. It implies that there is something particularly pleasurable about hearing a song based on Chinese melodies performed by a Chinese American musician. Indeed, such audience reactions can form a double-edged sword for performers, as they offer an opportunity to connect with audiences and broaden their appeal while also reinforcing discourses of musical authenticity. The enduring belief that different types of music originate from, and therefore belong to, a certain group or place allowed for an easy identification between Cara's Chineseness and Chinese music in the United States.[48]

One of the most successful classical musicians to market his Chineseness as a form of ethnic capital is pianist Lang Lang. His "Russian soul" notwithstanding, the pianist frequently drapes himself in visible signs of Chineseness in concerts and public events, appearing in Chinese-style clothing, programming Chinese compositions, and playing encores of Chinese folktunes with his father on the *er-hu* (a Chinese two-stringed bowed instrument). Regardless of whether Lang Lang's explicit Chinese references represent a sincere desire to express ethnic/nationalist pride, savvy marketing, or a combination of both, it is clear that the pianist successfully packages an East–West vision that plays on pleasurable performances of difference to broaden his appeal. In his analysis of the promotion and translation of Lang Lang for U.S. audiences, music scholar Eric Hung aptly acknowledges that "in the current market, orientalism sells, and Lang and his marketing team have exoticized him throughout his career to ensure that he maximizes his stardom."[49] Beyond his public presentation, Lang Lang also narrates his life story (in interviews and his memoir) through a familiar framework of clashing East–West polarities: China represents a childhood of hardship, lack, discipline, and monomaniacal parenting while the United States signifies magnanimity, openness, creativity, and freedom.[50] By constructing himself as a cultural ambassador bridging East and West—an individual who retains pride in his Chinese roots and embraces the gifts bestowed upon him by the West—the pianist fulfills dominant desires for exoticism and orientalist difference while also allowing the U.S. classical music establishment to construct itself as free of racial constraints.

At the same time, some Asian and Asian American musicians express ambivalence about positioning themselves (and being positioned) as cultural mediators or ideal interpreters of works by Asian composers. As discussed in the previous chapter, narratives of music as an international or universal language hold particular appeal to racialized groups seeking to claim inclusion in a musical tradition not necessarily viewed as their own. And yet, the hegemonic belief that geography, cultural heritage, and blood allow an artist to grasp the ineluctable essence of a culture—an innate mode of understanding that cannot be taught—continues to hold sway among classical music professionals. These discourses are often powerfully (and ambivalently) repeated by Asian and Asian American musicians themselves, who are familiar with hearing their artistic accomplishments filtered through coded beliefs and supposed compliments about native sensibility.[51] Take, for instance, the observations of Wen:

> It makes me feel great actually, seeing all the Asians in music. But at the same time . . . the tradition is still Western, from Europe. And I do have some friends from Europe, and their playing, it's really in their blood. Like this one friend of mine, her father was a baritone, her mother was a violinist, so she just grew up in this environment, and the way she plays, she doesn't even have to think about how to play right, she just plays it right. There's a certain kind of style, I don't know, kind of noble, kind of a European style, that's just in her playing. So in a way, I feel that Asians taking over, there's a certain sense of that lacking—it's less something completely born with. I mean it's very politically incorrect to say, because I'm an Asian myself. And it's hard to say, because there's also a lot of Asian musicians who are incredible musicians, so in a certain way this is not true.

While the cultural capital that her (presumably white) European friend possesses is cultivated and acquired, it is nonetheless perceived and narrated as intrinsic to her being. The slippage in Wen's language between racial, cultural, and familial inheritance highlights the obfuscation of white dominance through beliefs about natural ability, inherent talent, and playing that automatically sounds and feels "right." And while her recognition that Asian musicians (including herself) are also "incredible musicians" creates some internal inconsistencies, such contradictions are in keeping with Bourdieu's articulation of the dynamism of a cultural field wherein competition for resources appears democractic but, in practice, reinscribes inequitable distributions of power. Here, it is useful to turn again to Ghassan Hage, who elaborates (drawing on Bourdieu) how the privileging of inherent capital "fosters the belief that no matter how much capital one acquires through active accumulation, the very fact of this acquired capital being an *accumulation* leads to its devaluing relative to those who posit themselves to have inherited it or to possess it innately without having to accumulate it. . . . Only those

"legacy."

who have the innate capacity to dominate can really be said to possess enough capital to dominate the field."[52] This "innate capacity"—an inheritance that accrues value as an essence one is born into—is not, in the final moment, an asset available for accumulation in classical music. And thus, despite the changing demographics of the field, white privilege continues to encompass the so-called natural order.

Asian and Asian American musicians have pursued different and often conflicting strategies to accommodate themselves to the racial logic of such discourses. Scoffing at intimations that he lacks an innate understanding of classical music, Taiwan-born violinist Ming, for instance, observed that given the intensity and focus of his training from an early age, the European culture of classical music represents his "native" language—the music in which he feels most at "home." He claimed other music modalities, even those with which he holds a presumed intimacy, as being alien to him: "Classical music is European culture. . . . Everything is based in Europe, like Western harmony, the instruments, the thinking process, it's all European. So when I listen to Chinese traditional music, I don't get it. It's so foreign to me. The concept is totally different." By prioritizing training and familiarity as integral to assimilating one's "thinking process" to a musical culture, he asserts his belonging in classical music. At the same time, in a move that speaks to the powerful grip held by discourses of musical authenticity, Ming contradicts himself in the same interview, observing the "natural" affinity he possesses for particular Chinese elements found in the works of Chinese composers: "Certain kinds of Chinese things [in music] I would feel very intimately and Americans could never understand. It's only natural you know." Here, it is worth emphasizing that the music to which Ming refers is not Chinese traditional music but, rather, Chinese compositions written in the Western classical music tradition. The emergence of China in the global culture of classical music and the acclaim gained by Chinese composers, such as Bright Sheng and Tan Dun, have led Chinese and Chinese American musicians to marshal claims of intimate understanding—whether sincere, strategic, or both—to promote their performances of such works.

Thus while musicians of various backgrounds perform and record the works of contemporary Asian composers, powerful metaphors of musical inheritance led some of my interviewees to express ambivalence about the interpretations of non-Chinese performers. Citing the

Butterfly Lovers Concerto (a widely performed Chinese composition) as an example, Keng-yuen asserted, "One can't say only Chinese can play it. That's totally wrong." At the same time, he contended that the recordings by non-Chinese violinists were all poorly executed: "[The *Butterfly Lovers Concerto*] has a lot of portamentos and slides on the violin, and how it's done is quite tricky.[53] You have to get the microtones and all that stuff. It's quite complicated. But once you have it in your blood, it's very simple. When you hear it, it's there. You feel it, and you feel the phrasing, and then you know how to bend the pitch." Discursively linking bodily essence with the ability to "feel" certain phrasings and pitch, Keng-yuen's description turns on metaphors of biology and blood.

At the same time, claiming musical authenticity for works by Asian composers represents a small advantage given the long history of European tradition valorized in Western classical music. Indeed, many of my interviewees replicated beliefs that compositions by contemporary Asian composers are of lesser quality—superficial blendings of East and West translated for U.S./Western audiences and tastes.[54] Keng-yuen, for instance, bluntly described the *Butterfly Lovers Concerto* as "stupid," asserting that "the music is terribly written." Regardless of the merits of such critiques, such perceptions may lead musicians (regardless of their ethnicity) to believe that developing convincing interpretations of Asian compositions does not require the same amount of research, study, and cultural immersion as performing canonical works from the Western concert repertoire.

Ideas about authenticity simultaneously function as entrenched beliefs and discursive tropes while also animating the different marketing strategies deployed by musicians as they navigate the commercial landscape of classical music. Despite feeling less trained in the business side of making music, my interviewees recognized the challenges facing the classical music industry and the ways in which performers are marketed, packaged, and sold. They acknowledged how race enters conversations about diversity, multiculturalism, and authenticity even while marshaling universalizing discourses to downplay the significance of race in this field of culture.

At the same time, as the classical music industry begins looking to East Asia as a potential source of revenue, Asians and Asian American musicians may find themselves increasingly called on to play the role of cultural broker. China, in particular, has emerged since the late 1990s as a potential site of opportunity for the classical music industry—a market for performances, a geographical region to expand institutional presence, and a population from which to recruit talented students and gain tuition dollars. Still, reflecting on a global era marked by transcultural sharing, Taiwan-born violinist Nai-yuan reflected: "You hope that everyone will not lose their identity. But as far as everyone being equal, it's still not equal in terms of your own background." Wary of the homogenizing effects of globalization and the unequal flows of power that structure such traffic, he questioned how implicit inequalities continue to structure the terms of acceptance and belonging that Asians and Asian Americans experience in this cultural field.

The Future of Classical Music

I honestly think that in some real sense, the future of classical music depends on developments in China in the next 20 years. They represent a vast new audience as well as a classical music-performing population that is much larger than anything we've had so far. You're looking at a time when, maybe 20 to 40 years from now, Shanghai and Beijing are really going to be considered centers of world art music. —Robert Sirota, president of the Manhattan School of Music

In the summer of 2009 I accompanied a small group of music performance faculty and school administrators on their first official trip to China. Planned in the wake of steady media coverage about the astonishing growth of classical music in China, the school sought to build relationships with music conservatories and faculty that they hoped would, in the longer term, facilitate future partnerships and student recruiting. Given its size and scope, China represented a space both formidable and full of promise. Cara, a violin professor with the school, offered the following view: "The feeling was like ten million violinists and thirty million pianists, and all the big name schools were already recruiting there. We had to get on board." The admissions director similarly affirmed: "China is seen as the 'golden key'—what's going to solve the problems we have. I think that's something that a lot of music schools are thinking now."[55] While China is, as the quote from Robert Sirota suggests, presumably decades away from embodying the future of classical music, music schools in the United States have nonetheless felt a quickening pressure to get on board or implicitly fall behind.[56]

Certainly the classical music industry has been grappling for years about how best to court audiences and markets in China specifically and East Asia generally, even if existing racial paradigms continue to color perceptions of what Asians (and Asian Americans) bring to classical music making.

Given that in the United States most elite music conservatories already actively recruit students from major cities in China, a sense of belatedness permeated the trip. The frustrations that the group encountered confirming appointments, feeling properly understood (linguistically and culturally), and navigating a foreign landscape compounded a disconcerting sense that merely being located in the United States did not, in itself, represent sufficient enticement.[57] Speculating on the misalignment of expectations, Cara reflected: "You can't just come in and think that everyone will want to go to your school because you're in America. They already have all the best conservatories recruiting at their schools." While music schools like Juilliard can depend on a global brand recognition to attract top students, lesser known schools must compete in order to attract the growing talent and financial pool located in China.

Listening in on a violin master class at Beijing's Central Conservatory of Music, one of China's top music schools, it struck me that I, too, had arrived with certain assumptions about what I would see and hear. Wide-ranging U.S. media coverage about Chinese musicianship and a rigid education system had primed me to anticipate a certain formality in playing and personality. For that reason, I found the easy conviviality of the violin studio—a few students wandered in late; others brought beverages and joked with their teacher—almost as striking as the mixed range of playing that I heard. If many violinists did not possess flawless technical chops, their musicality did not sound, at least to my ear, especially stilted or forced. Discussing my observations with Cara, she similarly reflected: "There's not that much difference in terms of the problems that students have. You go to China and the perception we [Americans] have is that they are all going to be technically brilliant but not play with that much feeling. So I was actually surprised that they were not all that technically perfect. And the students have the same problems as my students [in the United States] have, like not thinking through their phrasing or being unsure about their own interpretation. I think a lot about how the students play, and the atmosphere of the studio depends on the teacher." What Cara intimated here is that while the challenges violinists confront in learning their craft may be universal, the racialization of these challenges is not. The entwinement of racial presumptions in what we hear, along with the hierarchical distinctions embedded in musical evaluations themselves, makes it difficult to disentangle what constitutes the musical performance itself. Nowhere was this point more clear to me than when, unmoored from the U.S. context and complicated by incomplete fluencies and cultural expectations, discourses about Chinese playing became harder to maintain. Moreover, whatever differences do exist in teachers and pedagogy may become less pronounced as Chinese-born faculty trained in the United States and Europe return to take up high-profile positions at top Chinese conservatories, lured by the high salaries offered by the Chinese government.[58]

Conversing with a Chinese-born conductor back in the United States, I asked his thoughts on changes in classical music training in China. Like other musicians who grew up in China, Bing repeated familiar shortcomings—a focus on solo performance rather than ensemble work, a subtle sense that foreign is better, and an emphasis on technique rather than musical expression. When I pushed further, he conceded that while many existing stereotypes have "cleared up a bit" given how "unbelievably good" young Chinese players are, he still found talk about the future of classical music in China to be overly optimistic. Given the long-standing hierarchies entrenched in classical music performance and pedagogy, he found it difficult to imagine a future when musicians from the United States would relocate to Asia to further their musical training or to establish their performing careers: "Before it was Japan. Then Taiwan and Korea. Now it's China. The numbers are there. But what does it mean to be there? What kind of future are we imagining? Will students from America go to Shanghai to study? I'm not so sure. Will they want to go to Tokyo? I'm not so sure." To be "there" implies a type of arrival, a process stuck in an act of deferral.

At the same time, given the staggering population of China and the enormous amount of capital invested by the Chinese government to train music students and create an infrastructure to support this talent, Bing also felt that Chinese dominance in classical music was an inevitability—a statement that did not inspire either feelings of pride or foreboding: "I don't feel anything. For me, it seems perfectly natural. You take one-fifth of the population and put the energy in classical music and of course so many of them will be good. It's only natural."

The significance of China as a source of revenue and the return migration of top Chinese players has begun to shift the coordinates of power and dependency that undergird long-standing Eurocentric discourses. Joon, a Korean-born cellist, mused that people in the United States do not fully comprehend the changes already under way: "This country's musicians don't really understand what's going on in China. There is a big energy in China. China is the country that [of all the Asian nations] will really come out."

I conclude this chapter by turning briefly to views about the place of China in the global culture of classical music because anxiety that ownership over one of the most elite forms of Western cultural capital is in the process of being transferred to Asians forms a critical backdrop to the contemporary racialization of Asian and Asian American classical musicians. Related, focusing on the dynamic of inclusion and tacit exclusion that marks Asian and Asian American belonging in the U.S. culture of classical music allows for a broader understanding of the maintenance and disruption of racial hierarchies and white privilege in an era of U.S. anxiety over waning cultural, economic, and global hegemony. When Asian Americans perform classical music, they manage and rework a range of intersecting racial and musical discourses that frame their participation in this cultural field. My interviewees recognized how their Asianness was used against them—to uphold dominant racial ideologies, to generate new stereotypes, and to bolster presumptions about innate capital and understanding. While recognizing how racial difference could be used for marketing, they, at the same time, continue to marshal the language of universalism and meritocracy to argue for the irrelevance of race in this field of culture.

Classical music represents a particularly trenchant site to investigate how race circulates in the United States given the color-blind beliefs embedded in performance pedagogy, in the critical apparatus, and in the narratives told by musicians themselves. As is clear, being present and successful does not ensure full belonging. The persistence and reformulation of racialized beliefs to accommodate shifting demographics underscore the intransigency of racial paradigms. The alignment of classical music with dominant ideologies about Asian Americans both enables and contains their success in this field.

For many middle-class Asian Americans who grew up taking music lessons, the rules and rigidity that mark the boundaries of classical music performance, the association of music lessons and practice with parental expectations, and the alignment of classical music with model minority pursuits led them to perceive classical music as an imposition or duty. Classical music did not necessarily resonate with their musical interests and desires. Nor did it provide them with the tools to express who they felt themselves to be. While this chapter focused on Asian Americans who pursued classical music as their chosen profession, others have used their classical music training as a springboard to pursue other musical pursuits. Still, as the following chapters show, the questions that Asian American classical musicians grapple with around race, authenticity, and sonic belonging haunt their involvement in other music fields, finding new expression and meaning in their participation in popular music forms both in the United States and abroad.

THREE

A Love Song to YouTube

Celebrity and Fandom Online

The way singer-songwriter David Choi tells the story, he was bored and tinkering around with his guitar when, in a flash of creativity, he composed a light-hearted ode to his latest object of infatuation, YouTube. It was in late December 2006, a few months after Google acquired the video-sharing platform but still during the early years of YouTube, and Choi enjoyed spending hours interacting with the website, even conducting searches, rather futilely at the time, for other Asian American singers. When he uploaded "YouTube (A Love Song)" onto his YouTube channel, fame, millions of views, and a performing career were far from the singer's mind. He had already posted two videos earlier that month, an acoustic cover of Corinne Bailey Rae's catchy pop hit "Put Your Records On" and a humorous, original song titled "Fart." While neither video garnered a great deal of viewer attention, Choi, just twenty years old at the time, enjoyed the process of creating content and participating in the creative musical community flourishing on the new online space. With its many double entendres about logging "in and out" to "please" YouTube, Choi's lyrics playfully captured the interactivity—the commenting, liking, responding, and sharing—that made this new social media space so pleasurable to its users. He hoped that some of his fellow YouTube addicts would find his song amusing but did not expect much more. Instead, soon thereafter, YouTube plucked Choi's song out of the hodgepodge of content scattered across the site and featured it on their official homepage. From there, bloggers reposted the video, users shared the video link through their networks, and messages began flooding the singer's inbox requesting more music and inquiring about albums and live performances. Within a week, "YouTube (A Love Song)" garnered over half a million views. The video has since accumulated over 2.8 million views and more than nine thousand user comments.[1]

Like other amateur videos uploaded during YouTube's early years, "YouTube (A Love Song)" holds many trademark DIY (do it yourself) qualities of intimacy and immediacy. Filmed in his bedroom in his parents' Orange County, California home, the video features Choi, alone on his bed with his guitar, singing rather earnestly and awkwardly to his computer (see fig. 3.1). The rough quality of the video enhances the viewers' sense that they are glimpsing a private snapshot of the singer—his unfiltered talent streaming directly from his sleeping quarters onto their own personal devices. The video's intimate aesthetic is further augmented by the medium itself, which provides a platform for individual artists to reach a potentially global audience through acts that can nonetheless feel and appear intensely private in their moment of creation.[2] Choi was (and maintains that he still is) "shy" and "uncomfortable performing in front of people."[3] What YouTube provided was an opportunity to perform without the concomitant anxiety of being onstage. As the singer explained, "The Internet thing is a little different because you're not performing in front of an audience; you're performing in front of nobody in a room in front of a camera." Moreover, even if the user imagines viewers on the other side of the camera, this audience is measured as the aggregation of individual views accumulated over time—moments of personal connection forged between one person singing to another person, often through small screens flickering close to their bodies.

With its grainy imagery, imperfect vocals, and out of sync audio, "YouTube (A Love Song)" carries the aesthetic markers that signify authenticity and realness. Such traits continue to be coveted by users even as the platform increasingly moves in the direction of professionally produced content. As cultural anthropologist Michael Wesch observes: "If you could name a core value on YouTube, it's authenticity. The strongest critique is to say that you're hiding behind something or you're not being real."[4] While what precisely constitutes authenticity is, as Lawrence Grossberg aptly contends, "itself a construction, an image,

3.1. Still from David Choi's video of "YouTube (A Love Song)."

which is no better or worse than any other," the belief that YouTube allows ordinary people to connect directly with an audience remains one of its central differentiating markers from traditional media.[5] That a video steeped in the vernacular of the ordinary, the amateur, and the everyday could go viral, reach millions of viewers, and launch Choi's solo performing career affirms the democratizing message promoted by the company. As a YouTube manager touted in a press release, "One of the greatest aspects of YouTube is how it has democratized the way in which videos are discovered and promoted. . . . On any given day, a video from a top-tier content creator or an ordinary YouTube user can become the next big thing."[6] The idea that YouTube embodies a new "frontier" of possibilities for ordinary users remains powerful despite the fact that the video-sharing platform has always been a commercial enterprise. Still, while it would be tempting to script an artist like Choi as a receptacle of raw talent just waiting to be discovered, such a description represents only a partial picture. Part of the reason the singer was able to capitalize on the surprise success of "YouTube (A Love Song)" was that he was not simply an amateur musician who posted a humorous song and stumbled upon a one-off hit. A motivated self-starter in his musical pursuits, Choi had already achieved some professional recognition for writing and producing music and in 2006 was working as a signed songwriter for Warner/Chappell music.

I begin this chapter with Choi—now sometimes affectionately dubbed, given his early adoption of the platform, the grandfather of YouTube —because he emblematizes how young Asian Americans have successfully mined the potential of YouTube to begin creating the conditions of their own visibility. As this chapter demonstrates, Choi is part of a larger cohort of young Asian American singer-songwriters who have turned to YouTube in an effort to circumvent and, at times, contest a racially stratified U.S. music industry. While they work in music genres and media platforms that hold very different histories, designations, and performance practices than those of the classical musicians investigated in the previous chapter, these singers, I argue, encounter a similar U.S. racial imaginary that shapes the boundaries of their musical participation. While the first part of the book analyzes how Asian "music moms" and Asian American classical musicians contend with and rework the meanings ascribed to their involvement in classical music, this chapter explores how young Asian American singer-songwriters negotiate racial and musical discourses that situate them on the outskirts of the U.S. popular music landscape.

At the same time, it is worth noting that many of the Asian American musicians I interviewed for this chapter enjoyed (or perhaps endured) a "love-hate" relationship with classical music during their youth. This fact should not, of course, imply that all Asian Americans grow up learning how to play classical music. I would argue that it instead highlights the class, generational, and ethnic backgrounds of these singers and the demographics privileged in the particular configuration of "Asian America" gaining visibility online. But I flag this detail, here, to underscore how for some of the YouTube singers I interviewed classical music represents part of the literal backdrop of their childhood as well as the figurative backdrop against which they make music. For instance, we can understand the remark made by Korean American singer Clara C. of feeling "boxed in" by classical music while growing up in the United States as indicative of an array of factors: the strict rules and parameters that govern classical music performance, the broader limitations that Asian American youth feel being stereotypically aligned with this field of high culture, a longing to express herself in the popular music that speaks most passionately to her and her peers, and the frustration that Asian Americans feel interacting with a U.S. popular music landscape that does not fully encompass who they are or imagine themselves to be. In what follows I examine how young Asian American singers use their music making, in general, and YouTube, in particular, to respond to the presumptive boxes placed on them in the U.S. context.

This chapter draws on a range of materials and sources: oral interviews conducted with YouTube musicians; attendance at concerts; surveys with Asian American fans; informal conversations with artist managers and concertgoers; and the vast archive of videos, music, images, and writing uploaded by, and posted about, these musicians on various blogs, online media, artist websites, and social networks, including YouTube, Twitter, and Facebook.[7] The larger network within which these performers are embedded partially enables this array of materials in my archive. The extensive amount of public information available about the YouTube stars discussed in this chapter creates an intense knowability and sense of accessibility about these artists, a trait that I argue represents a large part of their appeal.

In the course of gaining popularity on YouTube, young Asian American musicians like Choi connected with one another, gathered a large and loyal Asian American following, and collectively created what the singer described as a "so-called Asian movement that started online, on YouTube." As he elaborated, "There's been a huge upsurge of Asian Americans on YouTube. And it's encouraging to see because there was no place for Asians before. . . . Social media has really helped this generation of Asian Americans have a platform to share music and just share who we are with the world." The "huge upsurge" to which the singer refers includes not just the musicians, filmmakers, and personalities whose online videos amass millions of views, but also the legions of young Asian American fans (younger, that is, than the mostly twenty-something artists) who actively support their favorite YouTube stars both on- and offline.[8] This chapter interprets the meanings that this apparent movement holds for its young Asian American participants. And while Choi likely did not mean to invest his casual turn of phrase the "so-called Asian movement" with nuanced meaning, I argue that it is nonetheless telling, as it registers the ambivalent meanings ascribed to race by this group of young performers.

With close to a million subscribers to his YouTube channel and over one hundred million total video views, Choi leads this so-called movement as one of the most popular YouTube musicians of all time.[9] Yet, in contrast to when he first began searching for Asian American singers online, the singer is now part of a larger cohort of young Asian American YouTube stars. Included in this constantly shifting and growing group are singer-songwriters such as A. J. Rafael (ilajil), Clara Chung (ClaraCMusic), Kina Grannis (Kina Grannis), Jennifer Chung (JenniferJChung), Jason Chen (Music Never Sleeps), Jane Lui (LuieLand), J. R. Aquino (JRAquinomusic), and Joseph Vincent (hoorahjencar); popular personalities and filmmakers such as Ryan Higa (NigaHiga), Kevin Wu (KevJumba), Tim Chantarangsu (Timothy DeLaGhetto), Freddie Wong (freddiew), and Wesley Chan, Ted Fu, and Philip Wang (Wong Fu Productions); as well as beauty and style gurus like Michelle Phan (MichellePhan), Jenn Im (clothesencounters), and Jen Chae (frmheadtotoe). Together, these creative content producers make up a dense, pan-ethnic network of Asian American YouTube stars.[10] They frequently appear together online; star in each other's music videos, sketch comedy skits, vlogs (video blogs), and short films; team up to perform covers and original songs; and promote each other through their YouTube channels and other social media platforms.

The overlapping web of connections between these performers represents more than just a personal clique of affiliations and friendships. They also signal a strategic use of YouTube's interactive platform. Through their collaborations, artists drive traffic to each other's YouTube channels, link their fan bases, and collectively grow their online presence. Offline, these performers frequently appear together in concerts, community events, panel discussions, and tours. Therefore, while this chapter focuses specifically on the efforts of Asian American singer-songwriters, it is important to emphasize that these musicians participate in a larger network of Asian American talent.[11] Together, these enterprising young artists are creating a public record of what Kevin Wu terms a "new breed of Asian Americans"—a millennial generation versed in digital technology, linked through social media, unapologetic about their right to self-definition and change, and determined not to let race or other barriers limit the scope of their imagination.[12] Ignoring, parodying, and stretching racial expectations, these YouTube stars pull apart long-standing myths attributing to Asian Americans a surplus of meekness, technicality, discipline, and foreignness or, on the other side of the coin, a deficit of cool, passion, creativity, and native understanding of American culture.

Like other independent musicians, Asian Americans have turned to YouTube and related social media to maneuver a place for themselves in a music industry and media landscape undergoing rapid transformation. The interactivity and intimacy of YouTube, the democratizing possibilities of the platform, the aesthetic priority placed on authenticity, and the changing relationship between fan and performer all represent aspects of what it means to be a YouTube musician, regardless of one's ethnicity. In this way, this chapter allows us to understand the distinct openings that YouTube offers and the creative labor involved in building, as media scholars Jean Burgess and Joshua Green put it, "a meaningful presence and an engaged audience in a participatory media space."[13] While I only investigate a microcosm of the vast array of content available on YouTube and the meanings it holds for a very specific youth demographic, I contextualize the broadening presence of Asian Americans online within larger shifts in media industry practices spurred by technological transformations, the interactivity of Web 2.0, and increasing audience fragmentation. Media scholar Henry Jenkins aptly terms this process "convergence"—"the flow of content across media platforms, the cooperation between multiple media industries, and the migratory behavior of media audiences who will go almost anywhere in search of the kinds of entertainment experiences they want."[14]

At the same time, this chapter poses specific questions about the nature and impact of Asian American success on YouTube. Why have Asian Americans sought and gained visibility on YouTube? How does race calibrate the emotional investment in and identification with the artists that their fans have? And what holds this pan-ethnic community of Asian American YouTube musicians together? In proposing some answers to these questions, I focus less on the challenges that Asian American musicians face breaking into the traditional music industry—a daunting prospect for any musician, regardless of their subject position—and more on how these young artists discuss their experiences with race and music making and their understanding of the place that Asian Americans (including themselves) occupy on YouTube and in the U.S. popular imagination. In so doing, I offer a window into how these young Asian American musicians reconcile their own stated desires to be viewed and heard as beyond race with an acknowledgment of how race filters perceptions about their musicianship. Being Asian American holds relevance to these musicians because it impacts their opportunities and reception as well as provides the conditions for their visibility on YouTube.[15] Reflecting on the confluence of extramusical factors that affect his music making, David Choi conceded: "You just want to be seen for your music, but unfortunately there are those social, psychological things that play a factor, like in everything in life." His remarks imply an awareness that music, like "everything in life," takes place in a context where the social, cultural, and historical converge in the creation of meaning.

While Choi voiced a desire to be seen on the basis of his music, he also expressed pride in how Asian Americans have seized the potential of YouTube to express their own everyday experiences. That he and other Asian American artists frame this collective process as a movement speaks to the enormous sense of empowerment that gaining some measure of agency over their own representation and distribution entails, particularly in light of the gatekeeping mechanisms that Asian Americans encounter in traditional media. As the tagline for *Uploaded: The Asian American Movement*—a feature-length documentary film that celebrates how young Asian Americans artists use new media to express themselves and find an audience—reads, this moment "is about a new generation finding its voice through new media."[16]

Given the extent to which my interviewees downplayed the importance of race in their music making, there may be, at first glance, something paradoxical about an "Asian American movement" organized around race while simultaneously eschewing its significance. And yet, as I argue, such a stance is in keeping with the uneven contradictions at the heart of color-blind and multicultural discourses. Many of my interviewees disavowed the centrality of race even while recognizing its effects, articulated ethnic pride while mobilizing discourses of universalism, and claimed that greater familiarity with the "Asian American face" in U.S. popular media would lead to broader acceptance even while critiquing the shortcomings of existing representations. As Ingrid Monson reminds readers in *Saying Something*, her influential study of jazz musicians, the conflicting viewpoints that coexist within a single person—and often within a single interview—underscore how such concepts as universality and ethnic specificity are "discourses upon which musicians draw in particular interactive contexts."[17] Like the comments of the classical musicians discussed in the previous chapter, Asian American YouTube musicians' assertions that race is incidental to their music making need to be contextualized within broader uncertainties about how best to craft belonging within a musical landscape that places Asian Americans outside of the authenticating links assumed between race and musical ownership. The racialization and limitations that these YouTube singers encounter in their musical endeavors drive their desire to be perceived as universal *and* to frame their growing visibility as an unprecedented racial moment for Asian Americans.

For this reason, when musicians told me that being Asian connects this loosely affiliated group of YouTube performers and their fans together, I interpreted this to be more than simply an essentializing statement. Rather, being Asian places these artists on the outskirts of U.S. popular culture, engendering a bond that—at least publicly—is characterized not by rivalry or antagonism, but a shared sense of purpose. By articulating music making to be both an individual and a collective enterprise, these musicians sought to convert their Asianness into a resource and community from which to draw support in a competitive music industry. The public performances of collaboration and friendship that link this panethnic network of Asian Americans artists and audiences together provide insight into why some would narrate their burgeoning online presence as a movement. Certainly this is not an Asian American movement that identifies with a historical Asian American identity, earlier political struggles, or even broader coalitions with other racial minority groups. Yet by choosing to identify collectively *as* Asian Americans, these young artists pooled their creative efforts, strategically capitalizing on the tools that YouTube provided to gain visibility and grow their audience.

Given the rapidly changing landscape of YouTube, this chapter takes a snapshot of a fast-moving object of study, analyzing how Asian American musicians availed themselves of the unique opportunities YouTube offered during its early years. The breakneck pace of transformation in digital technology, Web 2.0, and YouTube is apparent in Choi's "grandfather" moniker, which registers how generations are marked in months and years rather than decades. Indeed, when I conducted my interviews in 2011, just six years after YouTube's launch, many of my interviewees already felt that the increasing focus on monetization and professionally produced content had profoundly altered the "psychology" of the site. Given the saturation of users, the enormous amount of resources expended on top-viewed videos, and the increasing prioritization of monetization and high production values, many of my interviewees wondered whether they could build a robust following if they were starting out in this transformed climate.[18] Therefore, while this chapter emphasizes how young Asian American musicians mobilized the potential of YouTube during its early years, it contextualizes this narrative within a broader recognition of change occurring not only on this media platform but also in the lives of this youthful demographic.

Being on YouTube

YouTube has already grown up so much. —Singer-songwriter Jennifer Chung

During the summer of 2007, Jennifer Chung, a young Korean American "soulful pop" singer, began uploading covers onto YouTube.[19] Having moved to a new city following her high school graduation, she was bored and missed her friends. YouTube represented a fun way to continue connecting with her friends. Yet, to her surprise, when she began posting covers—songs by popular artists she loved, such as Mariah Carey, Christina Aguilera, and Sara Bareilles—requests from "random people" began to trickle in. A few months later she gained even more visibility after a cover of Alicia Keys's hit "No One" was reposted on a hip hop website under the generic heading "Asian Girl Singing Alicia Keys"; that video eventually garnered over five million views.[20] When I asked why she thought that particular video resonated with viewers, Chung speculated that her image—a young, fresh-faced Asian girl sitting in front of a bed piled with stuffed animals and a comforter adorned with stars and moons (see fig. 3.2)—created a disconnect with her unexpectedly strong voice. Despite describing her singing on that video as being "really average," Chung mused, "I think people expected it not to be that good." That is, the appearance of a sweet-looking Asian girl tackling (with some success) the expressive vocal inflections of Keys muddled seeing and hearing, creating a moment of pause that led users to repost and forward the video to others.[21]

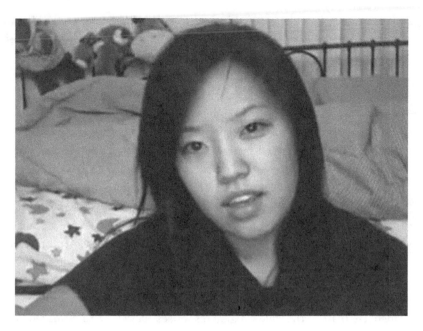

3.2. Still from Jennifer Chung's video of her cover of
Alicia Keys's "No One."

Chung's narrative resonates with stories that other YouTube musicians tell of their early experiences on the site—the unanticipated
broadening of their audience beyond friends and family, the video that
unexpectedly creates a connection with viewers, the intimate and yet
public nature of uploading videos, and the burgeoning sense that You-
Tube allows transgressions, racial and otherwise, that are not yet fully
embraced in traditional media. As Filipino American, pop-rock singer
A. J. Rafael commented, while YouTube is "important," it's not the
"main thing, so it's where you can have things that are not normal." On
the one hand, the uniqueness of YouTube stems from its many "abnor-
malities." The platform contains, for example, a diverse proliferation
of singers covering, composing, parodying, and performing songs in
all manner of genres and languages. As singer-songwriter Jason Chen
optimistically suggests on his YouTube channel, YouTube materializes
how "music is colorblind and languageblind." And yet, on the other
hand, a cursory glance at the comment section for any popular video
underscores the extent to which normative expectations are assertively,
if not viciously, reinforced and patrolled by users.[22] That is, uploading

content onto YouTube is a highly public act that invites the immediate and unfiltered reactions of an anonymous online community. Indeed, in the comment sections for videos by popular Asian American YouTube musicians one finds a stream of racialized commentary: outright racism, surprise (sometimes phrased affirmatively) that an Asian sings so well and/or without an accent, declarations of shared racial or ethnic pride, homophobic retorts in response to racist commentary, entreaties for the singer to ignore all the racist haters, and contentions that race has no place in discussions of music. In this morass of commentary, rhetoric of a "colorblind and languageblind" America collides with virulent xenophobia, racism, sexism, and homophobia. The sheer negativity of some comments "really sucks," as Jennifer Chung laments, "because it makes the good ones feel insignificant." And while the comments posted in response to YouTube videos should not be viewed as representative (only a small fraction of YouTube users actively comment on or upload videos), they nonetheless frame the public context in which these videos circulate.[23] The wide-ranging responses elicited by YouTube videos underscore the interlocking host of assumptions, antagonisms, investments, and desires placed on the bodies of performers, interrupting reveries of color-blind listening or music making.

Reflecting on their experiences of being on YouTube, a number of my interviewees marveled at how much they *and* YouTube had, as Chung put it, "grown up so much." Not only did many of these musicians begin uploading videos on YouTube while they were still students in high school or college, a period of tremendous personal transformation for individuals, but YouTube was then a fairly new and still-forming space. As early adopters, their maturation entailed shifting their understanding of YouTube from being just for fun (admittedly, the attitude of most users at the time) to being a critical part of their business platform in promoting their music and brand.[24] These young artists capitalized on their early success to establish and grow a fan base and "grew up" alongside YouTube by teaching themselves the basics of recording, editing, mixing, and production; upgrading their equipment; exploiting the interactivity of the platform (for example, by embedding links, using pop-up texts and annotations, and collaborating with other popular artists); and creating more polished content on their YouTube channels. Part of the success enjoyed by these Asian American YouTube musicians can be attributed to their skillfulness in adapting to the changing landscape of YouTube and their savvy in expanding upon and monetizing their YouTube fame. And while the musicians I interviewed did not claim to have any special knowledge of the alchemy of factors that makes particular videos gain popularity, they conceded that, unlike in the early years, videos with high production values are increasingly becoming a prerequisite to maintaining viability in the crowded and professionalizing landscape of YouTube.[25] As Choi observed, his original music videos tend to get "pretty viral because they're done really well. Production is a huge thing on YouTube."

While professionally produced videos frequently attract more viewers, the Asian American YouTube stars I interviewed continue to post stripped-down versions of covers and original songs from their homes. Not only were these videos simpler and cheaper to film and edit, but they also engendered what some singers described as a more authentic and meaningful interaction with their fans. "I feel more fulfilled," singer-songwriter A. J. Rafael reflected, "when people know my original songs that I'm singing in my own home and that I didn't spend a lot of money and time to make a professional-looking video just to get hits. That might be one of the reasons why I'm not growing as fast as a lot of other YouTube artists anymore. But for me, it's more satisfying, for my heart, and I feel way better about it." In Rafael's view, the balance between the pressure (and desire) to maximize growth and the discomfort he felt in accommodating changing expectations was tied not just to his personal fulfillment, but also to the broader inequalities he felt were increasingly reflected on YouTube. Commenting on the amount of capital, economic and otherwise, spent on top-viewed videos, Rafael questioned whether democratizing narratives about YouTube still held true.[26]

> People are spending a shit load of money on YouTube . . . with HD videos and people editing the crap out of their videos, the playing field, it's more uneven now. Because on You Tube at first it was just guitar or piano and voice and [your] singing and that was amazing to people. People loved showing people that. But now people love seeing videos that are edited, and the lighting has to be perfect, and a lot of them are lip-synced for people to get the angles, things like that. And I think it's uneven now because not everybody has resources like that. . . . But it isn't bad either. It's getting more people involved and making it easier for videographers and artists to make a living and stuff like that. So in that case, it's not bad, but it is a little uneven nowadays.

The unease that Rafael expressed about professionalization speaks to many of the uncertainties that my interviewees articulated about the shifting landscape of YouTube. Can artists lacking major resources and connections still build a significant online presence, or is the site increasingly structured to reward corporate and commercial interests? And does the shift toward professional-looking content help independent artists by creating opportunities and potential for revenue, or does it reinforce the hegemony of traditional media by replicating its exclusivity and standards of quality? Such questions highlight the "peculiarity" of a platform that, as Pelle Snickars and Patrick Vonderau put it, has constantly been "negotiating and navigating between community and commerce."[27] The preponderance of narratives detailing the empowerment that audiences and artists feel on YouTube often elides the fact that little has shifted in "the structure of ownership within the media system itself."[28]

The conflict that artists like Rafael see in changes on YouTube taps into a broader ambivalence around such labels as "YouTube musician," "YouTube sensation," or "YouTube star." Many musicians I interviewed chafed at popular associations linking YouTube with viral videos like "Charlie Bit My Finger," desiring distance between themselves and such amateur family fare.[29] "I want to be known," pop-folk singer Clara C. emphasized, "as somebody who produces content of quality, and people like it, and that's why I have a following." In this context, the shifting preference shown toward professional content on YouTube helped align the singer with a level of quality that she felt more properly reflected her artistry.

The multiple meanings attached to YouTube reflect its slippery "double function as a 'top down' platform for the distribution of popular culture and a 'bottom-up' platform for vernacular creativity."[30] The site was acquired by Google for $1.65 billion in 2006, and the challenge of monetizing it through advertising dollars in the years that followed has elicited a range of strategies aimed at attracting more professional content and professionalizing the promising "vernacular creativity" already on (or coming onto) the site.[31] Revenue-sharing programs, such as YouTube's Partner Programs, created in 2007, and the growing proliferation of media companies that work with YouTube allow popular users to earn revenue on advertisements placed on their videos.[32] YouTube itself also funds a variety of projects to support and develop professionally produced content—from providing resources and training

programs for top (and potential) YouTube stars to nurturing relationships with media companies ranging from start-up studios to major
media corporations like Disney.[33] And as part of a broader plan to keep
viewers on the site for longer periods, in 2012 YouTube financed a slate
of original channels aimed at attracting national and global audiences
for a variety of niche interests.[34] The growing number of partnerships
forged between new media and traditional media on YouTube highlights the multidirectional traffic in these relationships, challenging assumptions that success still represents (or always necessitates) crossing
over into traditional media platforms.

The rapid rate of transformation on YouTube creates an environment of both opportunity and insecurity for young enterprising artists.
As Gerald Ko, the only musician I interviewed who held an unrelated
full-time job (as a pharmacist) observed, even popular YouTube stars
cannot rest comfortably on their laurels: "YouTube is a very unstable
atmosphere. Because of that no one can feel safe and secure that what
they're doing now is going to continue to pay off." By highlighting some
of the shifts that have taken place on YouTube since its creation and
Asian American performers' reactions to these shifts, this section contextualizes the particular challenges and openings that performers
encounter using this "unstable" platform to promote their music and
brand.[35] At the same time, the early embrace of YouTube by many of
the Asian American musicians I interviewed allowed them to utilize its
democratizing potential and to consolidate a community of Asian American artists and fans. And, as the next section shows, the touchstones
of friendship and support at the core of this community stem from the
particular intimacies fostered through the medium of YouTube.

Building Community

It was a breezy summer evening in Monterey Park, California—one
of a number of "Asian" suburbs in Southern California—and the outdoor amphitheater in Barnes Park was nearly filled to its five-hundred-
person capacity with young Asian Americans who looked to be in their
teens.[36] The predominantly Asian American crowd had gathered to
watch a showcase of popular Asian American YouTube performers—
from singer-songwriters A. J. Rafael, Joseph Vincent, Jennifer Chung,
and Andrew Garcia to Korean Canadian rapper J.Reyez and the sketch

comedy duo JustKiddingFilms—perform in a charity benefit to support a local high school's choir program.[37] The casual vibe of the outdoor setting and the affirmative tone of the concert, dubbed Dreamchasers to encourage young Asian Americans to pursue their dreams in the arts and to shine a spotlight on artists already doing just that, extended to the individual acts as well. The artists displayed an easy camaraderie, appearing onstage at different moments to sing backup for fellow performers and joking with and about each other during their performances. As in their YouTube videos, the performers projected an air of approachability, friendship, and informality—directly addressing and thanking their audience and maintaining a spontaneous and even, at times, unrehearsed feel to their acts. And while the audience remained fairly calm and seated for most of the show, it was clear from the cheers, the signs and cards, and the long line that snaked backstage to meet the artists following the performance that many were devoted fans.[38] This concert, like many others featuring a group of artists, had tiered ticket pricing where the most expensive VIP seats also provided fans with access to signed merchandise and an artist meet-and-greet following the show. Thus while performances like Dreamchasers help materialize offline the sensibility of the Asian American YouTube scene, they also provide opportunities for fans to interact "in real life" with their favorite stars.

While no specific sound connected the performances, the majority of acts that evening fit squarely within the broad umbrella of pop.[39] The final act of the night, Joseph Vincent, a Filipino American singer-songwriter and heartthrob (judging by the cheers from the crowd) who first gained national attention in 2010 through his appearances on *The Ellen Degeneres Show*, closed the evening with a rousing medley of original songs and covers by such artists/groups as Maroon 5, Bruno Mars, and 'N Sync. Watching these musicians take the stage, what was striking was that they did not appear to be enacting or accommodating to any prescribed or expected sense of ethnicity. They were simply young people who love, write, and perform popular music. Their embrace of American popular music and YouTube projected, utterly naturally and without fanfare, an understanding of themselves as Asian Americans who are a constitutive part of U.S. society.

Indeed, spend enough time watching the videos of these young YouTube musicians and it is easy to feel like you are dropping in on a fun, tight-knit community where everyone is connected by one degree, where most people are Asian American, and where race is both visible and yet incidental to one's creative endeavors. These musicians express little interest in making music marked thematically or sonically as "Asian American," as evoking "Asian" musical traditions, or as making any broad claims about racial identity. Rather, through their music and videos, these artists rework the familiar sounds of the U.S. pop landscape into their own image (and that of their young Asian American fans). Casting other Asian Americans in their videos and supporting a network of other Asian American artists through their work, these performers collectively project a worldview that places Asian Americans at the normative center. Being Asian American becomes less a marker of difference than a shared aspect of identity that does not require additional explanation, commentary, or translation. In this way, these musicians help normalize what Christine Balance (drawing on the late José Muñoz) terms "feeling Asian American."[40]

While the growing Asian American presence on YouTube has created a networked community of performers and fans connected virtually, it is also physically located in southern California, the geographical hub for YouTube artists more generally.[41] Many Asian American artists grew up or attended college in southern California while others moved to the area to participate in the overlapping YouTube and Asian American scenes. Their close geographical proximity allows these artists to gather both professionally and personally. The multiracial landscape of southern California and the visible presence and denseness of Asian Americans in the cluster of urban/suburban communities that make up southern California help account for the sense of ease and comfort with being Asian American projected in these YouTube videos. That is, the accessibility of majority nonwhite and/or Asian American spaces helps mitigate feelings of racial difference that Asian Americans experience in interacting with a U.S. media landscape still described by my interviewees as polarized between whiteness and blackness.[42] As artist manager Tom Ngo (who produced and emceed the Dreamchasers concert) reflected, the demographics of Monterey Park, where he grew up, allowed him to feel grounded in a local community despite the absence of Asian Americans in the popular media he consumed: "I've never really had the thing of like I have to act white or black to fit in. I was always myself, even though I was influenced by media, TV, the books I read. I think it stems from how comfortable you are with yourself." While Ngo's remarks simplify racial identification into a black-white binary, they also register its continued salience, particularly in the mainstream media choices available to young Asian Americans.

Tellingly, none of my interviewees would admit to rivalry or tension within the close-knit community of Asian American YouTube artists. Regardless of whether we take these professions of solidarity at face value—as with any group of young artists, interpersonal and professional conflicts likely arise and breakups (romantic and otherwise) have sometimes become public—the consistent public articulation of friendship and support is striking.[43] Describing the closeness among this network of artists, Clara C. drew on the discourse of family and the attendant feelings of affection, loyalty, and reciprocity: "The Asian American YouTube community is really tight and connected. We all appear in everybody else's videos and songs. It's actually really great because music is something that can be so cutthroat and competitive. But in the YouTube world at least, the majority of us are very familial and nice and supportive." She attributed this support, in part, to having built a significant presence on YouTube when it was still "this big gray area that was growing but we didn't know what to do with it . . . with being labeled as YouTube stars and stuff like that. So I think we all bonded together because we were uncertain about what was coming next."

Asian Americans working in other creative fields also have drawn on the discourse of family to construct and imagine coalition. As Thuy Linh Tu keenly observes in *The Beautiful Generation*, Asian American fashion designers have used the language of kinship to describe their relationship with Asian garment workers.[44] While such rhetoric enacted a sense of connectedness and responsibility among the various actors, it also allowed Asian American designers to leverage resources and accrue small benefits in an industry in which they enjoy few advantages. For Asian American YouTube musicians, the articulation of a "family feeling" similarly allows them to aggregate resources and consolidate networks of support and accountability in the face of daunting odds not just of gaining fame, but of simply making a living in their chosen profession. However, unlike Asian American designers who, as Tu notes, do not necessarily perceive themselves as connected as a racialized group (despite or because of presumptions otherwise), Asian American YouTube musicians link their fates, thereby rendering music making as both an individual and a collective enterprise.

While uncertainty about the emerging platform of YouTube provided the initial bond between Asian American musicians, these familial attachments were bolstered by recognition of their shared location on the sidelines of mainstream popular culture. This helps account for the "automatic connection" that singer-songwriter A. J. Rafael described feeling when he meets other Asian American musicians: "I mean I would feel connected with a white person who does the same thing, but there's something about like 'Hey, we're struggling together in this because there's no stage for us, there's no platform for us.' Record labels and companies, they never give us a platform." In this sense, maintaining a sense of pan-ethnic collectivity is, as singer-songwriter Dawen put it, a simple matter of pooling resources, for "separated there is no power. But if we all come together as Asian American, we become something of worth." By collaborating on projects, appearing together at shows, and publicly supporting each other through their social networks, Asian American YouTube stars connect their efforts, drive interest and traffic to each other, and collectively grow their audience.

As young independent artists who lack the social capital of industry or family connections to facilitate their path in music, this peer network provides both material and emotional benefits.[45] Reflecting on the friendships forged among Asian American artists, A. J. Rafael commented: "I think it's more than we just love to hang out with each other kind of thing. It's also because we have to show that we're something to be reckoned with. I think it's great that we all have each other in each other's videos and we all have shows together because we have to stick together like that. Because if it's just one Asian American trying to make it out there and stuff, I don't think it's going to work. I think we need that support group of like other actual artists who are like us." Put differently, these musicians frame success in both individual and collective terms. Such a stance emerged repeatedly in my own interviews as well as through the artists' public personae as projected in concerts, social media activity, and media profiles. For instance, in a *New York Times* article on Legaci, the Filipino American R&B group chosen from YouTube to perform as backup singers for Justin Bieber (himself the epitome of YouTube stardom), Josh Kun quotes singer Delphin Lazaro as stating that the band hopes to begin the process of achieving mainstream acceptance for Asian American singers: "We want to open that door, and then we'll bring everyone with us."[46] While not all

Asian American YouTube musicians measure success as crossing over into traditional media, what is worth noting in Lazaro's statement is the rhetoric of reciprocity he draws on to frame individual achievement within the context of broader community goals.

A deeper longing to prove that a market exists for Asian American performers, despite a culture industry that has historically suggested otherwise, undergirded many of the iterations of mutuality and support I heard my interviewees make. Take, for instance, the following remark by Jennifer Chung: "I mean, mainstream media doesn't think that there's really a market there, but obviously there is." Here, her rejection of this "mainstream media" viewpoint—a denunciation buttressed by the robust fan base generated by Asian American YouTube stars—contains a broader refusal to accept as defensible the continued state of Asian American invisibility. And while my interviewees did not frame it as such, I would argue that their remarks reveal an awareness of the importance of gaining recognition as a market. For to be visible as a market in a neoliberal economy is to embody true signs of power and worth, markers that might finally yield to Asian Americans their long-sought-for recognition as "real" Americans. As sociologist Lisa Park demonstrates in her study of the children of Asian immigrant entrepreneurs, economic participation represents a benchmark for the maintenance and reproduction of citizenship—a yardstick to measure the "shifting boundaries of belonging, entitlement, and participation of Asian Americans in the U.S."[47] This connection between market visibility and cultural belonging accounts for the critiques my interviewees marshaled about mainstream representations of Asian Americans and the optimism they expressed about their burgeoning presence on YouTube and social media. As Chung hopefully contended, the visibility of Asian Americans online should pique broader interest: "I'm sure mainstream media is feeling like they have to listen."

Indeed, the flourishing and in many ways unexpectedly vibrant presence of Asian Americans online as artists and consumers has garnered attention from mainstream media outlets such as the *New York Times*, the *Washington Post*, the *Los Angeles Times*, and National Public Radio. Much of this coverage shines a spotlight on the growing number of Asian American (and nonwhite) artists who are successfully using YouTube to bypass the often tacit barriers they face in the mainstream music and film industries and on audiences who are eschewing traditional media in favor of representations they find relevant and empowering.[48] The potential to tap an Asian American youth market has also attracted the attention of market analysts searching for ways to exploit the growth of the Asian American demographic and the robust migration of young Asian Americans to online media platforms. Such a connection emerged, for instance, at a Kollaboration San Francisco show I attended in 2011, an Asian American talent competition and artist showcase held annually in multiple cities across North America.[49] During the performance, a spokesperson from the Nielsen Company, one of the show's corporate sponsors, greeted the predominantly Asian American crowd by telling them what many may have (at least intuitively) already known: that of all ethnic groups, Asian Americans spend the most time online, the most time on YouTube (and, conversely, the least amount of time watching television) and that this is an audience demographic that matters.[50] Put differently, young Asian Americans spend the most time interacting with and consuming media in which they have the greatest visibility. The migratory behavior of Asian American audiences to media platforms that present content meaningful to their lives helps undermine the belief that Asian American audiences are too ethnically splintered or assimilated (i.e., indistinguishable from a white audience) to represent a market. And to exist as a market within the cultural and economic context of neoliberalism suggests that the tastes and interests of Asian Americans might actually matter. This should not imply that an Asian American audience did not exist before YouTube or that Asian Americans were not engaged in making popular music of every sort before YouTube.[51] At the same time, while Asian American artists have gained recognition through independent routes, few, as music scholar Christi-Ann Castro concedes, "have experienced enough success to be considered mainstream."[52] YouTube provided a media platform for Asian Americans to connect with each other to an unprecedented extent and at a record pace and to link their efforts publicly as a group within a single space. As Gerald Ko reflected, YouTube is the only space where one can encounter "so many Asians doing American music."

For this reason, when Asian American YouTube musicians mobilize the language of family, I understand them not to be essentializing their bonds to one another but locating them, instead, within a shared purpose and practice of community. This imagination of community extended beyond the immediate network of Asian American musicians and performers to their fans as well. Clara C., for instance, described her fans as "family"—a supportive network that she depends on for love, loyalty, and economic and emotional sustenance. On the one hand, such an articulation is not unique to Asian Americans. Many popular artists claim to have the best fans. Moreover, the rhetorical nod to family by YouTube artists is in keeping with the intimate scale of their videos and the structure of the platform, which together create the conditions for the strong affective links between fans and performers. On the other hand, what I argue distinguishes Asian American YouTube musicians' claims of loyalty, friendship, and support is the degree to which they publicly model for their fans the process of coming together as a pan-ethnic community; as one respondent to the survey I conducted noted: "These musicians found and established connections with other artists who produce their music, direct videos, and create merchandise. It's a network of Asian American musicians who look [to] and support each other." By including fans in this extended family, performers allow consumers to feel that they, too, are critical members of the Asian American YouTube community. Such a gesture also helps configure consumption as a form of politics; through their clicks, shares, comments, and purchases, fans, too, are participating in what they might also feel to be an emerging Asian American movement online.

Here it is worth emphasizing that as with any family formation, the feeling of empowerment that accompanies inclusion can simultaneously map the borders of exclusion. As Dorinne Kondo aptly reminds, tropes like home and community are far from innocuous given their "enmeshment in networks of power."[53] It is clear that the Asian American YouTube community privileges and normalizes a specific configuration of Asian American youth: primarily East and Southeast Asian, second-generation, English-speaking, middle-class, heteronormative, suburban, and California-based.[54] These specific attributes reinforce existing hierarchies already enforced within (and beyond) Asian American communities. I raise this not to undercut the affective power that comes from feeling visible, gaining traction as a market, and/or finding stars who seem relatable and accessible, but rather to acknowledge how this articulation of community replicates norms that can be equally alienating to young Asian Americans excluded from this particular embrace of family.

Unlike mainstream celebrities, whose fame in the traditional entertainment industry facilitates their large following online, YouTube stars actively build and cultivate their following through that platform. They regularly interact with other members of the YouTube community, invite and respond to feedback from their fans, and create original content designed specifically for the site.[55] These artists directly engage with the participatory and reciprocal dynamics of YouTube (and related social media, namely, Facebook and Twitter) to build their brand. They accept the grind involved in keeping up with their social media channels as part of the daily labor that entails being (or aspiring to be) a YouTube celebrity. Joseph Vincent maintains: "It's a daily thing. I mean it's what I do, and I don't have any other day job so this is basically my career. So I put time into it. . . . I go every day. I see what people are doing, what people are interested in, and I try to start thinking up what's the next cover I need to do, or I started writing my own songs now so I spend time thinking about or planning how to push that."

The fame that YouTube stars like Vincent enjoy illustrates how the advent of social media and the increasingly fragmented media landscape have ushered in a star system based on public displays of closeness, access, affinity, and relatability rather than distance and difference.[56] In the process, a new type of artist–fan relationship has emerged. Clara C. explained it this way: "YouTube artists have a different kind of fan interaction than, say, somebody who's more mainstream and with a label. Because when you're under a label, you're kind of not really expected to respond. But we're independent. We make our own fan base, and we're in charge of pruning it and making sure that we maintain that relationship. It's definitely more personal." For Clara, the distinction between YouTube and mainstream artists lays not just in the agency that YouTube artists hold over their representation, image, and music, but also in the work expended to cultivate and expand their fan base. The singer translated the accountability she felt to her fans into, for instance, a willingness to meet them after shows, to respond (as much as possible) to personal messages and tweets, and to use contests and giveaways to generate personalized opportunities for direct fan interaction. Such activities allowed her to forge a close and loyal bond to her fans, a perception validated through comments by Asian American survey respondents that describe YouTube stars as "easier to relate with," "connected more deeply with their audience," and "more willing to do things with their fans and spend more time with them."

While the labor musicians invest in the reciprocal dynamics of new media encourages fans to feel an intimate connection, there is also something particular about YouTube that enables viewers to consume in ways that feel personal, immediate, and even private. Singer-songwriter Jane Lui described her experience of being on YouTube this way: "You are in your room, and someone else is in their room listening to you, and I'm looking right in your eyes, and you get to see my life, like where I put things, what my room looks like. And it's just this direct communication. There's no middle at all. It completely closes the distance between artist and audience." For Lui, YouTube changes the scale of intimacy, inviting a sense of closeness, accessibility, and interactivity between artist and viewer. The intense loyalty of fans, the feeling of connection and community, and the relatable quality of YouTube artists all emerge out of the affective bond generated through user-produced videos. Thus despite their mediation through technology, these artists seem intensely knowable and accessible.[57] Artist-manager Tom Ngo noted as much, reflecting: "You kind of see how everyone lives. You almost feel like you know them, digitally of course. And it's brought everyone together because although Asians are still a minority in the States, the Internet has kind of made us closer." Dispersed across the nation and consuming content on personal devices (often alone and in private spaces), Asian American youth are able through YouTube to imagine and enact membership within a larger community that is connected virtually and, at times, coalesces at live events.

For Asian American youth accustomed to interacting with a popular media landscape that does not fully represent lived (or aspirational) realities, uncovering relatable representations and like-minded fans can feel empowering. While the challenges posed by the absence of role models and the proliferation of harmful stereotypes are neither new nor unique to this generation of Asian American youth, their affective impact should not be discounted. Familiar with how the U.S. media landscape can limit imagination of self and community, Asian American YouTube stars recognize the significance of their collective presence for their predominantly young Asian American fans. Clara C., for example, recounted how she participated in a range of musical activities grow-

Ing up: piano and violin (enforced by her parents), guitar (in church), and flute (in high school band). Yet when it came to the popular music she loved the most, she internalized the absence of Asian Americans: "I loved music, but I had already accepted that it would never happen. Why? Because what I see on TV is not what I am." These remarks underscore how listening to and consuming popular media is not a color-blind process. For young Asian Americans socialized into identifying with non-Asian protagonists and encountering Asian Americans in limiting, if not cringe-worthy, roles, the act of feeling seen and heard is no small matter. As Clara put it: "I think it's as simple as when you see someone like you, it makes you feel empowered. It makes you feel recognized." The closeness forged between the singer and her Asian American fans is thus enhanced by the projection of sameness, the recognition of self in the artist, and, with it, affirmation that their tastes, their desires, and their ways of experiencing the world matter. A. J. Rafael made a similar observation, noting that "most of the fans we have are Asian American, and they look up to us because we are like them, and they have finally found somebody who they can relate to. And they love going to shows and stuff because they look to us as heroes."

While the YouTube musicians I interviewed did not begin to make music with a particular desire to represent Asian Americans or to become heroes to an even younger generation of Asian Americans, they accept the position they collectively occupy within a changing media landscape. They further believe that their generation of YouTube stars empower their fans differently from earlier generations of Asian Americans who attained success through traditional media. As A. J. Rafael reflected: "Older than me, actors like John Cho or Sandra Oh, they're famous and stuff, but I feel like the personalities on YouTube, like Happyslip [Christine Gambito] or Kevjumba [Kevin Wu], they're more empowering.[58] We're relatable. I feel that the difference between us and other celebrities are that we empower a whole generation." Not only do YouTube stars project "relatable" personas that are often based on a "real" self, but gaining visibility on YouTube is also a seemingly more accessible process than breaking into the Hollywood film industry or getting signed to a major record label, a distant prospect for any individual, regardless of race and other social factors.

If YouTube artists empower their fans, these fans are also empowered by the active role they play in discovering, supporting, and promoting unsigned, independent artists on YouTube. The interactivity of this process can, as Joseph Vincent explained, lead fans to feel a sense of ownership and pride over the milestones an artist achieves: "Your fans and supporters feel like they kind of own you. They're the ones who brought you up, so they feel like they're responsible for your success as opposed to, let's pick someone like 'N Sync, or other pop stars where the record companies said 'Here's a new act we have and you guys are going to love them.' As opposed to these kids who are like 'Hey, we found this guy. We love him and we're going to build him up.'" Put differently, there is collective ownership over this growing Asian American visibility online: artists directly cultivate their fan base as much as fans feel a shared sense of ownership over them. Indeed, many of the comments that appear beneath YouTube videos position the viewer in the role of the critic—discerning listeners who recognize the value and talent of unsigned artists despite the lack of commercialized marketing and promotion surrounding them.

Representing the Asian American Face

Alongside the growing presence of Asian Americans in new media, the door to visibility has begun to crack open in mainstream media as well. Television shows like *Glee* and *Grey's Anatomy* contain Asian American characters, Hollywood films like the *Harold and Kumar* trilogy provided top billing to Asian American actors, Far East Movement or FM reached the top spot on the Billboard Charts in 2010, and Asian American dance crews regularly dominated MTV's reality TV competition *America's Best Dance Crew* during its run from 2008–2012. Despite such gains, however, many of my interviewees felt mainstream representations reproduced existing racial patterns, a recognition that simultaneously thwarted and propelled their desire to acquire entry into traditional media. In our interview, A. J. Rafael repeated what I have often heard him say in live performances: that since America is still unaccustomed to seeing Asian faces in mainstream media, Asianness continues to be *the* defining aspect of a performer's identity. As he put it, "When people talk about Harry Shum they always say the Asian guy on *Glee*. But what would be awesome would be in a couple years, if someone like him is on *Glee,* they don't say the Asian guy but the awesome dancer on *Glee*." Rafael's desire to "normalize" the Asian American face—to have Asian Americans characterized by their individual subjectivities and talents—echoed his own yearning to uncouple his music making with his Asianness. In his view, YouTube represented a critical step toward broadening the available images of Asian Americans and making the Asian face a more recognizable, and thus unremarkable, aspect of the U.S. media landscape. As he elaborated: "I think we're creating our own thing where it's just a face that you put out there so people can get used to you." Here, Rafael articulates a position forwarded by other artists as well: that unfamiliarity lies at the root of limiting depictions of Asian Americans in mainstream media. Confining race to the visual level—as the embodiment of a shared set of phenotypical codes—he suggests that the proliferation of faces in new media that are visibly marked as Asian will help normalize their presence, paving the path toward wider acceptance.[59] Rafael's observation registers both the sense of resentment that stems from mainstream invisibility and the sense of optimism accompanying increased visibility.

Given the frequency with which the YouTube musicians I interviewed used "face" as rhetorical shorthand for race, it is unsurprising that vexed questions about the erasure of the Asian face in mainstream media emerged as a frequent theme in my interviews. Pop-soul singer Dawen interpreted the racial obfuscation of Asian Americans as indexing the extent to which "America is not ready for an Asian American face." As he noted, while singers such as Bruno Mars enjoy remarkable solo careers, they are not necessarily perceived, marketed, or even known to be Asian American. Put differently, their mixed-race heritage enhances their multicultural appeal—the pleasure of otherness and difference—while diffusing the potential burdens accrued by their Asianness. David Choi similarly mused: "There's a lot of halves that are doing really well, but straight up Asian, not yet. There is yet to be a single artist to be at number one, you know, a straight up Asian-looking person." His comment should not suggest that such "halves" are somehow less authentically Asian American or not included in the Asian American YouTube scene. Multiracial Asian Americans such as singer-songwriter Kina Grannis and actor/musician Chester See frequently collaborate with other Asian American YouTube stars. At the same time, these artists' racial ambiguity allows their Asianness to remain opaque in ways not fully available to "straight up Asian-looking" people.[60]

Choi's observation should also not discount the ways that so-called straight up Asians can also deploy strategies to mask, mute, and/or otherwise redirect attention away from their Asianness. Music scholars such as Oliver Wang and Deborah Wong deftly demonstrate how, in the mid-1990s, Asian American rappers such as the Mountain Brothers sought to deflect their Asianness by avoiding explicit references to ethnicity in their music and lyrics and concealing their ethnic background in promotional materials not aimed toward Asian American audiences.[61] In a different vein, Elizabeth Pisares reveals how in the late 1990s, the racial ambiguity of Filipino American singer Jocelyn Enriquez allowed her to be misrecognized as Latina and/or African American, thus placing the singer's mix of Latin freestyle, house, and R&B music more squarely within normative linkages between race and genre.[62] And in our interview, A. J. Rafael commented how the Jabbawockeez, the predominantly Asian American crew that won the first season of *America's Best Dance Crew* in 2008, literally veiled their Asianness behind white masks in their path toward, or perhaps as a condition to secure, national success. (Not wanting to sound overly critical, however, he also added that the dance crew "takes off their masks at the end of the show, which is cool.")[63] What these varied examples reveal is how gestures of invisibility accompany moments of Asian American visibility—a contradictory interplay that my interviewees intuited as interrupting any easy narrative equating Asian American presence with full belonging.

Indeed, a number of my interviewees used the chart-topping success of Far East Movement (see fig. 3.3) as occasion to reflect on the costs of acquiring mainstream success. Many popular Asian American YouTube musicians feel a personal connection with the group, having performed at International Secret Agents (ISA), a series of concert events that FM founded with Wong Fu Productions in 2008 to showcase the "new generation of Asian American talent breaking through to mainstream media."[64] The name International Secret Agents itself plays on the idea that the creative potential of Asian America remains hidden in plain sight—online, underground, and/or obscured through dominant narratives about Asian Americans. While David Choi, who describes the members of FM as his friends, articulated pride about the group's success, his remarks nonetheless reflected some unease about their public image. "I'm really proud that [Far East Movement] made it to number one," he told me. "The first Asian American in history or the world to be number one on the Billboard in America, even though they wear, you know, shades and it's kind of hard to tell what they are." When I

3.3. Far East Movement at a music video awards show in 2011.
Photograph by Vervegirl Canada.

asked whether he thought the sunglasses were designed to divert attention explicitly from their ethnicity, Choi was adamant: "Of course not. I don't think that's why they wear shades." Such denials notwithstanding, however, the singer continued to hedge his remarks: "But you can't really tell if they're Asian; you know what I mean? I don't know. But I'm really proud that they made it to number one." His reluctance to critique the group directly is in keeping with the family-like rhetoric of support and collaboration that exists within this Asian American YouTube community.

The equivocations in Choi's language and his refusal (or inability) to pin down what he means mirror the ambiguities in FM's own racial performance. While the group's name announces some type of explicit affiliation with the Far East, they do not make music identified either sonically or lyrically as Asian. Moreover, although their large sunglasses partially deflect their "straight up Asian-looking" faces, the ubiquitous presence of these accessories ironically draws attention to their eyes, to the very Asian features that are purportedly undercover. There may be something subversive about highlighting what one wants to remain hidden—a tongue-in-cheek statement on the reliance of visual cues that make race palpable and a paradoxical instance of masking Asianness in full view.

While the members of FM contend in media interviews that their signature shades represent a practical convenience (i.e., to hide the bags under their eyes from partying in clubs all night long), a nagging uncertainty about their potential additional racial function emerged in a number of my interviews.[65] Linking FM's style to the broader context of Asian American acceptance, Joseph Vincent lamented: "It just sucks because I don't know if they [FM] have to, but they're all wearing sunglasses, you know what I mean? It's still difficult. The transition is still not there completely." That is, in his view, despite breaking barriers, FM measures the distance separating Asian Americans from mainstream integration. If FM's signature sunglasses and colorful clothing create a uniformly cool look, they also contribute to an overall look and sound that downplay their ethnicity and individuality—a visual homogenization that mirrors the sonic homogenization of their processed voices.

Less a specific critique of FM, I understand the observations of musicians like Choi and Vincent as emerging out of a shared uncertainty about what full acceptance of Asian Americans would (or should) look like. If FM demonstrates that, with the proper marketing and promotional resources, an Asian American group can attain mainstream success, the group also suggests the need to deflect being seen and heard as "too Asian" when aiming to reach a broad public. A. J. Rafael contended: "There's always that compromise that you have to make with the mainstream because I don't think FM would have made it if they were going around saying 'Hey, we're Asian" or doing songs about Asian American power. I mean just like straight up, they made good party music."[66] The singer's observation speaks to unsettled questions that he and his peers continue to grapple with in their own music making: How might one make music that is universal in appeal and yet does not erase his/her Asian American subjectivity? And how might one embrace one's ethnic heritage in ways that speak to, rather than alienate, a broad listening public? There is a certain irony in Rafael's intimation that making songs about Asian American power or hyping "Hey, we're Asian" somehow constitute Asian American music making, for this limiting and even anachronistic mode of identity politics holds little interest to him or his peers. At the same time, what Rafael's remarks underscore are the limitations in the options he feels are available to him and other Asian Americans desiring to express the full range of their subjectivities through their music making.

The conundrum that Rafael articulates is exacerbated by his sense that as Asian Americans he and his peers enter musical genres and spaces in which their belonging is already contested at best.

> I don't think Asian Americans have their set kind of music thing. Maybe now people look at Asian Americans and think of YouTube and having ukuleles and stuff like that. But I don't think we have our thing like African Americans; they have their set culture that everybody can, I mean you definitely kind of know what to expect, you know what I'm saying. And you know how like white Americans, they have their thing going on. But I feel like Asian Americans don't—no one even knows what they're doing, and they're so involved trying to be white, and a lot of them are trying to be black. So it's a mix of Asian Americans just trying to be like everybody else I feel like. I mean that's what I'm thinking. And that's why it's been harder for us to find—I mean for other people's perceptions on us to be, you know, not like we're just trying to copy other people and stuff.

The equivocations that pepper the singer's language—his reluctance to delineate precisely the "set kind of thing" that defines "white" or "black" culture and his reliance on discursive placeholders such as "You know what I'm saying"—index the sensitivities that accompany discussions of race in a post–civil rights era of heightened racial awareness. Rafael's black and white observations about music no doubt gloss over a host of racial complexities. At the same time, they underscore the entrenched racial and ethnic shorthand that exists for different musical styles, popular understandings based not merely on racial essentialisms, but also on a music industry that has historically used race—from the race of the musician to the perceived race of the sound—to structure genre distinctions.[67]

Historicizing the construction of "pop" and the "mainstream," music scholar Tamara Roberts writes: "Despite the long history of cross-racial and interracial musical practice in the United States, the popular music industry has from its beginning been divided into racialized genres and executives have capitalized on perceptions of racial difference in marketing artists. From the early twentieth-century distinction of black 'race records' from white 'hillbilly records' to the current divisions between, supposedly, white rock, black hip-hop, and, more-or-less, brown world music, race has been the central organizing category for how popular music is cultivated, sold, and consumed."[68] The consolidation of a "musical color line" from a heterogeneous mix of sounds and styles in the early twentieth century, a historical process that Karl Miller insightfully calls "segregating sound," continues to materialize itself in the remarks made by Asian American artists.[69] Shifting between race, region, style, and sound in the U.S. popular landscape, these correlations are admittedly fraught and unstable but continue, nonetheless, to exclude Asian Americans and render them as non-American/ethnic others. Put differently, Asianness is figured as absence—outside the authenticating links connecting race and musical ownership but illusively present in the stereotyped sounds that serve as proxies for Asia and Asian bodies. And while popular music encompasses more than the black-and-white polarities referenced by musicians like A. J. Rafael, the lingering suspicion that there exists no music genre to which Asian Americans can claim as their "set kind of music thing" compounds the challenge of sonic belonging. Moreover, it goes without saying that the resulting perception of imitation—of "trying to copy other people" rather than drawing on original resources or traditions—plays on dominant tropes about the derivative nature of Asian Americans, allowing for the easy transfer of these traits onto their music making practices.

In an attempt to move beyond these questions of mimicry and musical belonging—questions driven, as Rafael emphasizes, by "other people's perceptions"—some of my interviewees sought to posit the act of singing as race-neutral and therefore more open to Asian Americans. Distinguishing between singing and rapping, they argued that non-black rappers encounter greater challenges working in a genre that is so closely associated both historically and culturally with blackness. For instance, Joseph Vincent reflected, "If you're a White guy or an Asian guy trying to do rap it's going to be a lot more difficult to break into that as opposed to a singer. People get used to seeing Asian Americans sing and use the guitar, and I think it's a smoother transition for Asians to go into some sort of singing than it is for rappers; you know what I mean?"[70] When I asked for greater elaboration, he offered: "Just to sing, you're not really trying to be anyone, you're just singing."

This is, on the one hand, a puzzling formulation given the extent to which the vocal aesthetics of pop music traffic in a dizzying range of racialized perceptions about whiteness, blackness, admixture, and difference. Put simply, while "just singing" may feel utterly natural—a mode of personal expression universally available to anyone with a human voice—it is neither ahistorical nor race-neutral. Much has been written about the complex historical, cultural, and economic dimensions of, for instance, black vocal stylings in American popular music; these histories, as Daphne Brooks trenchantly observes, continue to impact "how we sound race and how we racialize sound in the contemporary popular imaginary."[71] Racialized scripts influence what we hear and the bodies we expect to produce those sounds. These YouTube musicians recognize this. Take, for example, Jennifer Chung's recognition of the discrepancies created by her Asianness and the soulful register of her music. Comments that she "sounds like a black girl," which Chung described as hearing and taking as a compliment, speak to the unforeseen coupling of race and sound in her music.

On the other hand, for Asian American popular musicians haunted by the specter of nonexistence and framed through dominant perceptions that place them at odds with their musical aspirations, imagining and articulating race-neutral spaces of music making may well represent a mode of self-preservation that allows them to continue in their chosen profession. Positing the broad umbrella of pop—itself a slippery category encompassing, as Simon Frith contends, more the amalgamation of the residual traces left over from other genres than a specific style—and "just singing" as less fraught in racialized battles of authenticity and ownership allows these Asian American singers to envision more room for their presence.[72] It provides them a way to imagine accessing the symbolic culture of a nation that continues to treat them as not fully American.

The bind, of course, is that claims of race neutrality often serve as proxies for whiteness, thus reproducing its centrality as a marker of universality. This is evident in Clara C.'s account of deliberately leaving off her last name "Chung" in materials she used to recruit her band members. As she recounted, "After we'd gotten a lot closer and more comfortable, [my band members] were like, 'I thought you were some white girl from your singing.' And I guess that's kind of how it should be. It should be just like blank. Not that I should be a white girl but that I should just be a blank slate."[73] Given the symbolic capital of whiteness, it is unsurprising that Clara connects the feeling of being appreciated on the basis of musical merit alone with her perception of the "blankness" and freedom that comes from sounding like a "white girl."[74] For her, whiteness signified a sound unsullied by racial specificity and extramusical assumptions—a pure state akin to a blank slate. At the same time, aware that her remarks could be interpreted as a desire to *be* white or a denunciation of multiculturalism and her Asianness, she also amended: "But I don't know. I'm all for diversity."

Here, we might frame Clara's observations as a longing for the privileges that whiteness bestows through its association with universality, choice, and freedom. At the same time, her comments reflect the difficulty that many young Asian Americans feel specifying how race impacts their musical opportunities. Similar to the classical musicians encountered in the previous chapter, YouTube stars correlated discrimination with direct acts of disenfranchisement. Thus, despite an acknowledgment that "there's racism everywhere," Clara claimed that within the realm of music she enjoyed equitable treatment: "No one's ever just turned away an ear because I was Asian. I've always been given a fair chance." Here, the singer draws on existing frameworks of color blindness and meritocracy, implying that, as Lisa Nakamura aptly observes, "The failure to overtly discriminate on the basis of race, and the freedom to compete in the 'open market' despite an uneven playing field . . . constitutes fairness."[75] And yet, as Clara's own example suggests, making accommodations to, and thereby partially reinforcing the conflation of whiteness and universality and the assumption that a race-neutral sound is best achieved through concealing one's Asianness also represents a limiting vision of freedom and fair chance.

This should not suggest that entrenched assumptions about Asianness did not trouble these young musicians. Rather, their remarks can be interpreted as strategies to negotiate a music business and racial climate in which acknowledging the presence of race can, on its own, be viewed as inserting race (and intimations of racism) where it was not previously salient. As young Asian Americans attempting to make a living through their music, adhering to a script (and fantasy) of color-blind listening allows them to appeal to as broad an audience as possible. And while I do not want to discount how music making can, for these young singers, feel like a respite from social boundaries and racial politics, I also want to place their remarks within the broader contexts in which they make music and, in particular, the racialized comments they regularly receive on their YouTube videos.

In a video blog titled "Ramblings on Race," David Choi responded to charges of ethnic insularity among Asian American artists, riffing on this question posed by a user: "David, do you only hang out with Asians? As a white kid, this gets kind of awkward when every video I watch with a guest has an Asian in it. Except for the one with Chester."[76] Leaving aside the particular irony that Chester See is, as noted earlier, multiracial Asian American, Choi engages in some long-winded reflection about the value of racial diversity before addressing the comment directly.

> In response to your comment it's awkward to see Asians with only Asians, of course it's a little awkward because . . . there are no Asians in entertainment, in media in America, so it's not normal to see it. So I apologize if you feel weird about it. But I know there are a lot of white YouTubers out there, especially the big ones, who only use white people in their videos as well and I watch it and am like 'hey, it's normal.' I don't care. I don't feel it's awkward because I'm used to seeing it in mainstream media—white lead roles with other white casts. I've seen that so it's not weird to me.

After some more meandering musings on race and the value of cross-racial friendships, the singer repeats the familiar stance that, in the final moment, he only cares about making music. Like other YouTube musicians, he refused to politicize the "abnormal" visibility of Asian Americans in his videos, claiming greater interest in sharing quality music than in broadcasting something that hints at racial commentary or politics.

While Choi does not theorize his remarks this way, his comments incisively point to the limits of color-blind narratives and their entwinement in racial hierarchies. For a color-blind framework suggests that race does not matter as long as people of color assimilate to the perspective of a presumed white viewer, seamlessly upholding whiteness as normative, central, and universal. Unused to this break in protocol, the violation of such norms can feel disorienting to both Asians and non-Asians alike. For the self-identified "white kid," the

"Asianness" of Choi's videos made his/her whiteness palpable, provoking feelings of unease and exposing the uncomfortable existence of white privilege. For Asian Americans, the projection of a worldview populated by Asian Americans can feel equally disconcerting. But subverting the script on what constitutes normal can, as my interviewees attest, also represent an empowering process for young Asian Americans.

Ambiguities in the remarks Asian American YouTube musicians make about the roles that race and Asianness play in their music making point to the challenge of balancing their desire to be viewed as universal and normative Americans while recognizing the markets in which they circulate, their shared position on the periphery of national popular culture, and the demographics of their core fan base. The particular appeal that these musicians hold for Asian American audiences and their inclusion in Asian American–themed events and performances depend on their racialization *as* Asian American. Asian American YouTube stars understand this, correlating the intense loyalty of their core fan base to the dearth of Asian Americans in popular music and the collective hunger (a longing they share) for representations that expand and complicate the meanings associated with the Asian American face. In addition, these artists recognize how, in material terms, branding themselves through the identity marker Asian American facilitates opportunities, albeit within a smaller intra-ethnic market.[77] This helps contextualize artist manager Tom Ngo's assertion that Asian American independent musicians hold certain advantages over other unsigned artists: "You know that with an Asian American act you'll bring in Asian American fans. Because even if these artists are basically unknown, the audience will come out and explore them because they're Asian and they don't see other Asians performing like that. But say this was a white guy playing the same type of music as say Jason Mraz. Well, the fan could just go to a Jason Mraz concert." From Ngo's perspective, Asianness provides these artists with a form of ethnic capital that allows them to mobilize resources and a community. "Community," in this context, is not an abstract concept, but one made manifest by the young Asian Americans who turn up at shows, purchase merchandise and music, share and repost videos, and register their support through YouTube and social media.

At the same time, this benefit is double-edged as it limits and sets apart Asian American acts on the basis of race, confining them to a niche market perceived as narrow. My interviewees often wondered how a racialized audience base limited their opportunities to expand to a broader market and questioned whether the awkwardness that non-Asians might feel circulating in predominantly Asian American spaces potentially impacts their audience. As David Choi commented: "When a non-Asian comes to one of my shows and are there in a sea of Asians, it's like how are they going to feel? They'll feel a little out of place." He used the visibility of non-Asians at his concerts as a benchmark to calculate the universality of his music, observing: "When I do see non-Asians at my shows . . . I feel really good because it shows me that non-Asians are, well those particular non-Asians, are just listening to the music as opposed to seeing who is singing it."

Capitalizing on the global reach of YouTube represents one strategy that Asian American YouTube musicians use to expand the racialized niche market they occupy in the United States, even if it continues to place them within a racial framework. Some artists explicitly attempt to profit from the capital they possess as Asian Americans in their perceived home markets in Asia and from assumptions (placed on them and chosen) of diasporic belonging. Singer-songwriter Jason Chen, for instance, makes use of his Mandarin speaking skills through a separate YouTube channel that houses his covers of Chinese pop songs by artists like Jay Chou, JJ Lin, and Leehom Wang and covers of popular U.S. songs that he sings in Mandarin. At the same time, performing and/or marketing themselves to audiences in Asia also produces certain ambivalences for Asian American YouTube musicians, particularly given their desire to achieve recognition *as* American and to contest the racial logic of their foreignness.

The complex politics of home emerged, for instance, in my interview with Clara C., who at the time was preparing for a tour that would take her to Japan, Singapore, Taiwan, the Philippines, and Korea or, as she put it, the "motherland." After a requisite nod to appreciating her "culture and [Korean] language," the singer emphasized her Americanness, noting that she knew very little about Korea, was very "Americanized," and wanted to reach audiences in Asia on her own terms rather than "compromise myself to their standards." For Clara, this entailed more than just continuing to sing in English. Her perception of the manufactured quality of K-pop songs and the prevalence of plastic surgery among its top stars conflicted with her own stated desire for "naturalness"—or in YouTube terms "realness"—in both look and sound. The broader implication that Clara rightly articulates is that pursuing a music career in Asia would require conforming her image, sound, and brand to the parameters of that specific pop music industry. And while some aspiring Asian American pop singers may view Asia as an attractive alternate market to make music, my interviewees rankled at frequently encountered presumptions that their roots and cultural affinities necessarily lie outside of the United States.[78]

As young independent musicians attempting to make a living and develop their own individual voice, they did not necessarily want to be branded, as singer Jane Lui put it, as an "Asian American artist" with a racialized fan base. She expressed unease linking her individual path in music to an identity marker whose collective meanings she did not necessarily control. And yet, as is the case for all artists, Lui recognized that she could not manage the investments—racial or otherwise—that fans placed on her: "I just want my audience to be anyone who likes my stuff. But then I realized you cannot control how [an audience] interprets you. And if they see your skin color as something that they want to connect to, that's absolutely fine. . . . But for me, that's not kind of my goal."

While not her "goal," Lui acknowledged that identification through "skin color" held powerful resonance for her as well, as it somehow managed to foster connections across the many differences in musical styles, upbringings, aspirations, and desires within Asian American communities in southern California. As she put it,

> You know, I think what's the most humbling thing about the Asian community that I have met in L.A. is that we all make such completely different music but we're able to sit in a room, talk about it, collaborate together because of our ethnicity. That ethnicity . . . really connects us together and makes us kind of forget about genres and borders, to just work together. That has been so humbling to me. So I totally think that there is not an Asian American sound, just like how there is not a Caucasian sound. I mean there are all kinds of genres in the white world. But I feel like the fact that we can look at each other

and connect in some like instinctual, you know, way about our skin color has allowed us to work together beautifully. I still don't know what it is, and it blows my mind every time I see it happening, where I connect and meet new, you know, Asian artists and it just clicks.

Lui's rhetoric of an "instinctual" connection may, on the surface, sound essentializing—a recourse to instincts stitched in "skin color" that links Asian American artists together. And yet, in her formulation, ethnicity represents more than a static bond. The willingness to sit, talk, work, and collaborate stems from an investment in creating a shared pan-ethnic collectivity—a belief that they are participating in something larger than themselves. This community does not simply emerge out of perceived sameness in skin color but, rather, through the labor and continual practice to make the language of kinship feel meaningful.

It is these artists' willingness to work together as a pan-ethnic coalition in the pursuit of common goals—making quality music, consolidating a market, navigating a competitive music industry, countering limiting racial representations, and demonstrating their complexity and humanity—that I came to understand as undergirding the language of a movement mobilized by many of my interviewees. Drawing a comparison to other social movements, Joseph Vincent reflected: "We're kind of like that movement during black oppression except less dramatic. And it's kind of like we're banding together, and we know that other Asian Americans are trying to do the same thing we're doing. So we're all moving up together, and it's strength in numbers as opposed to just trying to be all out for yourself." Given that the civil rights movement arguably represents *the* dominant framework to discuss social movements in the United States, it is understandable that Vincent draws on this association, even if he feels it inadequately captures the "less dramatic" situation confronting Asian Americans. His hesitation in claiming equivalence with "black oppression" may also stem from his middle-class upbringing and the frequency with which he, like my other interviewees, downplayed the significance of race in their lives and mobilized whiteness rather than blackness as a comparative marker. At the same time, what emerges in Vincent's vaguely formed reference to the "movement during black oppression" is a belief in collective purpose and presence. As he elaborated: "It's really about time that people see [Asian Americans] as more than someone who just works hard and is diligent and is quiet. And I think that's what's happening right now, like these past five, six years. We're actually emerging and being seen as something more than just someone who can do math problems, or someone who could just do well in school, or someone who is going to be intimidated if you come off aggressive towards them." Singer Dawen made a similar observation, placing at the center of this movement an assertion of alternate frameworks of love, desire, coolness, and beauty: "You never feel as Asian Americans that we're 'the shit.' But it's time. We need to think of something Asian as beautiful."[79]

Desires to yoke the personal to the political and upend racist frameworks of beauty and self-worth have a long history in movement politics, even if these young musicians do not explicitly make such connections. Indeed, if a political center exists at all within this network of Asian American YouTube stars and fans, it may lie less in tackling racial inequalities or institutionalized racism than in laboring collectively to showcase and normalize the "Asian American face." These young artists engage in a form of politics that uses collaboration and shared endeavor as touchstones. And yet, embedded within the process of coming together *as* Asian Americans was a simultaneous desire to downplay the centrality of their Asianness, to insist on the universality of the themes and emotions contained in their music, and to gain visibility as Americans. The racial ambivalence at the center of this movement speaks to the conflicts that young Asian American musicians face participating in a popular media landscape in which Asianness continues to be marked through absence and misrecognition. This knowledge leads artists to undertake additional labor to link their efforts, aggregate resources, and form community. Taken together, their narratives underscore the dynamic of limitation and possibility that Asian American YouTube musicians experience pursuing their music making in a changing media landscape.

Conclusion

Listening to "YouTube (A Love Song)" years later, with the knowledge of the visibility that Choi and other Asian American performers have gained through YouTube, it is hard not to hear the song retrospectively as a statement of agency—a love song to the opportunities that the platform has given young Asian Americans to find each other, to feel seen and heard, and to materialize something that might be called a pan-ethnic Asian American community. While my interviewees acknowledged the barriers that Asian Americans encounter in forging a path within a competitive music industry, they also affirmed the capaciousness of singing, the color blindness of talent, and the faith that race need not shape the scope of their musical imagination. They expressed optimism about the ways in which Asian Americans capitalized on the democratic potential of YouTube to express themselves in a multiplicity of ways: to be the heroes of their own narratives, to cast themselves as subjects of desire and love, to engage with a community actively seeking self-expression, and to demonstrate that Asian Americans have not only an abundance of talent, passion, and creativity but also an audience willing to support their efforts. As my interviewees repeatedly told me, their cohort of creative content producers represents a new generation of Asian Americans whose collective output is lessening the burden of representation placed on any single artist. These young YouTube musicians matter because they amplify what racial politics and Asian America look like for the even younger generation of Asian Americans who constitute their core fan base.

At the same time, despite the openings yielded by YouTube and new media, it still remains, as Choi bluntly stated, "hard to make it in America as an Asian American." As the next chapter shows, this recognition leads some Asian American musicians to circumvent the United States entirely in search of opportunities abroad. Thus while it is possible that a musician like Leehom Wang, the subject of the next chapter, might have remained in the United States if YouTube and related social media had existed when he first began his musical career, it should be noted that Asian Americans' "reverse migration" to Asian popular music markets continues well into the "post-YouTube" era. Popular YouTube teen singer Megan Lee, for instance, relocated with her family to Korea to pursue a career in K-pop after achieving success on *MBC Star Audition* in 2010, an *American Idol*–style reality competition show (many such music competition shows in South Korea feature Korean Americans among its contestants). And since our interview in 2011, singer-songwriter Dawen relocated to Taiwan to pursue opportunities in the Chinese popular music scene and released his debut Mandarin album *Hello* (*Nihao*) with Universal Music in 2013.[80] While these are individual journeys for these singers, paths likely inflected by personal motivations as well as musical interests, they manifest a broader pattern of viewing Asian markets as spaces of opportunities. The next chapter maps the possibilities, as well as challenges, that Asian Americans encounter in their musical migrations to Asia.

FOUR

Finding Sonic Belonging Abroad

Reimagining Chinese American Subjectivities through Diaspora

In the fall of 2011, Wong Fu Productions, a trio of Chinese American filmmakers best known for their music videos and short films on YouTube, posted an exciting announcement on their blog: they were headed to Taiwan to direct a music video for the global pop star Leehom Wang. Realizing that some of their fans might not grasp the immensity of their upcoming collaboration, Wong Fu Productions provided this short primer: "For those of you who do not know who Leehom is, it's ok, we forgive you, haha. He's by far one of all of Asia's top stars. He's a multiplatinum singer who's been selling out arenas for over a decade, an actor, and a director among his list of accomplishments. What's cool is that he was born in the USA, so he speaks perfect English too. He's like Justin Timberlake, except JT has only 2 solo albums and Leehom has had 14, haha."[1] Their casual online language notwithstanding, a distinct sense of pride emerges in their description of Wang, a singer who rivals pop stars like Justin Timberlake with the scope of his fame and accolades in Asia but who, like them, was "born in the USA" and "speaks perfect English."[2] While the members of Wong Fu Productions were longtime fans of the singer (and had even featured his music in the closing credits of an early film), the idea that Wang—a celebrity whose star wattage and geographical home base seemed so distant from theirs—was not only familiar with, but also an admirer of, their small-scale YouTube videos seemed almost implausible. They were certain a friend was pranking them when the message from Wang and his team landed in their e-mail inboxes.

Still, that Wang would reach out to Wong Fu Productions is not necessarily surprising given his longstanding investment in exploring the nuances of Chineseness and Chinese American identity in his artistic endeavors. The singer shared not only a similar subject position with the members of Wong Fu Productions but also an awareness of the paucity of popular representations in the U.S. media landscape framed through that perspective. Speaking to Philip Wang and Wesley Chan, the two members of Wong Fu Productions who traveled to Taipei for the music video shoot, Wang explained: "I love watching your skits. You guys do some crazy, ridiculous stuff. It's really unique. You don't get to see that type of genre of work in other places. And you guys have really touched upon a nerve that I share, because I'm an ABC [American-born Chinese] as well."[3] Thus, while the massive stardom that Wang enjoys in global Chinese markets stands in stark contrast to the niche celebrity occupied by YouTube stars like Wong Fu Productions, the particularities of their fame and professional trajectories are similarly shaped by the racial limitations that Asian Americans encounter in the U.S. media landscape. Neither Wang nor Wong Fu Productions enjoys mainstream popularity in the United States.[4] Despite working in divergent commercial, linguistic, and cultural milieus, these artists recognize how their Chinese American background impacts the contours and reception of their artistic work, even if an examination of ethnicity is not necessarily at the core of their creative pursuits. Tapping Wong Fu Productions to direct the music video for "Still in Love with You" ("Yi ran ai ni"), an up-tempo love song that Wang wrote to be included in an album of greatest hits, allowed the singer to register his support for the Asian American talent flourishing on YouTube and provide the young filmmakers with a visible platform to expand the diasporic reach of their audience base.

While chapter 3 examined how young Asian Americans capitalize on the democratized access of YouTube to navigate, circumvent, and, at times, contest their racial and musical inheritance in the United States, this chapter assesses the choice that aspiring Asian American pop stars make to leave the United States in order to pursue recording contracts and musical careers in Asia. Investigating the seemingly unnatural career path of a pop singer whose attainment of stardom is conditioned on gaining fluency in linguistic, cultural, and national contexts not quite but also assumed to be his own, this chapter uses Wang's phenomenal celebrity in Asia to analyze how and under what conditions Asian Americans achieve success in their presumed homelands abroad. Although the professional and strategic decision that Asian Americans make to bypass the U.S. popular music industry is conditioned by U.S. racism, discourses of diaspora—those placed on them and/or adopted by choice—naturalize these reverse migrations as a form of cultural return and homecoming. As one of the most popular artists working in Mandopop (Mandarin-language popular music) and a pop star with pan-Asian appeal, Wang represents an ideal case study to investigate how the growth of Asian popular music industries and markets, coupled with a racially stratified U.S. media landscape, have begun reconfiguring overseas homelands as spaces of mobility, promise, and opportunity for Asian Americans.[5] The singer's ubiquitous presence in Chinese markets underscores the absence of an Asian American pop star of equivalent popularity in the United States while it also projects what is possible by "crossing over" into culture industries abroad.

How did Wang, a singer born and raised in Rochester, New York, and only marginally fluent in Mandarin before enrolling in language classes as an undergraduate at Williams College, emerge as one of the industry heavyweights of Mandopop? What "nerve" does Wang share with other ABCs, and how does it become translated, commodified, and transformed in Chinese contexts? And how do Chinese Americans rework, manage, and even profit from their discrepant fluencies by participating in a foreign musical landscape in which racial similarity rather than difference marks the terms of their membership? Following Wang's unlikely musical journey from the suburbs of Western New York to global pop music stardom in Chinese-speaking markets, this chapter traces the commercial and state interests, emotional resonances, and multiple mediations that constitute diaspora. On the one hand, the singer smoothly integrates into a transnational popular music industry already adept at marketing a diverse mix of ethnic Chinese artists as belonging to a shared pan-Chinese community. Wang skillfully conforms to the linguistic, aesthetic, and political parameters placed on mainstream Mandopop artists, crafting a public performance of self carefully attuned to nationalist narratives of self-improvement and Chinese pride. As a singer who aims for the broadest audience possible, his music fosters

the imagination of a community of Chinese listeners sutured and uni-
fied despite imperfect translations across linguistic and national territories, and the contested and often contingent geopolitical relationships between China, Taiwan, Hong Kong, the United States, and the
broader Chinese diaspora.[6] On the other hand, the singer's more than
decade-long career in Asia makes visible the continual learning and
practice necessary to forge diasporic belonging, despite the essializa-
tion of such labor through biological invocations of shared ancestry
and blood. Through his music, Wang both reinforces and complicates
long-standing Chinese metaphors, such as falling leaves return to roots
(*luoye guigen*)—also the title of one of his popular songs—gesturing, at
times, to more capacious understandings of diaspora that would fully
allow for his inclusion.

To understand more fully how Chinese Americans have successfully
pursued careers in Mandopop, this chapter provides background of the
economic, cultural, and geopolitical contexts of the transnational music
industry and the central role occupied by Taiwan. I then turn to the
L.A. Boyz, one of the earliest Taiwanese American groups to gain commercial success in Taiwan's competitive music industry, and analyze
how their music and marketing reflected and helped mold perceptions
of ABCs. Given Wang's prolific musical output, in addition to his vast
film and television work, this chapter focuses primarily on songs and
albums that thematize Chinese American subjectivity and the manifold meanings of Chineseness in a globalized era. Through songs such
as Wang's hip hop remake of "Descendants of the Dragon" (2000) and
what he coined "chinked out," a musical aesthetic explored on the albums
Shangri-la (2004) and *Heroes of Earth* (2005), this chapter investigates
how the singer incorporates a Chinese American perspective into his
music. Finally, I extend my analysis to Chinese American fans of Wang,
examining how they use their fandom both to claim greater familiarity with their roots and Chinese heritage and to counter U.S. views of
Chinese pop music and by extension Chinese culture as somehow less
than and second-rate.

Indeed, it is worth noting that when Chinese Americans singers and
fans turn to Mandopop, they carry a familiarity with, and may even
partially share, prevailing U.S. perspectives of the music as corny and
banal; highly commodified and industry driven; teeming with attractive

(and possibly surgically enhanced) singers who lack talent; and overrun by cheesy, 1980s-style ballads.[7] Many Americans do not possess a clear impression of Mandopop, and those who do often deride it (and Asian pop music more broadly) as a cloying replica of American pop. Travel guidebooks warn that "overexposure to the saccharine confections of mainstream Cantopop [Cantonese popular music produced in Hong Kong] and Mandopop may be like drinking gallons of extra-sugary Fanta."[8] Articles appearing in the *New York Times* similarly concede that Mandopop is "sappy by Western tastes," a sonic landscape akin to "saccharine easy-listening."[9] The prevalence of such views helps account for the ambivalence that Asian Americans, including the YouTube singers discussed in the previous chapter, sometimes express being associated with, let alone pursuing a professional career in, Asian popular music industries.

Still, as Wang himself suggested in a talk for a British audience at the Oxford Union, such judgments may well reflect the shortcomings and arrogance of American/Western listeners, their inability—indeed, refusal—to consider the meanings, pleasures, and values that millions of Mandopop fans derive from the music they love: "Western ears aren't familiar with and therefore don't really understand how to appreciate Chinese music."[10] Acknowledging that he, too, initially perceived Mandopop songs to be "lame" and "cheesy" upon his arrival to Taiwan, the singer concedes that this early impression spoke less to the quality of the music than to his own ignorance about the sounds, rhythms, lyrics, and song structures that connected powerfully with Chinese audiences.[11] Learning to listen, as he put it, with "local ears" necessitated deconstructing his own cultural assumptions and the broader hierarchies that racialize seemingly personal matters of taste and quality.[12] In his self-proclaimed role as a "cultural ambassador of Chinese pop"—a transnational figure with intimate understanding of both American and Chinese viewpoints—Wang markets himself as ideally positioned to broker cultural misperceptions and to champion the vibrancy of Chinese music. This chapter argues that "chinked out" represents the singer's own musical attempt to speak back to reductive U.S. assumptions about Chinese Americans and to contest the presumed dominance of U.S. culture industries, particularly in an era marked by glib proclamations about the rise of China.

The Transnational Landscape of Mandopop

If Mandopop invokes such descriptions as lame or corny in the U.S. context, these associations contrast sharply with the powerful influence it wields in Asia as the stylized sonic embodiment of modernity, cosmopolitanism, and transnational lifestyles. Following Hong Kong's reunification with China in 1997, Taiwan emerged as the geographic and cultural hub of Chinese popular music—"the centre of global Chinese cool as well as producer of global Chinese pop stars."[13] As the commercialized pop music genre that dominates Chinese-speaking markets, Taiwan's Mandopop enjoys phenomenal popularity in China, Taiwan, Hong Kong, Southeast Asia, and the greater Chinese diaspora.[14] The extent to which Taiwan's pop music industry fuels the listening tastes and popular imagination of a massive Chinese listening public underscores the thorny nationalisms that lay submerged—erupting only on occasion—in the lighthearted sounds of Mandopop. In his cogent analysis of the cultural and political work of Mandopop, Marc Moskowitz concedes: "It is nothing less than astounding that Taiwan, which houses 23 million people, can dictate the musical tastes of a nation of 1.3 billion. Taiwan is under the shadow of the PRC's economic, military, and political might . . . but it dominates China's popular culture to such a degree that it is not surprising that the PRC government seems to worry that Taiwan is the proverbial tail wagging the PRC dog."[15] While the influence that Taiwan holds in Mandopop will likely diminish as China develops a stronger infrastructure for producing, distributing, and promoting its own stable of local singers and songwriters, for the time being, Taiwan represents the music industry powerhouse for Chinese audiences.[16]

Taiwan's popular music industry operates in a relatively open society, having flourished alongside the process of democratization and liberalization that followed the lifting of martial law in 1987. At the same time, given China's status as a market powerhouse, Taiwan's Mandopop artists seeking to maintain their commercial viability and corporate endorsements are careful to acquire approval from the Chinese government. For this reason, singers avoid broaching issues related to Taiwan's official status and other potentially sensitive political issues, focusing instead on topics ranging from shared cultural traits to such personal emotions as love, longing, loneliness, and heartbreak. Moreover, when Mandopop artists do investigate social issues, they highlight such themes as intergenerational conflict or domestic violence and locate *interesting.* the responsibility for change in the actions of individuals rather than, for example, the political leadership of the state.[17] Such an emphasis is visible in the music of Wang, who promoted environmental aware- *individual* ness in his 2007 album *Change Me* through a neoliberal emphasis on *responsibility* personal responsibility and self-improvement, highlighting what young people can do—from recycling to reducing personal consumption—to inspire change in their local communities.

While Taiwan's Mandopop skillfully promotes and markets a flexible pan-Chinese identity, singers nonetheless do find themselves inadvertently caught, at times, within contentious cross-straits politics between Taiwan and China.[18] Take, for instance, the popular Taiwanese aboriginal singer A-Mei, who was banned by the mainland Chinese government owing to suspected loyalties to the Taiwan independence movement after performing the Taiwanese national anthem at President Chen Shui-bian's inauguration ceremony in 2000. Yet, when A-Mei refused to speak up against the ban, contending that "I am just a singer" and "we all know that singers should not be involved with politics," her "apolitical" stance drew criticism from the pro-independence faction in Taiwan, who felt that A-Mei should defend her loyalties to her country more vigorously.[19] The singer's popularity and stated desire to sidestep politics provided little insulation against the geopolitical tensions in which her music circulates. While mainstream Mandopop stars generally refrain from broaching any potentially charged political topics in their music and media interviews, it may be that Chinese Americans can more easily distance themselves from cross-straits conflicts given their upbringing in the United States.

The transnational market for and sensibility of Mandopop reflects the economic growth experienced in Taiwan (and Asia more generally) during the past few decades and the emergence of Asianness as a desirable commodity and Asia as a market for the circulation of popular culture from Taiwan, China, Hong Kong, Japan, Singapore, and South Korea.[20] The multidirectional traffic of popular media and "trans-pop-consumers" in Asia highlights processes of globalization guided less through East-West distinctions (and a dominant U.S. anchor) than through a cross-pollination of cultural influences within East and Southeast Asia.[21] As Koichi Iwabuchi observes, the diffusion of global power in the circulation of popular culture in Asia makes it increasingly necessary to "recenter" globalization to include consumer markets and cultural brokers that may not reside in the West (and the United States). Such a shift prompts an understanding of Asian popular media as reflecting local modernities, which, despite their strong entwinement with U.S. cultural influences, "dynamically rework the meanings of being modern in Asian contexts at the site of production and consumption."[22]

Alongside its divergent inter-Asian cultural influences, Taiwan's Mandopop also contains a wide variety of ethnic Chinese artists who hail from Taiwan, Hong Kong, China, Malaysia, Singapore, and North America. This diverse mix reflects the international markets within which Mandopop circulates. Transnational celebrities like Wang serve as bridging figures who help augment the imagination of a global Chinese community joined together through shared popular culture consumption. The singer, in turn, speaks of his audience through globalizing frameworks, asserting: "The place where the Chinese people live is the place for Chinese language songs. There is no national boundary in music."[23] While such a statement conveniently disavows political tensions, uneven power relations, and territorial divides, it also makes tangible a vision of cultural Chineseness—the belief, as Sau-ling Wong puts it, that "a purely cultural Chinese diasporic identity is possible, one divorced from political economy and transcending nation-states."[24] Put differently, the consumption of Mandopop across disparate Chinese territories enhances the notion of an "imagined community" of Chinese listeners dispersed across time and space, converging, reinforcing, and commodifying discourses about the potential for music and Chineseness to transcend borders. As the sonic embodiment of Chineseness, Mandopop positions itself as the culture industry that produces, sells, and markets Chinese music for an enormous global network of Mandarin-speaking Chinese people to consume. And as U.S. perceptions (or lack of knowledge) of Mandopop make evident, Chinese popular music is not marketed with U.S./Western tastes in mind. This segregation of markets means that while Mandopop stars do sell out shows in cities like Los Angeles and Las Vegas—places where Chinese people live or enjoy visiting—they continue to remain largely unknown outside of Chinese immigrant / Chinese American communities in the United States.[25]

Finally, it is useful to note how widespread piracy and illegal downloading in Asia (though clearly not exclusive to that region) create a synergistic relationship between multinational corporations, state entities, and artists seeking to increase their celebrity status and generate alternate revenue streams for their music. While Mandopop artists depend on securing corporate sponsorship to achieve commercial success, corporations, in turn, expend top marketing dollars on pop stars who have acquired the blessings of state-run media. The interdependency between artists and corporate support explains the slew of corporate endorsements maintained by Mandopop stars.[26] For unlike in the United States, where blatant celebrity endorsement for commercial brands is often pejoratively viewed as selling out, the fame and popularity of an artist in Asia are measured by the vastness of the products that the artist promotes.[27] In this "chaotic" economic landscape, the line demarcating commerce, promotion, and music is often unclear.[28] The entwinement of a company's image and its celebrity spokesperson means that both mutually constitute the public face of their respective brands.

Given the extent to which CD and MP3 sales represent unreliable, if not old-fashioned, barometers for measuring an album's success, Chinese popular music industries have established alternate modes of acquiring revenue, including live performances, advertising deals, product endorsements, sales of mobile phone ringtones, corporate-sponsored music videos, and KTV (karaoke) licensing fees.[29] The elaborate shows that Mandopop stars stage to promote their albums reflect the economic realities of Mandopop specifically and music industries more broadly, where live performances and personal appearances increasingly represent the most profitable channels to generate income.[30] In addition, the enormous popularity of KTV among Mandopop listeners means that ease of singing becomes part of the criteria that music producers and audiences use to evaluate a song's value. Understanding this context also helps to contextualize why slow ballads with relatively uncomplicated melodies and vocal ranges dominate the Mandopop landscape.[31] Industry pressure to predict and generate hits is apparent in Wang's albums, all of which contain a reliable stable of slow love songs regardless of the particular style or influence adopted for that album. Tellingly, the singer's fans regularly cite love songs as their favorite style of music adopted by the singer.[32]

As a savvy artist who aims for the broadest audience possible, Wang continually adapts to the political, cultural, and commercial demands placed upon him as an artist working in a changing media environment. He capitalizes on his long-standing celebrity and track record of commercial success to seek innovative ways of distributing content and connecting with his audience, from the revamping of his official website in 2013 to begin selling music directly to listeners to his deft utilization of social media platforms such as YouTube, Youku (a Chinese video hosting site similar to YouTube), and Sina Weibo (a Chinese microblog similar to Twitter).[33] More than thirty-six million fans follow Wang's updates on Sina Weibo, revealing both his skillful adoption of new media platforms and the extent of his cultural reach in Asia.[34] Still, how did a Chinese American singer from the suburbs of Western New York accumulate such a massive scale of fame and fandom in Chinese popular music? To answer this question we need to trace the footsteps of earlier Chinese Americans who turned to Taiwan's music industry as a site to pursue their musical dreams. As the next section shows, groups like the L.A. Boyz capitalized on and powerfully molded perceptions of ABCs in Chinese popular music, paving the path for other Chinese Americans to follow.

The L.A. Boyz and the Construction of ABC Identity

When Wang's first album debuted in 1995, he stepped into a Chinese music scene already versed in marketing and selling ABCs to Chinese-speaking audiences. Just three years earlier the L.A. Boyz—a trio of Taiwanese American teenagers from Orange County, California—took Taiwan's pop music scene by storm. Composed of two brothers, Jeffrey and Stanley Huang, and their cousin, Steven Lin, the L.A. Boyz served as foreign but still familiar vehicles to repackage U.S. hip hop culture into a hodgepodge of colorful clothing, dancing, and clean-cut fun.[35] With their low-slung pants, backward baseball caps, and trendy Cross Colours jackets, the group with "straight-up Taiwanese soul" hailing "direct from LA" danced their way into the hearts of young (mostly female) Taiwanese fans.[36] Best known for their coordinated choreography and songs rapped primarily in English, with a sprinkling of Taiwanese and Mandarin thrown in for good measure, the L.A. Boyz projected an image of American modernity, athleticism, and youthfulness rendered cool through their citation of hip hop iconography while also made accessible through their emphasis on shared ethnic heritage.

Often credited with introducing hip hop to Taiwan, the L.A. Boyz's breakout hit "Jump" ("Tiao") hit the airwaves in 1992, replete with a mishmash of goofy English lyrics and bragging rights based on possessing such assets as intelligence, athleticism, and managerial expertise.[37] Flaunting an image of masculinity that traded on their attractiveness, sociability, and cool, the L.A. Boyz flaunted qualities that Asian American men are perceived as lacking in the United States. As the trio boasted in "Jump": "super good looks, super like a man, super cool, super fit, super fast, super slick, super in tennis ball, super in basketball, super in management, super intelligent." As these lyrics suggest, the themes explored in their music steer clear of any potentially controversial content associated with hip hop in the U.S. context—from racial oppression to urban violence, drugs, or explicit sexuality. And while their lyrics may strain credibility, particularly from a U.S. perspective, it is worth emphasizing that the appeal of the L.A. Boyz lay less in the precise content of their lyrics than in the overall marketing of their brand through a framework of diasporic closeness intersected with foreignness, hybridity, and cool. While the L.A. Boyz began their careers in Taiwan with only a spotty grasp of Mandarin and basic fluency in Taiwanese (a local Chinese dialect distinct from Mandarin, which the trio grew up speaking in their home), most of their fans did not fully understand the English included in their songs.[38] What linked the L.A. Boyz and their fans was less a common spoken language than what Paul Gilroy describes in a different context as a "playful diasporic intimacy," a sense of fraternity brokered unevenly through the shared consumption of cultural productions across diasporic communities.[39]

In their translation of hip hop for a Taiwanese market, the L.A. Boyz decontextualized the music and culture into an innocuous form of dance, fashion, and speech—a mode of posturing layered onto a catchy beat. While the trio aligned themselves with Los Angeles (and, by dubious proxy, areas like Compton and South Central), they disassociated themselves from the costs of blackness, disenfranchisement, and racism. As Jeffrey Huang acknowledged in the *Los Angeles Times*: "We don't rap to rebel, we just want you to dance." Besides, as he continued, "When it comes to Asians, there's really not that much to rap about."[40] Huang's generalized claim that Asians lack the proper source material from which to rap may speak to the race and class distance that he personally felt from the origins of hip hop as a teenager hailing from the suburban streets of Irvine. At the same time, it also emphasizes the broader incongruities, at least in the U.S. popular imaginary (and particularly in the early 1990s), of tethering an Asian American body with rap.[41] But as rappers pursuing a musical career in Taiwan, at a safe remove from entrenched politics of racial authenticity and actual African Americans, the L.A. Boyz found a credible space to capitalize on their status as Americans, borrow freely from black cultural referents, and make brash, albeit empty, claims of "doing damage to all rappers even as I speak."

As relative newcomers to Taiwan when their album debuted, it is unlikely that the three teenagers were versed enough in the local politics, culture, or language to make any type of significant observation about life in Taipei. Moreover, as youth navigating a foreign music industry early in their career, the L.A. Boyz likely did not possess much agency over their musical content and image. In this sense, their marketing can be interpreted as reflecting the interests of a foreign music industry attempting to extract maximum value from a novel ABC teen-idol group before their fame receded. Rather than expressions of everyday realities encountered in the United States, the L.A. Boyz projected a Taiwanese fantasy of life enjoyed by overseas Chinese in the "land of opportunity." That is, the group represented Taiwanese manifestations of the American Dream—prodigal sons returned home to share their gifts and tales from abroad. As Chih-ming Wang reflects about the place that Asian Americans hold in the Taiwanese popular imaginary, "[Asian Americans] show up as models of success who speak and act with the aura of America. But they do not exist as mere images on the screen; oftentimes they exist in our family as our 'American' cousins and relatives whom our parents cannot stop singing the praises of and looking up to. . . . They are hardly ever seen within the history of racism and struggle but perceived to be the embodiment of transnational success and positive hybridity, finely mixing the East and West."[42] For the L.A. Boyz to ruminate on such topics as racism in the United States—the race and class legacies of hip hop and the racial barricades that confine not only African Americans but also, in different ways, Asian Americans—would pierce the "aura of America" these gleaming young men embodied in Taiwan. In this sense, the L.A. Boyz held aspirational appeal as familiar— if not familial—incarnations of what is possible in the United States. If hip hop represented a rebellious vernacular to Taiwanese youth, a stance no doubt enhanced by its association with the edginess of black culture, the L.A. Boyz signified sanctioned and sanitized defiance at best. Taiwanese media praised the trio as "good examples for young people," singling out their admirable ability to "both study and sing."[43] This may be why, as I discuss later in the chapter, the stated intentions behind Wang's "chinked out" music, which highlighted the racism and discrimination that Chinese face in the United States, failed to resonate fully with Chinese audiences, even though the music itself was a commercial success.

While the L.A. Boyz did not achieve fame that extended far beyond Taiwan's borders and disbanded a few years after their initial success—replaced in that competitive music landscape with yet a newer teen-idol boy band—they helped establish a successful formula for infusing hip hop into the commercialized framework of Taiwan's existing pop aesthetic.[44] More significantly, they smoothed the path for other Chinese Americans to begin envisioning homeland as a viable market to pursue recording contracts and fame. For while being Asian American does not represent an asset in the U.S. music industry—the challenges explicated by Asian American YouTube musicians in the previous chapter illustrate that well—being an ABC in Chinese popular music could signify a certain amount of cultural capital. If, within the confining categories of the U.S. music industry, Asian Americans are unable to assert ownership or musical authenticity in any popular music genre, in Chinese contexts they could gain recognition as L.A. Boyz—no hyphenated identity necessary—who possess native knowledge and intimate understanding of American culture. In short, crossing over into Chinese pop allowed the L.A. Boyz to claim elusive qualities rarely, if ever, granted to Asian Americans in the U.S. cultural context: authenticity and soul.[45] As a Chinese American record producer based in Taiwan contended: "I don't think that someone who has only listened to Western music can give you Western music with its soul—that comes from being in the environment and having grown up in it and really knowing the culture. You might be able to imitate it, but you won't get the same kind of 'soul.'"[46] Such a remark paradoxically redeploys the same logic used to delegitimize the musical authenticity of Asian Americans in the United States and leaves intact the presumed isomorphism, as Akhil Gupta and James Ferguson notably put it, of "space, place, and culture" that limits the full inclusion of Asians and Asian Americans in U.S. popular music as well as other forms of music.[47]

As one of the earliest Chinese American groups to achieve commercial success in Taiwan's popular music scene, the L.A. Boyz helped concretize an image of ABCs as embodying a particular combination of lack and privilege—lack of literacy in Chinese language and culture but the privilege of U.S. education, "insider" access to American popular culture, and American-accented English. While ABC is an identity marker with limited circulation in the United States outside of Chinese communities—used primarily by the immigrant generation to indict subsequent generations as hollow bamboo (read: assimilated, Americanized, and emptied of Chinese culture and roots)—it is a familiar acronym imposed upon and adopted by Chinese Americans abroad to make their subjectivity legible in Chinese contexts. Thus even if there exists no homogeneous or authentic Chinese identity against which the cultural and linguistic incompetence of ABCs can be measured— the heterogeneous dialects of, and forms of being, Chinese around the world speak to this impossibility—the purported hollowness of ABCs translates into a range of negative stereotypes. For instance, in Taiwan, ABCs have a reputation of being rude, loud, and spoiled: "Locals often stereotype ABCs as being rich and arrogant, with a poor command of Mandarin. They are often boxed in certain roles on TV dramas as bumbling homecoming kings."[48] While these negative shortcomings— whether the source of jokes in TV dramas or portrayed as cute in the case of the L.A. Boyz—are often made visible in the cultural realm, they also are inextricably linked to historical and geopolitical relations of power: the continuing preeminence of U.S. empire, the hegemonic reach of English as an international language, and Taiwan's postwar economic and political reliance on the United States.

At the same time, the growing economic prosperity of East Asia has produced an affluent middle and upper-middle class with access to foreign travel, education, consumer goods, and popular media. Such changes make any Chinese American claims (whether real or perceived) of economic and/or cultural superiority increasingly misguided. Put differently, the coordinates of power and privilege that historically marked the relationship between overseas Chinese and local Chinese communities have begun to shift in relation to the strength of modernizing Asian nations. At the same time, the advantages that Chinese Americans possess in light of their U.S. upbringing still hold special value in Taiwan given the entrenchment of its political structure and popular culture within American influence, ideas, and sensibilities.[49] U.S. hegemony in Taiwan reflects not just the international dominance exerted by a global superpower, but also the particular role that the United States played in the postwar period as the promoter and, albeit ambiguous, protector of a capitalist democracy sustained under the long shadow of China. China, which officially views Taiwan as a "rogue" island that is part of its national empire, continues to exercise considerable political and economic weight to prevent Taiwan from gaining official international recognition. As a sovereign but not quite independent state, Taiwan is triangulated between two empires—China and the United States. The geopolitical relationship of power and political dependency between Taiwan and the United States impacts the perception of ABCs in Taiwan.[50]

Still, while ABC identity acts as a signifier of privilege upon which local Chinese can graft various claims of arrogance and emptiness, the category also signposts the inevitability of diasporic belonging: one's ethnic destiny as an "American-born Chinese" to remain Chinese or *huaren* regardless of birthplace. The use of the word *huaren* rather than *zhongguoren* in discussions of Chinese diasporic communities is significant. While *huaren* refers to people of Chinese descent and emphasizes shared racial ancestry and cultural heritage, *zhongguoren* links Chinese identity nationally, politically, and territorially to mainland China.[51] Untethered from the U.S. context, the signifier Asian American becomes linked less with a history of shared exclusion and racial oppression and more with diasporic discourses of origin and descent. As Sau-ling Wong concedes, "The concept of *Asian Americans* doesn't travel well, and for good reason. Explicitly coalitional, more anti-essentialist than it has been given credit for, it grew out of a specific history of resistance and advocacy within the United States."[52] As the pan-ethnic category Asian American gains legibility through its accrual of a new set of descent-based connotations, it comes to signify the potential of transnational mobility and capital rather than minority status. For the idea of Asian America, as Chih-ming Wang notes, "when it is perceived in Asia, suggests a distinct combination of both 'America' as a symbol of modernity and 'Asian' as a transnational metaphor of flexibility and convertability. Taken out of its local history, 'Asian American' becomes a desirable and accessible identity in Asia."[53] As an aspirational symbol as much as an actual identity, *Asian American* invokes a hybrid subjectivity that imbues ethnic belonging with the privilege of international/American upbringing and understanding.

While the coupling of Chinese Americans with Chinese homelands (and normative Americans with whiteness) replicates a politics of exclusion reinforced by U.S. racial politics, such linkages also enable new forms of inclusion based on perceptions of shared Chinese cultural heritage.[54] As a contradictory sign of lack and privilege, ABC identity thus straddles the shifting terrain of inclusion and exclusion, a dynamic that resonates with the racial position that Asian Americans occupy in the United States. This may be the reason why Wang claims to feel most at home with other ABCs: "I've got a lot of people asking me whether I feel more American or more Chinese, and I say the group that I most identify with are the ABCs." The feeling of not quite belonging in the racialized landscape of the United States is comparable to ABC subjectivity in Taiwan. At the same time, living and touring in Asia allow the singer to place ABC identity within a global context, reframing it as one of many hybrid ways of being Chinese in the world rather than a stigmatized marker of racial difference. Chinese Americans in Mandopop capitalize on their in-between status, drawing on notions of diasporic belonging, cosmopolitanism, and transnational hybridity to tap into expanding Chinese markets. Wang's carefully choreographed public persona draws on the positive attributions placed on ABC subjectivity in Asia to market and expand the reach of his brand.

The Public Persona of Leehom Wang

Walk into a public space in cities such as Taipei, Hong Kong, or Beijing and it is difficult not to encounter some aspect of Wang's celebrity—his air-brushed visage splashed on billboards and buses, his music playing in a commercial, or his smiling face plastered on any number of products for sale.[55] His familiar presence in the cultural and economic landscape of these global Chinese cities speaks both to the wide reach of his fame and the particular set of demands placed on celebrities in Asian entertainment industries. As the singer observed, Asia "is a very multimedia pop culture. Your fans need to hear you and see you in films and commercials. My philosophy is that I have to try to be a good entertainer."[56] Thus while best known for his music, Wang, like other popular entertainers in the Asian popular music industry, works in a multitude of realms. Since his breakthrough album *Revolution* (1998), he has been at the top of the Chinese music charts, releasing on average one new album a year and embarking on elaborate promotional events and concert tours to market them. Given his long-standing endorsement deals with numerous multinational brands—McDonald's, Coca-Cola, Nikon, Head and Shoulders, and Sony Ericsson, to name a few—Wang turns up in commercials throughout Asia. As an actor he has appeared in several high-profile Chinese films, including Ang Lee's *Lust, Caution* (2007); *Little Big Soldier* (2009), costarring Jackie Chan; the romantic comedy *Love in Disguise* (2010), which he also wrote, directed, and scored; and *My Lucky Star* (2013), costarring Zhang Ziyi.[57] And finally, the singer participates in a wide range of philanthropic projects, from UNICEF to World Vision Taiwan, an aid relief organization.

The dizzying scope of Wang's activities complements the singer's public persona as a dedicated workaholic willing to stay up nights on end to finish his projects. He is known and beloved by his fans for his impressive work ethic, his uncompromising desire for perfection, his sterling academic credentials, his clean-cut yet sexy image, and his unstinting devotion to music. Promoted by music industry executives early in his career as a pop idol with marquee good looks, Wang has since transformed into a quality idol who also possesses a deep reservoir of musical talent.[58] He composes, arranges, and produces all of his own music, writes most of his own lyrics, and plays almost all the instruments on his albums, including the violin, piano, guitar, drums, bass, and a vast array of traditional Chinese instruments.

Wang's privileged upbringing in the United States augments his image as a multitalented, quality star. As the child of upwardly mobile, post-1965 Asian immigrants, he holds many of the stereotypical trademarks of high-achieving, middle-class Asian American kids: he began playing the violin at the age of six and enrolled at the preparatory division of the prestigious Eastman School of Music, he excelled at school (fansites often mention that he received a perfect score on his SATs and turned down Ivy League institutions to attend the smaller Williams College), and he faced parental pressure to follow the career path of his father and brother, both medical doctors.[59] Yet Wang "broke the mold," as he put it, by defying his parents in order to follow his heart and pursue a more precarious career in music.[60] During a summer visit to Taipei as a teenager, he joined a talent contest and caught the interest of music producers. Sidestepping the U.S. music scene entirely, he launched his career in Taiwan. He released his first album in Taiwan in 1995, at the age of nineteen. As an undergraduate at Williams College, Wang flew back and forth between Taipei and Massachusetts to record and promote his albums. After years of transcontinental travel and a brief stint at Berklee College of Music following receipt of his bachelor's degree, Wang relocated to Taipei to pursue his already burgeoning musical career.

These biographical details are key in helping shape Wang's persona as an inspirational role model who works hard, listens to his heart, and possesses a wide range of talents. As a 2006 article that appeared in the Singaporean magazine *Teens* highlighted, being smart and winning academic and musical accolades imbue Wang with the necessary ingredients to be a desirable heartthrob. In a sidebar to their cover story, *Teens* broke down the "numbers that make up Leehom's life" this way:

17/5/1976:	Leehom was born in Rochester, New York, U.S. He sang his first tune at age 3 and subsequently learned to play the violin and piano.
2:	He has two brothers: the older one is a doctor while the younger one is a student. Most of his family and relatives are in the medical field.
19 years:	He trail blazed his way into the Taiwanese music scene with a best selling album, *Love Rival Beethoven*, whose title track became a hit.
23 years:	Leehom became the youngest winner at Taiwan's Golden Melody Awards when he bagged the Best Male Singer and Best Producer trophies.
1,600 points:	His reportedly high score during the SATs meant he was accepted into prestigious universities such as Princeton and Yale. But he eventually went to Williams College to further his studies in music.
260,000:	His concert in Taipei in March this year holds the record for the most number of tickets sold.
1,800,000:	No. of copies *Heroes of Earth* has shifted.[61]

Thus, while Wang's winning looks no doubt serve as a major factor for his popularity, his music, marketing, media coverage, and commercial endorsements also profit from a public performance of diligence, passion, and achievement. These traits carry positive associations for his fans, who cite his upstanding character, his willingness to follow his dreams, his academic and musical prowess, and his dedication to promoting

Chinese music as key reasons for maintaining devotion to their star.[62] The positive image conveyed by Wang resonates with qualities associated with other popular Chinese stars as well, underscoring the appeal that marketing strategies such as his holds for fans in Chinese contexts.

In their investigation of online Chinese fansites for the popular Cantopop singer Leon Lai, Yiu Fai Chow and Jeroen de Kloet observe that, in contrast to other fan cultures, Chinese fans often praise their star's strong work ethic: "Besides his good looks, Leon's most remarkable character trait is his hard work, perseverance, and constant attempt to seek improvement and honour."[63] The scholars link the pride that Lai's devotees feel about their singer's diligence and determination to the belief that such characteristics are necessary to achieve success and accrue wealth in a global economy. Moreover, the accolades that Lai accumulates reflect back onto the character of the fans—their well-chosen tastes and their own mediated participation in bringing honor to Hong Kong.

Here it is worth emphasizing that the public persona that Wang and other Chinese singers craft to bolster their mass appeal in Chinese contexts also contrasts greatly with the marketing of pop stars in the United States. For while hard work, practice, and dedication are necessary to achieve prominence in any musical field, it is clear that a celebrity image built around such traits would hardly be successful in the United States, especially for an Asian American singer. Not only is being studious and overachieving generally perceived as uncool and incompatible with mainstream pop stardom in the United States, but the model minority stereotype embeds these qualities as seemingly natural to, if not at the core of, the Asian American character. In this way, details like perfect SAT scores or prowess on the violin become imbued with racial significance, representing racialized markers from which Asian American pop aspirants seek distance rather than affinity. Moreover, as discussed in chapter 2, even in classical music, where diligence and discipline carry positive attributions, Asian Americans can quickly become exemplars of excess, pathologized as possessing a work ethic that veers toward deviance. Outside of the U.S. context, however, such qualities as diligence and sacrifice symbolize flexible traits that hold value in globalized economies rather than Asian characteristics used to discipline the "deficiencies" of other racial minority groups, highlight the perpetual foreignness of Asian Americans, and typecast Asian Americans as uniformly privileged and therefore exempt from racism. Transnational figures like Wang thus expose the ideological utility of model minority discourses—their function as cultural narratives that uphold U.S. racial paradigms.[64] That his marketing strategy replicates model minority presumptions of Asian Americans and would not hold mass appeal to U.S. audiences is of little concern to Mandopop singers like Wang, for whom the coveted marketplace is China. Within the Chinese transnational markets that make up Wang's audience base, the United States, with its comparatively tiny Chinese American demographic, represents only a peripheral market.

In his music and media appearances, Wang enhances his public image by promoting the values that derive from hard work and determination. For example, the singer graciously thanked his fans in his acceptance speech at Taiwan's 2006 Golden Melody Awards (a major music award show in Taiwan, akin to the U.S. Grammys) by humbly pledging to continue striving to be worthy of their support. Extolling the virtue of practicing to achieve self-improvement, the singer reflected: "I think I wasn't very good at singing before but I am determined to practice every day and practice makes perfect. . . . I will continue the hard work."[65] His remarks dispel any notion that the so-called fluffier genre of pop does not require craft and technique or that musical talent is somehow intrinsic to one's being. Expanding on these thoughts on his official website, the singer posted copy of the speech he would have given barring time constraints, where he linked the principles of diligence and self-improvement to the collective goal of raising the global profile of Chinese music: "[Chinese artists'] competitors should not be each other, but rather, the international artists who have historically set the standard in popular music. I know if we put in the hard work to improve our skills, we will be one step closer to making Chinese pop music a worldwide phenomenon."[66]

Through his remarks the singer correlates the need for practice and improvement with the nationalist project of elevating the status of Chinese music on the world stage. Such a public performance of self coincides with what Aihwa Ong describes as a shift in Asian growth zones toward promoting citizenship and belonging through neoliberal ideals of self-improvement and market-driven individualism. As Ong observes, "In East and South Asian environments, neoliberal ethics of self-responsible citizenship are linked to social obligations to build the nation."[67] Responsibility lies with the individual to acquire the flexible skills and knowledge needed to accumulate capital and contribute to the growth of the nation. Traits of hard work and practice are extolled in globalized economics, where they are seen as serving the larger project of building the nation. Here we see how the particular modes of achieving success implied in the model minority trope overlap with global narratives of modernization and upward mobility.[68]

Wang's public image as a good role model allows him to prosper in a music industry that depends on both corporate support and state approval. As Anthony Fung notes, in more closed nations, like China, both the state and the market determine which cultural products gain popularity: "Popular music that is allowed to operate in China first has to meet the regime's political agenda before it is circulated to the public."[69] The Chinese government's selection of Wang as a torchbearer and a performer at the closing ceremonies of the 2008 Beijing Olympic Games—he was, quite notably, the only Taiwan-based singer to perform in the official ceremonies—provides evidence of the singer's exemplary standing in China. In Taiwan, Wang is similarly lauded for bringing pride to that country as well. In 2009 the Taiwanese education ministry selected the singer to launch a broader "character-building plan" that would "cultivate the nation's moral character, quality, and taste."[70] And the following year, the mayor of Taipei selected Wang to represent that city at the Shanghai 2010 World Expo, observing that "with his great image, high popularity and international profile, Wang is a one in a million pick for goodwill ambassador." Such official state endorsements attest to Wang's marketing and brand as a quality idol who possesses industriousness and musical talent, follows his heart and passion, and reflects positively on Chinese people around the world.

The success that Wang enjoys in Asia depends on a public image of quality seamlessly integrated into his music, commercial sponsorships, television and film work, and media appearances. He narrates the accolades he receives as part of a broader desire to raise the international profile of Chinese music and to celebrate pride in Chineseness. At the same time, while his belonging in Mandopop depends on his diasporic incorporation, the singer also uses his Chinese American subjectivity to explore the meanings that his particular calibration of Chineseness holds in national and transnational contexts. Through an exploration of the complex politics of diaspora and belonging, Wang's music prompts a reconsideration of the United States as the assumed, desired, or only home for Chinese Americans. In the process, his music sheds insight into the increasingly critical role that Asia plays in the making and remaking of Asian American subjectivities.

Becoming a Descendant of the Dragon

The construction of Wang as part of a global Chinese community unevenly stitched together through shared ancestry and roots is, on the one hand, a shrewd marketing tactic that transforms him from a semi-foreign artist tied to a particular place (given his status as both an ABC *and* a Taiwan-based singer) into a pan-Chinese singer who appeals to an enormous PRC audience and beyond.[71] On the other hand, Wang's articulation of the ineffable sense of belonging he felt upon his arrival to Taiwan appears undeniably sincere, underscoring the deep affective allure that the promise of diaspora invokes, particularly for racially marginalized communities in the United States. While all diasporic formations contain profound emotional resonance, part of the specific power of the Chinese diaspora lies in the enormity of its scope and size, long-standing myths lauding a glorious ancient past, the escalating status of China (and the popularly termed smaller dragons of Taiwan, Hong Kong, and Singapore), and the potential of belonging to a collectivity on the basis of strength rather than disenfranchisement. As cultural critic Ien Ang elaborates,

> By imagining oneself as part of a globally significant, transnational Chinese diasporic community, a minority Chinese subject can rise, at least in the imagination, above the national environment in which (s)he lives but from which (s)he may always have felt symbolically excluded. I would contend that much of the current popularity of "Chinese diaspora" among ethnic Chinese around the world is fuelled precisely by this emotive desire not just to belong, but to belong to a respectable imagined community, one that instills pride in one's identity precisely because it is so much larger and more encompassing, in geographical terms at least, than any territorially bounded nation.[72]

In media interviews, Wang similarly connects his racial minority status in the United States with the palpable sense of belonging he experienced coming to Taiwan, noting: "Growing up in the States, I was always a minority. I was trying to fit in, especially when I was an adolescent. But going to Taiwan for the first time was an incredible feeling. I think it must be . . . belonging. I couldn't fit in then because I couldn't speak Chinese, but it's still a feeling."[73] While Wang overcame the literal linguistic barrier of not speaking Chinese that limited his early interactions, he nonetheless continues to confront and rework authenticating beliefs that link proper modes of being and speaking Chinese and that equate the lingering traces of an ABC accent with shortcomings in his Chineseness.

This feeling that Wang calls belonging first finds musical translation in his hip hop–infused remake of "Descendants of the Dragon" ("Long de chuan ren"), a popular song written by Taiwanese composer Hou De-jian and first recorded in 1978 by singer Li Jian Fu (a relative of Wang's).[74] Wang's interpretation, recorded in 2000, includes a new verse, sung and rapped in English and Mandarin, that describes his parents' immigration to New York and his racial inheritance as a "descendant of the dragon." The updated lyrics appear, at first glance, to present a classic immigrant narrative of a young couple that arrives with few resources and achieves success through hard work and strength of character.

> Now here's a story that'll make you cry.
> Straight from Taiwan they came,
> Just a girl and a homeboy in love.
> No money, no job, no speak, no English.
> Nobody gonna give 'em the time of day.
> In a city so cold, they made a wish.
> And then they had the strength to graduate with honors.

The cultural capital that his parents bring with them from Taiwan as upwardly mobile subjects pursuing higher education degrees notwithstanding, Wang highlights hardships encountered negotiating a new language and new land. Yet rather than end the verse with his parent's settlement and assimilation into the nation, the singer shifts back to Mandarin and emphasizes the failure of migration to dissipate the pride and longing that Chinese people feel as "descendants of the dragon": "Many years ago, on a quiet night, my family arrived in New York. Nothing can destroy what is in our hearts. Longing for home every day and night. I grew up in someone else's land. After I grew up, I became a descendant of the dragon." Becoming Chinese, as Wang's lyrics suggest, involves a process of retrieval, reclamation, and cultural homecoming.

Constructing himself as a "descendant of the dragon" who was raised in a foreign land, the singer taps into intersecting discourses. If U.S. racial ideologies restrict Chinese Americans' ability to claim full belonging, Chinese mythologies reinforce beliefs of ethnic descent through common origin and blood. The entwinement of U.S. and Chinese discourses in diasporic invocations of roots exposes the extent to which these narratives are neither natural, freely chosen, nor wholly imposed.[75]

In Wang's updated verse, his parents' achievements in the United States reflect less on the attributes of the host country—from oft-cited virtues of meritocracy to the American Dream—and more on the ability of Chinese people to compete and thrive globally. Less a nation of immigrants integrating new arrivals into a shared cultural space, the song reconfigures the United States as one of many sites for the territorial settlement of Chinese communities. Framed through processes of migration and global diasporas, the United States represents one (albeit powerful) node in a network of territories wherein ethnic Chinese take up residence—no longer, as Arjun Appadurai suggests, "a closed space for the melting pot to work its magic, but yet another diasporic switching point."[76] And while such a narrative of migration can feel uncomfortably close to affirming dominant discourses of Asian Americans as unassimilable, sojourners, and perpetual foreigners, it is important to recall that Wang's primary audience is not located in the United States. With its small Chinese population, the United States is not marketed to in any specific way.

Drawing on long-standing Chinese discourses that trace lineage to the Yellow Emperor, "Descendants of the Dragon" narrates Chineseness as embodied physically through shared racial features—"black eyes, black hair, yellow skin"—emotionally through the love one feels for the Chinese nation, and psychically through the spirit of the dragon that flows in the mighty Yangtze and Yellow rivers and in the hearts of Chinese people around the world (regardless of their place of birth or settlement). While the song conflates race with China—the physical topography of the land and the spiritual connection to the dragon—it also premises diasporic incorporation through cultural bonds. Such a move, as Yiu Fai Chow observes in his astute analysis of Chinese patriotic songs, is in keeping with the broader tradition of nationalistic songs to draw on idealized and imagined memories of the motherland but to fuel diasporic longing through the "cultural logic of inclusion."[77]

If embracing Chineseness involves the individual act of excavating what lies deep within one's heart, Wang also suggests that it entails collective recognition that the slumbering dragon is awakening. In a series of journal entries penned in 2000–2001, the singer drew upon nationalist beliefs that the new century belongs to the Chinese people.[78] Written as letters addressed to his fans (whom he variously encourages to study hard, try their best, and follow their heart and passion), the entries marked an attempt by the singer to redirect media attention away from his personal life and toward his music and to engage directly with his audience. Describing "Descendants of the Dragon," Wang wrote:

> It is a remake of my uncle, Li Jian Fu's 1980 classic, which became a song associated with pride for being a member of the Chinese race. I believe this song has taken on a new meaning over the last 20 years as Chinese people now have spread across every corner of the earth. Many people have said that the 21st century will witness the "awakening of the dragon," the rise of Chinese people in the global community. I too believe this to be true. How could it not be with such an immense population combined with the improvement of global information technology? The remake of this song is intended to encourage taking pride in who we are and creating a general awareness of this pride regardless of where we live or may have grown up.[79]

Here the singer connects renewed feelings of Chinese pride with increasing economic prosperity and the emergence of global technology that facilitates communication between Chinese communities around the world. Narrating the ascent of the Chinese people as inevitable, he harnesses himself to the "awakening dragon"—which encompasses China, Asia's "smaller dragons" (Taiwan, Hong Kong, and Singapore), and overseas Chinese communities—and sonically represents this future through the scale and grandeur of his vocal arrangements. As Wang details: "I also sung twenty-something tracks of vocals and background vocals so I could sound like a strong chorus of voices singing. 'They are all the descendants of the dragon!' I thought, 'I need to make it sound big!' To me, this song is about having a positive attitude towards the future of Chinese people. The strength and the power of a billion and a half lives were on my mind as I approached this song's production."

If the sound of a chorus of voices joining and multiplying in unison conjures an image of multiple Chinese dragons surging and rising, it also produces a feeling of transnational connectivity that allows the singer (and his listeners) to hear and imagine their collective strength. More significantly, the "diasporic intimacy" marketed and commodified in patriotic songs like "Descendants of the Dragon" gives Wang access to success on the level and scope of China's growing dominance. The "bigness" sonically resonating in the "twenty-something tracks of vocals and background vocals" layered onto each other also marks the vibrating boom of China's consumer marketplace and the potential purchasing power this population represents in global capitalism.[80] At the same time, the chorus of voices is also literally a single voice, Wang's own, permeating each moment of the song. His voice, reproduced to represent Chinese people scattered across the globe, symbolically denotes the privileged position the singer occupies—as a celebrity, an affluent border crosser, and a cultural ambassador—in conversations about the meanings of Chineseness in a globalized era.

As a bold declaration of pride in becoming Chinese, "Descendants of the Dragon" forecasts Wang's interest in exploring a Chinese sonic identity that he feels would properly reflect the "rise of China" in the new millennium. Ruminating on U.S. views of Chinese music, he reflected: "It would be a shame if an American pop artist were to travel to Asia and find that our pop music sounds the same as theirs, just with Chinese lyrics." Here, Wang gives credibility to U.S. dismissals of Chinese pop music as shoddy versions of the "real thing." Yet he uses this perspective to call for a transformation of Mandopop, issuing a challenge (that he then sets out to achieve) to create a "more internationally recognizable Chinese pop music sound." And while the singer's comment can be viewed as authenticating beliefs about the derivative quality of Chinese popular music, it also carves out a rationale for his interest in exploring Chinese musical modalities. Situating his music squarely within Chinese-speaking markets and audiences, he transforms his outsider status as a Chinese American who grew up in "someone else's land" into a source of inspiration that fuels his ongoing experimentations in Chinese music. And in the process, he ambitiously announces his desire to shift global presumptions of the United States as pop culture hegemon.

Wang's commitment to creating an identifiably Chinese sound in Mandopop resulted in two albums, *Shangri-la* (2004), which incorporated the music of ethnic minorities from China, Tibet, and Mongolia; and *Heroes of Earth* (2005), which drew on the traditional high arts of Beijing opera and Kunqu (one of the oldest forms of Chinese musical theater). Both albums emerged after a period of study and travel that Wang undertook searching for musical sources that he felt to be specific and original to Chinese culture. These albums, both of which present musical explorations framed by his subject position as a Chinese American, tapped into ongoing debates about the impact of cultural globalization on processes of homogenization and localization.[81]

In the liner notes to *Shangri-la*, Wang theorizes the premise of his album as twofold. First, despite a rapidly growing Chinese presence in the global economy, "the world's understanding of Chinese people, pop culture and music still lags behind. As much as we hate to admit it, we are still faced with age-old stereotypes and unjust prejudices that need addressing." Second, he contends that "Chinese pop music does not have a strong enough sonic identity. Instead of being purely karaoke driven, instead of covering or imitating other countries' popular songs, we can focus on developing our own sound, drawing from the rich sources that abound in Chinese culture." While Wang gestures broadly to the world's stereotypical understandings of Chinese people, he links his remarks specifically to the racism that Chinese Americans encounter living in the United States. He connects the project of creating a strong Chinese musical identity to the nationalist goal of raising the global profile of Chinese people and to the more abstract objective of countering U.S./Western hegemony. In this way, his efforts can be interpreted as participating in two related strands: Chinese nationalism and Asian American cultural politics. On the one hand, the release of *Shangri-la* and *Heroes of Earth* coincided with a renewed moment of intense Chinese nationalism visible in the lead up to the Beijing Olympics; the popularity of kung fu films, such as *Yip Man* (2008); and the commercial success of such musical trends as "Chinese Wind" (*Zhongguo feng*), a blending of Chinese traditional elements with Western pop genres (a category that includes the music of Wang).[82] The singer's experimentation with Chinese traditional music—along with his many bold declarations of Chinese pride—thus participates in and helps fuel existing market-driven nationalism about China's growing stature on the political world stage. On the other hand, as an assertive, masculinist voice that speaks back to U.S. racism and hegemony, Wang's resistant stance finds echoes in Asian American cultural politics, from writers like Frank Chin to jazz musicians like Jon Jang and the late Fred Ho.

Describing his project as "chinked out," Wang reframes his minority subjectivity as a source of symbolic capital that energizes Chinese music and produces an international sound that properly reflects the dynamism and complexity of Chinese culture.

> Derived from the historically derogatory racial slur "chink," used to put-down Chinese people, "chinked-out" repossesses the word, turns its negative connotations upside-down, and uses them as material to fuel the new sound of this music. The term describes an effort to create a sound that is international, and at the same time, Chinese. In this album, I decided to implement some of China's most precious and untapped resources, the music of its "shao shu min zu" (少數民族), or ethnic minorities, concentrating on the regions of Yunan, Shangri-la, Tibet, Xinjiang and Mongolia.

While Wang's decision to label his efforts "chinked out" fueled controversy among Asian Americans—some of whom objected to his use of the derogatory term and the implied parallel between the reclamation of a racial slur by a privileged Chinese American pop star in a foreign context and the repossession of the "n-word" by African American hip hop artists—it is worth emphasizing that the term *chink* does not hold the same valence in China, Taiwan, or Hong Kong.[83] Most of his Chinese-speaking fans in Asia, lacking familiarity with both the term and the social and historical context from which it emerged, did not fully understand or care about the nuances of Wang's use of the word. Wang himself noted as much, observing: "I realize that people [in Asia] don't really know this term because they don't have a discrimination problem. But if people go abroad and are not aware that they are being insulted, I don't want people to be ignorant of that. I want people to know that there exists this kind of understanding of Chinese people in the world."[84] By using the foreign phrase "chinked out," Wang thus positions himself as a bridge to those in the Chinese-speaking world who may not recognize the types of prejudice that Chinese face in their global travels and migrations. He redirects attention away from ABC as a symbol of privilege, emphasizing instead how racism informs the perception of Chinese people in the United States.[85] This should not imply that China and Taiwan also do not have a "discrimination problem," as evidenced by the racism practiced by the dominant population toward its indigenous populations, the ethnic minorities whose music Wang celebrates, exploits, or both, in *Shangri-la*.[86] Still, as a singer who makes music marketed toward a mass Chinese audience, he steers clear of such potentially sensitive topics.

Given that his primary audience is in Asia, Wang is exempt from industry pressures to translate, market, or otherwise cater his efforts for a Western/U.S. audience, whose consumption of Chineseness can readily lapse into orientalist embrace. As Deborah Wong perceptively observes, in the imprecise exchange of audience reception Asian American artists in the United States can find themselves unwittingly consumed by the very frameworks they seek to contest: "Given the susceptibility of American audiences to orientalist pleasure—their willingness to give themselves over to it—I must ask what happens when performers think they are saying one thing and audiences hear something else entirely, and whose responsibility it is to redirect the reading."[87] This bind is particularly salient for Asian American musicians who draw on recognizably Asian sounds and instruments in their music—signifiers that risk placing them in the aural register of orientalism and stoking (and fulfilling) U.S./Western appetites for exoticism and commodified visions of Chineseness. The ease with which, as Shu-mei Shih notes, "an anti-Orientalist gesture can slip into a reconfirmation of Orientalism" helps explain, for example, the distance that Asian American YouTube musicians maintain from Asian musical traditions and the long-standing debates that have ensued over the international accolades garnered by prominent Chinese artists in the United States/West.[88] Still, while some scholars have argued that Wang self-orientalizes through sounds and visions that enhance the imagination of impermeable East-West polarities, it is worth emphasizing that "chinked out" operates through a structure of closeness—of proximity rather than distance from the ethnic minority cultures and traditional Chinese arts that influence his music.[89] Such a dynamic resonance resounds in the argument that Thuy Linh Tu makes about Asian American fashion designers who deploy a cultural logic of intimacy to navigate Asian cultural influences in an industry well known for capitalizing on orientalist commodifications of "Asian chic."[90] In interpreting the meanings of "chinked out," it is significant to take into account not only Wang's Chinese American subjectivity but also the contexts in which it circulates. That is, "chinked out" may reflect a host of motivations for and responses from Wang and his Chinese listeners—an exploration of ethnicity, an excavation of tradition, a romanticization of lost and distant pasts—but it does not suggest racial difference or exoticism in quite the same ways that it would for U.S./Western audiences.

At the same time, in a manner not entirely dissimilar to U.S. practices of multiculturalism, *Shangri-la* culls from indigenous populations in a celebratory manner that leaves certain political topics unsaid, from the treatment of ethnic minorities by the Chinese state to ongoing political tensions between China and Tibet. The impression that heterogeneous minority communities in China coexist in a state of harmonic national cohesion—a multicultural narrative sustained through such state-driven pageantry as the opening ceremonies for the Beijing Olympic Games—is a fiction that *Shangri-la* helps corroborate.[91] While it is unsurprising that Wang sidesteps any critical commentary to avoid attracting negative attention by the PRC government, he also deflects questions of appropriation by constructing himself as a Chinese American gaining knowledge about Chinese musical traditions through the position of shared appreciation and a collective search for cultural roots. This perspective is reinforced in the music video for the title track, which depicts the singer as a journeyman traveling across time and space conscientiously studying, transcribing, searching for, and fantasizing about the different ingredients that constitute Chinese music. Here Wang's public image as a high-achieving student, whose diligence at mastering Mandarin rivals his passionate study of music, enhances this representation.

Through the term *chinked out*, Wang invokes the experience of being Chinese American in the United States and the racialized hierarchies of power that frame global understandings of the relationship between East and West more broadly and the United States and China/Taiwan specifically. As he explained in Chinese media outlets: "The word 'chink' is a derogatory racial slur used by white people to insult Asians. I grew up in New York and I heard that said to me."[92] Yet, while in the United States *chink* fixes one in a static position of inferiority and marginality, on the Chinese international stage being "chinked out"—reformulated as a verb and practice—enacts a process of transformation to strength, pride, and cool. Imagining himself as "chinked out" allows Wang to reject the reductive assumptions placed on Chinese Americans in the United States. As he recalls: "When I was growing up, people would come up to me and say, 'Oh you're Chinese? You know kung fu? You like Bruce Lee?' and I think that's too bad. That's one of the reasons that I've done 10 albums in Chinese, and not one in English."[93] Comments such as these depict his conscious decision to pursue a career in Mandopop. Moreover, "chinked out" allows Wang to challenge the assumption that the United States represents the only viable or desirable culture industry from which to achieve international success. As he advocates, by focusing on creating a uniquely vibrant Chinese sound, Chinese popular music can compete on the world stage on its own terms.

While Wang frames "chinked out" explicitly through his Chinese American subjectivity, the questions he raises and his musical experimentations are not entirely new. Indeed, the process of searching for inspiration from classical Chinese arts, the music of ethnic minorities, the grand topography of rural China, and evocations of a mythic/mystical Shangri-la strongly resonates with the work of earlier Chinese artists. In his study of Chinese popular music, Nimrod Baranovitch observes that the "root-seeking" cultural movement in China during the 1980s reflected a desire "to reestablish a renewed sense of identity and to mediate the conflict that many Chinese intellectuals faced in the post-revolutionary era, being deprived of history and tradition after the Cultural Revolution, cynical about communism and the whole revolutionary ethos, and suddenly flooded with Western culture."[94] This exploration, which registered cultural longings to create a "usable past," fueled broader debates about how best to assemble, construct, and authenticate a collective Chinese identity.[95] These conversations are clearly ongoing. What is worth emphasizing, however, is that while the quest for roots and cultural belonging might appear to be the obsessive fixation of ABCs—an identity crisis of sorts stemming from their in-between status in both Asia and the United States—"chinked out" also strikes a chord in questions about root-seeking and Chineseness already long in the making in Chinese contexts.[96] Indeed, "chinked out" placed Wang in contemporary discussions about how best to adapt ancient traditions of Chinese opera into modern styles that would bolster its commercial viability, appeal to youth, and also preserve artistic integrity.[97] The popularity of Wang's "chinked out" style led to various, high-profile collaborations, including an invitation to compose the theme song for a Chinese television series aimed at introducing traditional Chinese opera to young people.[98] There is a certain irony that a Chinese American projection of Chinese culture becomes subsumed within contemporary cultural efforts and debates about how best to preserve the sacred traditions of Chinese opera for a new generation of young Chinese people.[99]

Wang continued his exploration of a "chinked out" musical aesthetic on *Heroes of Earth*, an album that assembled an impressive ensemble of Asian musical heroes, including K-pop sensation Rain, Chinese American rapper MC Jin, and Beijing opera singer Yan Li. Explaining his desire to infuse the album with a sense of confidence and masculine swagger (that is, outside of his trademark love songs), the singer observed: "I wanted to make the chinked-out style more hip-hop yet more Chinese, and borrowed musical elements from traditional Chinese music like Beijing opera. Many characters in Beijing opera like General Yue Fei and Emperor Qian Long conquered the earth with their might and attitude. And I found the same attitude in rap, with its tough, edgy lyrics."[100] The cover image for the album—which features Wang clad in a military-inspired jacket, his face partially shadowed by a bejeweled black cap (see fig. 4.1)—visually complements the assertive stance and posture projected in the album. Drawing a parallel between the "strong self-esteem" evoked by contemporary rappers and the military and political strength that allowed "ancient heroes" to rule the world, *Heroes of Earth* envisions a future that once again belongs to the Chinese people.[101]

The palpable sense that the Chinese people are on an accelerated pace to reclaim a position of stature and prominence in the world is best exemplified on the title track, "Heroes of Earth" ("Gaishi yingxiong"), a song overflowing with self-congratulatory rhetoric and repeated declarations that "future is here," the "great heroes are coming," and the "world is their stage." Opening with shout-outs to Homeboy productions (Wang's production studio), Xiang Yu (a military general from the Qin dynasty whose story is frequently retold in Beijing operas), and his "homeboy Jin" (MC Jin), the song draws a continuous line between myths of China's glorious past and the escalating stature of Chinese people worldwide. Given the masculinist vision of accruing power and

4.1. Cover image for the album *Heroes of Earth*.

demanding respect projected in "Heroes of Earth," it is not surprising that all of the ancient and contemporary heroes namechecked in the song are men whose imposing skills foretell a shift of global power "back" to the Chinese people. In the song, Wang acts as a bridge connecting old and new—Beijing opera and American rap, classical arts and modern styles—infusing his diction and singing voice with inflections drawn from Beijing opera and rapping in Mandarin (with a smattering of English thrown in) in some of his songs.

That Wang reaches out to MC Jin is consistent with the personal and professional interest he shows in promoting and affiliating with other Chinese American artists. At the same time, the singer also draws on his collaboration with the rapper to bolster his own credibility as an ABC who draws musical inspiration from hip hop. We see this in Wang's description of Jin to the Chinese press, where he repeatedly emphasizes the rapper's top-notch credentials as "the top American freestyler" and the "Chinese rap master who triumphed over all of his competitors in an American rap competition."[102] Jin's most notable success, being undefeated in a series of freestyle battles against mostly African American competitors on the cable network BET's *106 & Park*, becomes vaguely de-racialized in its depiction as an "American rap competition." Moreover, while Jin's victory is particularly impressive coming from the United States, the place from which rap originates, his achievement is framed through his Chineseness. His success overseas in the United States reflects back on the ability of the Chinese to compete and triumph against the best on the international stage.

Although Jin raps in English (with a splash of Cantonese thrown in) on "Heroes of Earth" he ultimately links his, and the fates of Chinese Americans more broadly, to Chinese communities in Asia.

> Yo, it's Jin and Leehom,
> It feels good to be home,
> I got the skills to be known,
> So I'm a chill on my throne,
> Yes, I keeps it blazing,
> From Shanghai out to Beijing,
> Stop in Taiwan back to Hong Kong
> Where they stay doin' they thing.

Moving seamlessly between interlocking global Chinese cities, Jin "keeps it blazing" in both the Chinese diaspora and Chinese popular music. Reimagining Chinese America through diaspora, Jin decenters the territorial and cultural space of the United States as the preferred home for Chinese America. And while such a vision of diaspora may feel empowering, particularly for racial minorities hungering for alternate spaces to find fame and belonging, it is a privileged vision—one that evokes an image of cosmopolitan globetrotters freely traveling across borders—and it also taps into a nationalist discourse of representing China / Chinese culture at its best. The challenges that Jin encountered in the United States—from the disappointing sales of his much-anticipated 2004 album *The Rest Is History* to the ways that his Asianness both marked and limited him in the racialized and gendered landscape of hip hop—become subsumed into a long narrative of Chinese achievement that spans "a couple thousand years." Interestingly,

Jin's inclusion on *Heroes of Earth* heralded the start of his own professional foray into Chinese markets. Not long after his collaboration with Wang, Jin released an album rapped primarily in Cantonese entitled *ABC* (2007) and relocated to Hong Kong.[103]

Here it is worth acknowledging that in the range of hip hop that exists in Chinese contexts, Wang, like other mainstream Mandopop stars, fits squarely within the aesthetic parameters of the Mandopop industry, where hip hop embodies an evolving archive of toughness, defiance, and stylized cool that draws from but simultaneously disavows its racialized and class origins in the United States. Mandopop versions of hip hop tend to capitalize on the sense of rebelliousness, internationalism, and youthfulness associated with hip hop as a way to sell both the artist and the vast landscape of corporate products linked with that artist's brand. In this sense there is a clear kinship between Mandopop and other East Asian pop music industries. In the commercialized hip hop found in Japan, for instance, Ian Condry observes how "corporate support has flowed more quickly to those who accommodate the marketing world's fetishization of blackness as hip, sensual, and rebellious or to those who deemphasize blackness in favor of Japan's traditionally lighthearted and inoffensive pop music realm. If one's only exposure to Japanese rap comes from television, radio, or the mainstream music press, one is likely to see the edginess of hip-hop promoted through racially coded imagery, often combining an outlaw stance with conspicuous, brand-name consumption."[104] A similar dynamic exists in Mandopop, where commercial artists—all of whom depend heavily on corporate endorsements to generate revenue—fail to deviate from stylized visions of blackness as cool. Moreover, that corporate support follows artists sanctioned by state-run media means that the gangsta persona articulated in Mandopop represents, at best, sanitized social commentary.[105]

This should not suggest that more politically oriented forms of hip hop do not exist in China, Taiwan, or Hong Kong. As a Chinese DJ opines in a *New York Times* article on hip hop in China, the underground hip hop scene reflects "real" hip hop more than pop stars who rap about love (romantic, nationalist, and otherwise) and "call it hip hop when it isn't."[106] Such a remark suggests the extent to which characterizations of "authentic" hip hop is "a contentious subject for musicians, producers and fans in China. Hong Kong, mainland and Taiwanese pop stars who have their own spin on hip hop dominate the mainstream. Many tack high-speed raps onto the end of their songs, even ballads, and consider themselves rappers."[107] While the article cites the "clean-cut and handsome" singer Jay Chou as representative of such a pop star turned part-time rapper, it just as easily could have pointed to Wang, who similarly raps about such seemingly subversive topics as national-ist pride and traditional Chinese arts. For instance, the song "Beside the Plum Blossom" ("Zai mei bian") ends with a tongue-twisting rap— 295 words in fifty seconds—in which Wang encourages young people to take the time to enjoy the introspective beauty of classical poetry and Chinese opera despite the quick pace of a technologically oriented modern world.

While contestations over notions of realness represent part of the discourse around the production of hip hop in Chinese contexts (often reproducing the familiar coupling of commercialism and inauthentic-ity), it is worth emphasizing that these debates, however unsettled, fail to traffic in assumptions of racial inauthenticity that have long con-fronted Asian American rappers in the United States.[108] Wang's loca-tion gives him a certain amount of freedom—a space to envision being "chinked out" and to imbue his musical performance with the tough-ness and "strong self-esteem" associated with African American rap-pers (at a distance from African American communities and U.S. racial politics).[109] Drawing influence from hip hop allows the singer to claim a certain amount of "edginess" within his "quality idol" designation.

At the same time, the scope of Wang's ambitions and intentions aside, the motivations he articulated behind "chinked out" did not fully translate in Chinese contexts. While *Shangri-la* and *Heroes of Earth* were both critical and commercial successes, the foreign phrase "chinked out" did not gain much traction with Chinese fans and media. Chinese media tended to categorize his music through the more familiar discourse of "Chinese Wind" (Zhongguo feng), describing his style as "Chinese hip hop"—a hybrid blend of Western packaging with Chinese elements.[110] And while Wang denied that he was merely placing a new name on a popular trend, the singer's turn to overtly Chinese sounds and ico-nography in Mandopop nonetheless built upon and bolstered a musical style with proven commercial appeal for Chinese audiences.[111] Thus, de-spite a promotional strategy that involved Wang repeatedly explaining the meaning of "chinked out," the category "Chinese Wind" proved a far more compelling and legible framework to understand not only his musical style but also his identity and upbringing in the United States. The foreign phrase "chinked out" was both too abstract and culturally specific for Chinese audiences who lacked previous encounters with the racial slur. Indeed, the untranslatability of "chinked out" as a phrase reflecting a specific overseas experience highlights the discrepant equivalences smoothed over in the shared Chineseness marketed, imagined, and commodified through Mandopop. Still, while the specific contextual meanings attached to "chinked out" did not resonate with his Chinese listeners, *Shangri-la* and *Heroes of Earth* successfully communicated Wang's desire to explore the sonic nuances of Chineseness in Mandopop and to develop a uniquely Chinese pop sound that would begin to challenge the cultural hegemony of the United States. The popularity of these albums helped establish Wang as one of the main cultural arbiters of "Chinese Wind" and enhanced his gleaming image as a multifaceted artist who strives to celebrate Chinese musical traditions and to promote Chinese music around the world.

Chineseness in a Global Context

In his exploration of the meanings of Chineseness within the context of globalization, Wang capitalizes on the internationalism and hybridity associated with his U.S. upbringing, his home base in Taipei, and a cosmopolitan lifestyle marked by constant travel, tours, and performances. In this sense the singer's spotlight on his own experiences growing up outside of Asia—in "someone else's land"—and his desire to become "chinked out" raised broader questions about the nature of roots, Chineseness, and belonging.[112] For Chinese American fans in particular, this process of questioning stereotypical assumptions of Chineseness and excavating roots and cultural heritage finds frequent correspondence with the reasons given for their fandom of Wang specifically and Mandopop generally.

In the forum section of Wang's North American fan club, Hom Sweet Home, his Chinese American and Chinese Canadian fans frequently describe their devotion to the singer as inspiring (or itself the result of) a deeper exploration and appreciation of their Chinese heritage.[113] A representative post might be the following, from "Hae," who observed: "Leehom really inspired me to return to my roots . . . he made learning Chinese fun and actually exciting. . . . I get to understand my culture and be proud of where I come from. Before I was a bit of a banana and too stuck with western styled life and didn't bother to really try to discover my own culture or even thought I belonged."[114] For "Hae," becoming a fan of the singer prompted a reconsideration of her roots, a process that helped shift her view of learning Mandarin—and, by extension, about Chinese culture—as something that is "fun and actually exciting." Another fan, "Je'maine," similarly commented that her parents supported her devotion to the singer because "lee hom motivated me to learn mandarin again. i'm an ABC like him but i gave up learning mandarin. so thanks to him, i requested to learn mandarin again." That Wang did not speak Mandarin while growing up is a particular point of inspiration for fans who themselves might be working to improve their Chinese language skills. While gaining deeper knowledge about Wang incentivizes fans to hone their Mandarin (to understand his lyrics better, to access articles about him more easily, and to follow his film and TV work more deeply), gaining language fluency is narrated as a choice, a chosen rather than imposed activity that is linked to self-discovery. Wang becomes a proxy for Chinese culture—a springboard for becoming "proud of where I come from"—as well as an inspirational model for how Chinese Americans might reconsider and return to their roots. As one of the administrators of the singer's North American fan club told me: "He's a great role model in discovering his own heritage and helping us discover it as well." Moreover, as she added, "It is nice to see Asian Americans succeed in the entertainment industry."[115] If there is a certain paradox that Chinese Americans—and those residing in North America more broadly—need to learn Mandarin in order to follow with greater depth the career of a Chinese American pop star born and raised in the United States, this point did not arise in the fan forum.

At the same time, as North American fans seek alternate formations of youth culture and cool beyond the commercial parameters of the United States, they participate in a broader trend of globalization and media convergence that media scholar Henry Jenkins terms "pop cosmopolitanism."[116] As Jenkins explains, for American youth who hold devotion to Asian media forms, their embrace of global popular culture represents a way to distinguish themselves from their parents, their peers, and the presumed parochialism of their local communities and to envision themselves as global citizens. At the same time, "pop cosmopolitanism" assumes attraction through difference and distance—

through the enjoyment and worldliness derived from accumulating knowledge about foreign global media unfamiliar to most Americans. Jenkins himself concedes that a fan's subject position can inspire different investments and attachments. That is, while the devotion that North American fans have for Wang specifically and Mandopop generally allows them to distinguish themselves from the (perceived) insular tastes of mainstream America and the "Western-styled life" of their peers, for the Chinese American (and Chinese Canadian) fans included within that group, their fandom can also have the powerful effect of producing feelings of belonging to a transnational Chinese community.

In this sense, Mandopop's relative lack of popularity in North America allows ethnic Chinese youth to claim fandom in a culture industry little known, if not misunderstood and disparaged, by their peers and yet enormously popular halfway around the world. Their devotion to Wang allows Chinese American/Chinese Canadian fans to recalibrate their own sense of minoritized subjectivity and to eschew, if not resist, the discourses that circulate about Asians (including Asian popular culture) in their home countries. Here we can draw a parallel to Jeroen de Kloet's observation of how Cantopop is "used by the Chinese diaspora as a tactic of distinction, to contest the dominance of Western pop icons, to claim their own cultural space beyond the surveying eyes of Western contemporaries.[117] It bears repeating that Chinese American fans, from Wong Fu Productions to individuals commenting on social media and fansites, frequently emphasize how cool it is that a global pop star like Wang is an ABC/Chinese American like them. As discussed in chapter 3, for Asian American youth to see versions of themselves in the popular media they consume is empowering, particularly given the anomaly of such experiences. But to find a musical space where a Chinese American singer is massively famous, undeniably marketable, and incontrovertibly accepted as sexy, passionate, and cool—Wang is, as many fans gush, "so perfect"—can prompt some Chinese Americans to claim this culture industry as part of their own roots and heritage, regardless of their level of language fluency and cultural knowledge. It can lead some fans to search, like Wang does, for sonic belonging in Chinese pop.

Yet, what it means to celebrate heritage or to excavate roots are unsettled questions for individuals beyond those we might label as Chinese American or ABC. While songs like "Descendants of the Dragon" and musical experiments like "chinked out" suggest that home is best authenticated through Chinese traditions and spaces, they also place the search for shared cultural roots within the context of changes wrought by histories of migration, colonialism, globalization, and urbanization. That is, being uprooted may well represent part of the modern condition rather than the unique concerns of Chinese Americans/ABCs. By highlighting such themes as the globalization of the Chinese language in his songs, Wang advocates a more capacious understanding of Chinese identity, one that allows ABCs and other diasporic Chinese to recognize their hybrid forms of identity as encompassing full and authentic modes of being Chinese in the world. In this way, his music gives sonic expression to what cultural anthropologist Andrea Louie describes as the slippery residue of diasporic formations. As Louie writes: "While identities based on shared territory and genealogical origins may appear to result only in the reinforcement of static, 'traditional' identities, these same relationships form the basis for the construction of new and often contrapuntal forms of Chinese identity."[118]

These "new and contrapuntal forms of Chinese identity" are celebrated in songs like "Cockney Girl," in which Wang marvels at the remarkable heterogeneity audible in China, Taiwan, Hong Kong, and the Chinese diaspora.[119] Celebrating the "special intonations" and "mysterious rhythms" he hears in the alluring accent of a British-born Chinese woman, the song contests the hierarchies—linguistic and otherwise—that identify certain (i.e., Beijing) Chinese accents as the most "proper" way of speaking and implicitly being Chinese. Wang frames the innovations produced by the globalization and localization of spoken Mandarin not as speech distortions requiring correction, but as sources of musical inspiration. As the singer reflected in an interview: "I am very interested in accents, especially the Southern accent, the Beijing accent, the Taiwan accent and the Guangdong accent. I had a performance in London a short time ago and met a British-born Chinese. His Chinese was very good, but he had a London accent. Now more and more people are learning Chinese, and more and more different accents have appeared. I think this represents a new auditory challenge. As a musician, I keep looking for new auditory challenges. No other language has as many different accents as Chinese does."[120] By highlighting the manifold Chinese accents located around the world, Wang reframes what might be perceived as linguistic deficiencies into opportunities for musical experimentation. Such a move also allows the singer to counter criticisms that he has faced throughout his career, particularly those that directly link his "ABC accent" to shortcomings in his song lyrics and, by extension, his Chinese identity.

Despite arriving in Taiwan with little familiarity with Mandarin, Wang quickly gained fluency in speaking, reading, and writing. Still, for some critics, lingering traces of an ABC accent betray the limits of Wang's belonging in Mandopop specifically and in Chinese contexts more broadly. For instance, when Chinese music journalists castigate the singer's lyrics for being superficial or one-dimensional, they often link those shortcomings directly to his ABC identity and the inherent difficulties ABCs face in expressing themselves and truly grasping the nuance behind words and phrases in Mandarin. As one music critic noted: "We all know that Leehom is ABC, which makes him have the same problems as other ABC singers have: lyrics cannot express what they want to say clearly. They cannot use words to precisely describe and express their ideas."[121] Other critics pointed to songs like "Hail to the Chinese" ("Huaren wansui"), which Wang composed to encourage the efforts of Chinese athletes during the patriotic buildup to the Beijing Olympic Games, as the overly compensatory efforts of an ABC who, emptied of his roots, compulsively seeks to fill that loss.[122]

In her critique of the essentialisms that structure understandings of diaspora, Ien Ang contends: "It is by recognizing the irreducible productivity of the syncretic practices of diaspora cultures that 'not speaking Chinese' will stop being a problem for overseas Chinese people. 'China,' the mythic homeland, will then stop being the absolute norm for 'Chineseness' against which all other Chinese cultures of the diaspora are measured."[123] By shifting the coordinates of authenticity mapped onto various dialects and accents, Wang similarly suggests that we hear the "contrapuntal" ways of being Chinese found around the world as a source of inspiration. This might well be a marketing tactic, a way to transform his linguistic limitations and nonnative-speaking status into a potential advantage.[124] As the singer contends: "I always think that for artists to take their shortcomings and turn them around and make them into what defines them as an artist is a real trick."[125] But underlying this "trick" might also be a genuine desire to claim and experience the powerful feeling of belonging. In celebrating the multiple forms of Chineseness located around the globe, Wang creates a place for himself and other Chinese Americans in the transnational sounds of Mandopop.

Conclusion

In an interview with the alumni magazine *Berklee Today*, Wang reflected that, despite growing up in the United States, he "never really had plans to launch an American career. I think I'm lucky that things started in Asia, because I was able to develop as a pure musician, to be known for my music and let the music speak for itself. In America, I'd rather be known for my music than as the 'Chinese artist.' In Asia, it's easier to let my music speak for itself."[126] His comments indicate an understanding that in the United States he would likely be typecast as the Chinese artist and be constrained by the stereotypical assumptions and expectations tethered to that label. For Wang, gaining freedom from that label was made possible only by participating in a pan-Chinese space—by incorporating rather than eliminating ethnicity as a marker of difference. That is, working in Mandopop allowed Wang to enter a musical landscape in which racial similarity marked the terms of his belonging. And while as an ABC Wang inhabits a particular Chinese subjectivity— one marked simultaneously by lack and privilege, familiarity and foreignness, inclusion and exclusion—he also uses his music to explore those shifting dynamics, to coin new terms, and to experiment with Chinese music modalities.

At the same time, as a mainstream artist who aims for the widest audience possible, Wang glides over questions about the contested meanings of Chineseness through his stylized grooves, his winning smile, his heartfelt love songs, and a carefully crafted image that emphasizes his upstanding character, sterling credentials, sincere disposition, and pride in being a "descendant of the dragon." While Wang's success likely facilitates much of the musical freedom afforded to him, he also fails to stray far from the parameters that would limit the commercial scope of his appeal. If pursuing a musical career outside of the United States allows the singer to be less encumbered by domestic racial politics, it also requires learning, adapting, and conforming to a new set of geopolitical, commercial, and aesthetic expectations. Moreover, by circumventing the United States to pursue a career in Asia, Wang does not challenge the racialized framework that constrains Asian Americans in the U.S. popular music industry—from perceptions that Asian Americans lack musical authenticity to beliefs that they are unmarketable to a mass audience—enabling it to remain intact.

What happens when Asian American artists leave the United States and enter geographical, diasporic, and cultural contexts also unevenly understood as home? Wang's remarkable career in Asia allows us to understand how the transnational landscape of Mandopop fosters, markets, and commodifies linkages between various forms of Chineseness. On the one hand, the notion that Wang's music can "speak for itself" in Asia is, for the most part, an illusion in light of the commercialism of Mandopop and the multiple constituencies that the singer serves (and is beholden to) through his brand. On the other hand, his commercial success does provide him with musical freedom and leverage. Moreover, participating in Chinese contexts allows Wang greater flexibility to explore questions of ethnicity and Chineseness while still remaining universal in his musical appeal. Returning to his roots, Wang explores their multiplicity of meanings and suggests new ways of imagining, consuming, and marketing being Chinese in the world. In the process, the singer achieves a level of fame, critical acclaim, fandom, and celebrity that is nearly impossible to imagine an Asian American singer ever achieving in the racialized space of the United States.

Enter the "Tiger Mother"

The almost instantaneous uproar elicited by Amy Chua's *Wall Street Journal* op-ed "Why Chinese Mothers Are Superior" and her memoir *Battle Hymn of the Tiger Mother* (2011) was, in many ways, expected.[1] With her brash and unapologetic claims about the reasons for Chinese success, Chua touched on several interlocking anxieties: waning U.S. cultural and economic hegemony, growing Chinese dominance, and proper forms of parenting in a neoliberal era of global competition. As the symbolic embodiment of these fears, Chua evoked a tiger on the loose—the threat of danger and difference run amok without proper management, domestication, and punishment. Parenting blogs reviled her mothering style as child abuse, disparaged the (narrowly defined) success achieved by Asian American kids as the product of excessive discipline and rote practice, and extolled the virtue of balance, sleepovers, and play. In the thousands of comments generated from Chua's op-ed, a panoply of responses emerged: critiques of the author's reliance on tired cultural stereotypes, racist generalizations about the authoritarian regime of China (where Chua, as some readers suggested, implicitly belongs), sweeping comparisons between Asian roboticism and American ingenuity, praise of "tiger" parenting for producing impressive results, and tales of harm suffered as a result of such despotic forms of parenting. Statistics emerged about the high suicide rates among Asian American women. Comparisons were made to other types of so-called ethnic parenting. Doubts crept in about the legitimacy of Chua's Chineseness, given her twice-removed status as the U.S. offspring of ethnic Chinese parents raised in the Philippines. Dispatches arrived from "real" Chinese mothers in China, Taiwan, and Hong Kong variously refuting and authenticating Chua's claims. And in the fray of this media frenzy appeared a personal rebuttal in the *New York Post*, penned by one of Chua's two daughters, defending her mother against charges of tyranny, child abuse, and the withholding of love.

This whirlwind of public debates thrust the Chinese/Asian immigrant mother into the spotlight. And yet, while at the center of this conversation she nonetheless remained spoken for by others—a shadowy figure upon whom to project suspicions, condemnations, and desires, a function she similarly holds in Chua's own memoir. Indeed, a haunting presence crowds the pages of *Battle Hymn of the Tiger Mother*—the immigrant generation of Chinese parents whose purported ability to enforce discipline and obedience in their children puts even the author's own stringent parenting tactics to shame. Chua apes these "true" tiger mothers. In her desire to reproduce their toughness, their "motivational" insults, their strictness and exacting expectations, she anoints herself to be their mouthpiece. And yet, a conundrum remains. As a tenured Yale Law School professor (married to the same), the author possesses ample cultural resources and class privileges. How could the author provide her children with the purported benefits of being "poor immigrant kids" while living in an environment of material comfort and plenty?[2] In her search for an answer, Chua turns to the violin and piano—the seemingly fetishized objects of desire of Chinese immigrant parents. "Classical music," as Chua contends, "was the opposite of decline, the opposite of laziness, vulgarity, and spoiledness" (22). To succeed in a cultural site that requires discipline, hard work, and practice *and* one in which Chinese immigrants invest tremendous energy and effort would successfully test the author's mettle as a tiger mother. And thus, in *Battle Hymn of the Tiger Mother*, the violin and piano become the sites where battle lines are drawn, where the campaign against "generational decline" is waged, and where the "bitter clash of cultures" clangs most cacophonously.

Who are these Chinese immigrant parents that Chua so desperately seeks to embody? For the most part, the author offers her own parents as ideal models to emulate. Described through the memories of Chua's childhood, her parents represent an effective combination of strictness, frugality, self-reliance, and discipline. Attempting to reproduce their winning parenting tactics, Chua calls her daughter "garbage" for disrespecting her, much like her father did to the author when she was a child. "It's a Chinese immigrant thing," she explains to her horrified "Western" friends, who helpfully note that she is, in actuality, not a Chinese immigrant (50). Chua glosses over these inconsistencies, much as she does the fact that in the present moment her parents embody rather diluted versions of "tiger" parents. As the author sighs, "America changes people" (18). Years of living in the United States have softened these once tough-as-nails immigrants, as their suggestion that she ease up on her children's music practice makes abundantly clear. Thus in her quest against "generational decline," Chua looks to her parents as envisioned in their early years, in the image she conjures up and calcifies of them as recent Chinese immigrants still hardened by the dislocating experience of immigration. She bases the Chineseness of her parenting techniques on this "insider" knowledge about Chinese immigrants rather than any claimed diasporic closeness with China. Indeed, Chua neither looks to nor expresses longing for an ancestral Chinese motherland, offering instead somewhat glib hyperbole that trades on stereotypical perceptions about the strange consumption and cultural practices of the Chinese. Rather, she romanticizes the difficulties that racialized immigrants face in being treated like they do not belong, for exclusion intensifies one's desires for betterment and success. Or as Chua puts it, to "feel like outsiders in America . . . is less a burden than a privilege" (19).

Yet when Chua finds herself face-to-face with her fetishized immigrant subjects, she feels distance rather than affinity. Waiting with her husband for her younger daughter to finish her violin audition for Juilliard's Pre-College division, she sees throngs of other anxious Asian parents. Here, in the company of supposedly like-minded parents, one might imagine Chua feeling right at home. Finally, a crowd of her peers! And yet, what Chua experiences is disidentification, not to mention a sinking feeling that, despite her best efforts, she is lagging behind: "In the waiting area, we saw Asian parents everywhere, pacing back and forth, grim-faced and single-minded. They seem so unsubtle, I thought to myself, can they possibly love music? Then it hit me that almost all the other parents were foreigners or immigrants and that music was a ticket for them, and I thought, I'm not like them. I don't have what it takes" (141–142). It is the ticket that classical music represents to these "grim-faced" Asian parents that differentiates Chua from the immigrants whose perspective she purports to embody and share with her reading public. These parents, even more than the "Western" parents (or rather, the middle- and upper-middle-class white American parents) that Chua derides in her narratives, are the "others" against whom the author compares.

What type of ticket does classical music represent to the anxious "Asian parents" Chua encounters? As I argued in the first chapter, for middle- and upper-middle-class Asian immigrant parents at Juilliard Pre-College, participating in classical music represents a vehicle to demonstrate their high levels of education, their cultural sophistication, and their erudite tastes—traits that racialized immigrants, for whom English is a second, if not third, language, are viewed as not possessing. Living in a monolingual nation where downward mobility, racism, and language discrimination represent a constant reality, Asian parents view their investment in a universalizing field of elite culture as a means of gaining cultural capital (including an appreciation for music) and flexible skills that would ameliorate those effects. In this context, while many Chinese and Korean immigrant "music moms" make sweeping generalizations about the work ethic of "Asians" and the laziness of "Americans"—descriptions echoed throughout Chua's memoir—their articulations represent more than claims of superiority. They speak, instead, to the class, race, and linguistic anxieties that racialized immigrants experience in the United States. But replace that context with Chua's reservoir of privileges as a hyper-fluent Yale Law School professor and one is left simply with a narrative of arrogance—empty, essentialist claims of Chinese superiority.

Chua's cultural fluency allows her to distinguish between the striving immigrant model marked as "Chinese" and the worldliness, intellectual curiosity, art collecting, and "good taste" (tastes that are cultivated but scripted as natural) implicitly marked as "white" and glimpsed in her memoir through her upper-middle-class Jewish husband and his mother. When Chua asks how the Asian parents waiting at Juilliard can "possibly love music," she voices the disconnect that she—and the broad U.S. public that makes up her implied readership—sees between those "unsubtle" foreign bodies and the élan, artistry, and grace of the Western high arts. This, of course, is a question that readers might pose to the author herself, one that she invites by reproducing in her memoir worksheets detailing "measure-by-measure instructions" for her children's practice sessions and demands such as "I'm going to count to three, then I want *musicality!*" (28). It is likely that Chua, similar to the "music moms" I interviewed, gained an affection and appreciation for classical music through her children's music training. Nonetheless, the suspicion that she articulates—and ironically performs—about "single-minded" Asian parents speaks to the barriers that racialized immigrants face attempting to accrue the full returns of elite cultural capital absent the proper accoutrement of race (read: whiteness). The extent to which Asian immigrant parents' intense involvement in Western classical music training has failed to grant them the image of refinement and erudition they seek to display is nowhere more apparent than in the cacophonous debates that ensued over "tiger parenting."

Chua's idealization of the immigrant generation is one reason why her memoir reads so strangely. Why romanticize the hard knock life of immigrants while in abundant possession of economic, cultural, and institutional resources? While second- or third-generation nostalgia for an ancestral homeland is a familiar narrative—a narrative, as I described in chapter 4, frequently framed as a search for roots, identity, and belonging—nostalgia for the immigrant generation is not. On the one hand, in this context of heightened anti-immigrant sentiment, such a gesture is irresponsible. To celebrate immigrant toughness as a privilege, cultural exclusion as a form of capital, and institutionalized racism and downward mobility as a personal challenge to succeed, turns racism into individual failure. Cultural values become proxies for racial embodiments that elide relations of power. On the other hand, this may be precisely the point. Chua's memoir is carefully marketed to tap into and alleviate existing concerns about immigration, race, and global competition, particularly from China. For the author, of course, is no outsider. She profits from a savvy racial performance that trades on her abilities to decode the strange and foreign ways of the Chinese for an American public. Her memoir reveals a high degree of fluency in the formulaic narratives, stock characterizations, and racialized anxieties that speak to the dominant culture. In true "American" fashion, race and class hierarchies are reduced to the individual: one's personality, work ethic, and effort.

The spotlight on Chua appears to have passed, nudged aside in favor of newer, more salacious media conversations and unrevived, for the most part, despite a more recent polemic on cultural traits and success (coauthored by her husband, Jeb Rubenfield) titled *The Triple Package*. But the legacy of *Battle Hymn of the Tiger Mother* lingers, visible in the addition of the term "tiger mother" into our everyday vocabulary. The referent "tiger mother" collapses race, class, immigration, and cultural difference into a frustratingly tidy bundle that serves multiple purposes. It domesticates ongoing anxieties about China (and other Asian "tiger" economies) and the place of racialized immigrants in the United States. It limits the discourses available to discuss the complexities of race, class, and power. And it stokes fears about the racial pathologies of the Chinese. For while Chua claims to have learned her lesson—a balance of "Chinese" and "Western" ways might embody a better route to pursue—she invokes the specter of other, more determined "tigers" still on the loose. They prowl about "grim-faced" and "single-minded," crowding our schools and universities with their overachieving ways, taking over elite fields of Western high culture where they implicitly do not belong, and seizing disproportionate slices of the American pie while maintaining their culturally foreign ways. How to stave off these tigers prowling about in the United States and encircling it, even more menacingly, from abroad? Chua's "tiger mother" introduces a powerful tool for legitimizing and managing the Asian threat writ large. The author updates the figure of the Asian parent to fuel as well as contain a range of anxieties in an era of globalization.

If the popularity of Chua's "tiger mother" concept underscored the enduring resilience of racial logics—particularly in light of its seamless adoption as shorthand for an array of beliefs about Asian Americans, social class, parenting, and immigration—it also highlighted the commercial payoffs of playing into its assumptions. Uneasy with the implications of the term "tiger mother," cognizant of its currency, and disinterested in catering to its appeal, young Asian Americans I interviewed creatively reworked their understanding of its meanings. Reflecting on the figure of the tiger mother, for instance, singer Joseph Vincent suggested that the focus that Asian parents place on practicing instruments and toiling away at the computer (presumably completing schoolwork) unwittingly created the foundations for the Asian American creativity flourishing online. As he reflected, "because of the tiger mom mentality, the Asian mom thing, Asian kids have to learn the piano and violin growing up. And Asian kids are not allowed to go out on weekends and stuff like that. So where do we spend the most time? On the Internet. So Asians took over the Internet, and that became one of the most prominent of media, social media." While the extent to which Asians have taken over the Internet remains debatable, Vincent's observation reflects a desire to reinterpret the meanings ascribed to the "tiger mother" and the results produced by her efforts. In the singer's reframing, the time, space, and access that young, middle-class Asian Americans have to digital technology and seemingly nerdy pursuits like learning the piano and violin provide them with many of the necessary tools for self-expression—the means to counter representations that do not speak fully to their own experiences and, in some ways, to the complexity of their parents' lives as well.

The prevalence that images of the model minority, the "yellow peril," and now the "tiger mother" hold in the popular U.S. imaginary, and the routes through which they are both dispelled as myths and upheld as somehow revealing certain truths about this pan-ethnic group, represents part of the racialized landscape that Asian Americans confront when making music. The case studies investigated in this book considered how Asian American music makers navigate this racial terrain, reimagining Asian American subjectivity through elite cultural practices, shared popular consumption, new media, and diaspora. Their music making exposes how music both muddles and upholds racial boundaries, even as universalism and color-blind intimacy continue to be endorsed as attainable and worthy goals. Working within these racialized structures, these music makers still manage to upend expectations, find and create new markets for themselves, shift the significations accrued to their Asianness, and chart new routes for Asian Americans to imagine home and belonging in shifting global, cultural, and musical landscapes.

ACKNOWLEDGMENTS

This book is built on the faith of others who often have believed in this project more than I have myself. My biggest thanks go to all the individuals who graciously agreed to be interviewed over the years, whose complex stories I hope to have captured, in some small part, in these pages. I am indebted to many others for immense guidance, friendship, and support. Sarita See helped me find my bearings in this project and this profession, June Howard stretched herself to provide inspired mentorship, and Susan Douglas, Jonathan Freedman, and Stephen Sumida encouraged me with their astute feedback. Nikki Stanton and Nhi Lieu know this work almost better than I do myself and are my constant cheerleaders in this profession and in life. Kim Alidio, Jason Chang, Paul Ching, Richard Kim, John McKiernan-Gonzalez, Larry Hashima, Janxin Leu, Teresa Macedo Pool, Anna Pegler Gordon, Michelle Seldin-Silverman, and Cindy Wu made Ann Arbor such a fun place to learn and grow. Tamar Barzel, Alisa Braun, Libby Garland, and Nick Syrett encouraged some of my earliest efforts. Adria Imada, Cary Cordova, Lucy Corin, erin Khuê Ninh, Cecilia Tsu, Thuy Linh Tu, and Julie Wyman have been wonderful friends in this profession. Jennifer Beckham, Erika Gasser, Laura Halperin, Kathy Jurado, Shani Mott, Nikki Stanton, and Carla Vecchiola, aka the Girl Turtles, saw me through graduate school and taught me just how much writing is a collective process. Michael Cohen, Nadia Ellis, Robin Hayes, Tori Langland, Susette Min, and Leigh Raiford, aka the Surplussers, helped me transform this project into a book through their collective brilliance, careful reading, and encouragement. So many of these pages were written at the East Asian Studies library at Berkeley, where Robin Hayes instituted the "program" and Nadia Ellis saw me to the finish line.

I am grateful to have landed at the American Studies Program at UC Davis, where colleagues Charlotte Biltekoff, Carolyn de la Peña,

Caren Kaplan, Ari Y. Kelman, Jay Mechling, and Michael Smith—and especially directors Eric Smoodin and Julie Sze—have provided a supportive environment for me to grow as a scholar and teacher. Thanks also to Kay Clare Allen, Aklil Bekele, and Naomi Ambriz for bringing order to my life. For institutional support, I am grateful to the University of Michigan's Rackham Graduate School, the Michigan Society of Fellows, the UC Presidents Postdoctoral Fellowship and my mentor Sunaina Maira, the UC Davis Humanities Institute, and the UC Davis Dean's Office. I also thank the Center for Ethnic Studies and Arts at the University of Iowa and Lauren Rabinowitz, Kent Ono, and Deborah Whaley for astute feedback. At Duke University Press, I am enormously grateful to Courtney Berger for believing in the promise of this project and being an ideal editor, to Christine Choi and Erin Hanas for their careful guidance, and to the anonymous readers of the manuscript for the time and care they took to give such thoughtful feedback. And for their impeccable work as research assistants, I thank Christina Owens, Sylvie Liao, and Yi Zhou.

An earlier version of chapter 1 appeared as "Interlopers in the Realm of High Culture," *American Quarterly* 61, no. 4 (December 2009): 881–903. An earlier version of chapter 4 appeared as "The 'ABCs' of Chinese Pop," *Journal of Transnational American Studies* 4, no. 1 (2012). An earlier version of the epilogue appeared as "On Tiger Mothers and Music Moms," *Amerasia* 37, no. 2 (2011): 130–136.

My mother has always encouraged me in all of my endeavors, even as she sometimes puzzled over their meanings. Both she and my father cultivated in me a love of music and learning at an early age, and while I wish my father could have seen some of the directions this eventually took me in life, this early influence remains powerful. My sister, no doubt more of a music expert than me, has been my constant sounding board and confidant in all things. I am, above all else, blessed to share my life with Arthur, who inspires me with his optimism, compassion, and calm. Aria came into our lives as I was finishing this book, but already her voice and laughter make music like no other.

Introduction

1. Chang, *Hunger*, 113.

2. Lam, "Embracing 'Asian American Music' as an Heuristic Device," 44. Also see Deborah Wong's Introduction to *Speak It Louder* for more on the theoretical limitations of "Asian American music," a category that, as she notes, Asian American musicians and producers themselves hold little interest in advancing or being grouped under.

3. As Small explains, the "fundamental nature and meaning of music lie not in objects, not in musical works at all, but in action, in what people do. . . . *To music is to take part, in any capacity, in a musical performance, whether by performing, by listening, by rehearsing, or practicing, by providing material for performance (what is called composing), or by dancing.*" Small, *Musicking*, 8–9; italics in original.

4. Cook, "Music as Performance," 208.

5. Nguyen, *Race and Resistance*, 11. For more on the cultural capital that the ideological framework of resistance holds in Asian American studies scholarship also see Koshy, "Morphing Race into Ethnicity"; and Chiang, *Cultural Capital of Asian American Studies*.

6. Ninh, *Ingratitude*, 9.

7. Ninh, *Ingratitude*; Lieu, *American Dream in Vietnamese*; and So, *Economic Citizens*.

8. Palumbo-Liu, *Asian/American*, 4.

9. For a highly influential examination of the contradictions in national and cultural belonging see Lisa Lowe's study *Immigrant Acts*. I would also point to the marshaling of cultural explanations to account for Asian American success in education research. As Jennifer Ng, Sharon S. Lee, and Yoon K. Pak observe in their review of existing education literature, the focus on cultural evidence reinforces dominant cultural myths about Asian Americans while eliding the intersecting roles of race and class: "Basing conclusions on specific Asian cultural practices and beliefs limits our understanding of how particular racialized groups in the United States adopt certain adaptive strategies to deal with racism and how education is seen as one of the few means to gain social capital."

Ng, Lee, and Pak, "Contesting the Model Minority and Perpetual Foreigner Stereotypes," 99.

10. This is, in part, not a dynamic unique to Asian American classical musicians. For example, Jewish and other white ethnic musicians in decades past similarly encountered racialized suspicions about the limits of their musicality, creativity, and success. As MacDonald Moore observes, by the mid-twentieth century, the growing presence of Jewish immigrants in classical music spheres engendered a feeling of "invasion" and "ethnic dissonance." Moore, *Yankee Blues*, 147. The redundancies in the discourse used to characterize Jewish musicians (as well as parents) and Asians/Asian Americans underscore the intractability and flexibility of racial paradigms, the function of elite cultural practices for upwardly mobile immigrant groups, and the gatekeeping mechanisms of Western classical music. At the same time, what I would argue distinguishes the current visibility of Asians/Asian Americans in classical music from earlier white ethnic immigrant groups is not just questions about the access Asians and Asian Americans have to whiteness, but also the staggering scope and scale of interest in classical music taking place in East Asia (particularly China) alongside ongoing conversations about the declining interest in and symbolic value of classical music in the United States.

11. Asian American studies scholars have aptly demonstrated how model minority and "yellow peril" ideologies rest on a racial continuum. As Robert Lee observes: "The model minority has two faces. The myth presents Asian Americans as silent and disciplined; this is the secret to success. At the same time, this silence and discipline is used in constructing the Asian American as a new yellow peril." Lee, *Orientals*, 190. Also see Gary Okihiro, *Margins and Mainstreams*, 141–142; and Colleen Lye, *America's Asia*.

12. Gorbman, "Scoring the Indian," 234.

13. Wong, *Speak It Louder*, 13.

14. Dirlik, "Race Talk, Race, and Contemporary Racism," 1370.

15. Feld, "Communication, Music, and Speech about Music," 91.

16. Fong-Torres, *Rice Room*, 75. While Fong-Torres speaks here of the power of rock and roll to experience transcendence from racial borders (and the politics this holds for minority populations, such as Asian Americans), it is significant that such an imagination depends on a narrative of rock and roll that downplays the complex processes of racial theft, admixture, and appropriation at the core of this music form.

17. Lipsitz, *Dangerous Crossroads*, 137.

18. Frith, "Towards an Aesthetic of Popular Music," 144.

19. Radano and Bohlman, *Music and the Racial Imagination*, 6.

20. Here I draw insight from Oliver Wang's astute analysis of the different strategies that Asian American rappers mobilize in order to participate in a

musical form that historically and culturally has been constructed as black and Kevin Fellezs's investigation of how Asian American jazz musicians negotiate a musical culture framed through black and white. As Fellezs observes, racial and normative jazz discourses converge to place Asian American jazz musicians outside of the musical tradition: "An Asian jazz musician is always seen as 'coming into' a jazz tradition from an external space." Fellezs, "Silenced but Not Silent," 77. Similarly observing how the racial politics and history of hip hop places Asian Americans at a distance, Wang reveals how Asian American hip hop artists attempt to claim belonging by upholding the "universalizing" tenets of talent and skill or by attempting to diffuse the potential liabilities of their Asianness by addressing it head-on. Wang, "Rapping and Repping Asian."

21. Ross, *Listen to This*, 5.

22. For a popular example of how other racial minority groups draw on the (implicitly white) cultural capital of classical music as a strategy to negotiate their race and class positioning in the United States see Brent Staples's description of training himself to whistle Vivaldi's *Four Seasons* while walking through Chicago's Hyde Park as a graduate student. As Staples observes, aligning himself with the elite culture of classical music distanced him from negative stereotypes associated with blackness, masculinity, and violence, a move that both reassured passersby and, in turn, helped him relax. Social psychologist Claude Steele uses Staples's description as his organizing anecdote in *Whistling Vivaldi* to illustrate how stereotypes impact perception and performance.

23. For more on how strategies of cultural accumulation by elite Asian subjects collide uneasily with U.S. racial regimes and hierarchies see, for instance, Ong, *Flexible Citizenship*.

24. Mireya Navarro, "Trying to Crack the Hot 100," *New York Times*, March 4, 2007.

25. Ramsey, *Race Music*, 38.

26. Vanweelden and McGee, "Influence of Music Style and Conductor Race on Perceptions of Ensemble and Conductor Performance."

27. Anthony Tommasini, "Can What You Know Affect What You Hear?," *New York Times*, March 18, 2007.

28. Joyce Hatto, a British pianist, retired in the early 1970s after an unassuming concert career and a diagnosis of cancer only to reemerge in 1989 with an extraordinary series of recordings (produced by her husband) that showcased the near entirety of the standard piano repertoire with astounding artistry, technical virtuosity, and musicality. Critics framed their praise of Hatto's CDs through the narrative of personal triumph—the indomitability of the human spirit and proof that genius can bloom even late in life. In the end, however, technology revealed plagiarism. A listener's iTunes library correctly identified one of Hatto's recordings as that of another pianist, a revelation that eventually exposed all of her recordings to be performances by other artists. Music critics hoodwinked by the affair felt humiliated. And yet, as Denis Dutton noted in an op-ed for the *New York Times*, such reactions were unjustified, for "music isn't just about sound; it is about achievement in a larger human sense. If you think an interpretation is by a 74-year-old pianist at the end of her life, it won't sound quite the same to you as if you think it's by a 24-year-old piano-competition winner who is just starting out. Beyond all the pretty notes, we want creative engagement and communication from music, we want music to be a bridge to another personality." Dutton, "Shoot the Piano Player," *New York Times*, Feb. 26, 2007.

29. This stands in contrast to Mari Yoshihara's investigation of Asian and Asian American participation in classical music in which she suggests that, in the "music itself," such categories as race and ethnicity recede into the background. As she observes: "Being a musician is the most significant mode for structuring identity, through which other categories like race, ethnicity, gender are played out. This explains why race is so frequently downplayed in the narratives they tell. Being a musician is the most important aspect of their identity." Yoshihara, *Musicians from a Different Shore*, 227.

30. Yoshino, *Covering*, 130.

31. Kun, *Audiotopia*, 26.

32. George Lipsitz deftly summarizes these sonic cues this way: "Gongs and specific string instruments signal 'Asia,' trumpets, congas, and maracas suggest 'South America,' and tom toms, vibrato, and familiar chord progressions simulate Native American 'Indian' territory. These stereotypes have almost no relationship to actual Asian, South American, or indigenous music; they are more a caricature of what such music sounds like to provincial Western listeners." Lipsitz, *Footsteps in the Dark*, xvii.

33. The pentatonic scale is a five-note scale commonly used in Asian traditional music.

34. Oliver Saria, "Cover Story: Far East Movement," *KoreAm*, October 2010.

35. Jeff Weiss, "Far East Movement Hits the Dance Floor," *Los Angeles Times*, Dec. 25, 2009. While the group originally called themselves Emcee's Anonymous as a way of downplaying their racial identity, they felt that the name signaled embarrassment rather than pride in their ethnic background. Band member Kev Nish (Kevin Nishimura) is quoted in the article as stating: "Emcee's Anonymous is wack—that's about being scared to own up to who you are. We respect and take pride in our culture." At the same time, as I discuss in greater detail in chapter 3, Asian American YouTube singers frequently expressed ambivalence about FM's visual image (in concerts, media appearances, and publicity materials), which consistently showed the group wearing sunglasses—a move that some of my interviewees interpreted as partially obfuscating their Asianness.

36. Evan Leong, "Far East Movement Feel 'Free to Geek Out' on New Album," MTV.com, Sept. 15, 2010, http://www.mtv.com/news/articles/1647920/far-east -movement-feel-free-geek-out-on-new-album.jhtml (accessed Oct. 14, 2010).

37. Banet-Weiser, "Branding the Post-feminist Self," 285.

38. Nakamura and Chow-White, *Race after the Internet*, 2. Also see Nakamura's *Digitizing Race* for more on the Internet as a visual medium in which race and other social categories circulate and find new meaning.

39. Melamed, "Spirit of Neoliberalism," 2.

40. Omi and Winant, *Racial Formation in the United States*, 55.

41. Prior to 1965 a quota system imposed an annual limit of two thousand Asians allowed to emigrate from the "Asia-Pacific triangle" (a geographic region extending from India to Japan and the Pacific islands). For an analysis of the impact that American immigration legislation in general and 1965 immigration laws in particular have had on the construction of Asian American communities see Hing, *Making and Remaking Asian America through Immigration Policy*; and Park and Park, *Probationary Americans*.

42. The tension between nationalist paradigms of "claiming America" and transnational frameworks of identity formation have been the subject of long-standing debates within Asian American studies. See, for instance, Wong, "Denationalization Reconsidered." Moreover, the residual connotations that haunt the term *immigration* can hamper recognition of the divergent routes undertaken by post-1965 Asian immigrants. As Sandhya Shukla writes: "Immigration remains in its most essential meaning a one-way process, from one country into another; the framework for the United States as destination significantly shapes the way that the homeland is constructed as necessarily a political and/or cultural space with fewer resources." Shukla, *India Abroad*, 11.

43. Appadurai, *Modernity at Large*, 31.

44. For an excellent examination of the complex cultural and social politics of Taiwan's Mandopop see Moskowitz, *Cries of Joy, Songs of Sorrow*.

45. Iwabuchi, *Recentering Globalization*.

46. As Henry Jenkins notes, the migratory behavior of contemporary audiences represents a core aspect of a changing media landscape. Jenkins, *Convergence Culture*. Still, as I analyze in greater detail in chapter 3, the fact that young Asian Americans eschew traditional media in favor of online media at rates higher than other racial groups highlights, in part, this population's hunger for cultural content and representations that hold relevance to their own lives.

47. For those who follow K-pop, the temporary banishment of Korean American singer Jay Park, former lead singer of the popular boy band 2PM, to the United States because of perceived slights against Korean cultural nationalism is well known. In September 2009, an errant comment that had been made years before on Park's Myspace page (where he dismissed Korea as "gay"

and "backward") became public knowledge, leading to public rejection of the singer and his subsequent removal from 2PM. The singer's repeated professions of remorse—his explanation that these were the immature comments of a lonely teenager adjusting to life in South Korea and to the rigors of pop stardom training—fell on the closed ears of outraged netizens. After returning to his hometown, Seattle, Park began uploading YouTube videos of his b-boy dance crew and covers of U.S. chart hits and interacting with the growing Asian American creative scene taking place both on- and offline. Yet, if lingering online traces led to Park's hasty retreat to the United States, it was social media and specifically YouTube that revitalized his career. His YouTube covers went viral, particularly in South Korea, where many of his fans began to reconsider their harsh stance. Park has since returned to South Korea to continue pursuing music and film opportunities. What this incident highlights is the tenuousness of diasporic inclusion and the new set of limitations—aesthetic, political, and otherwise —that Asian American artists confront when making music and pursuing celebrity in global pop music markets in Asia. While this book focuses on Chinese Americans in Mandopop, connections can be made to the experiences of other artists attempting to use diasporic inclusion as a basis through which to seek and gain commercial opportunities in "ethnic" homelands abroad.

48. See, for instance, Ong, "Experiments with Freedom."

49. For more on the imbrication of corporate and state support in Chinese pop music see Fung, "Western Style, Chinese Pop."

50. Jun, *Race for Citizenship*, 132.

51. This should not discount how the idea of "Asian values" circulates in Asia, which I discuss in chapter 4.

52. Ang, *On Not Speaking Chinese*, 12.

53. The emphasis on Chinese contexts and Chinese Americans (and East Asians more broadly) that is evident in this book is, on the one hand, a reflection of the demographics of the musical scenes I discuss; this is particularly true of Western classical music training. On the other hand, in focusing on the deployment of diaspora in Asian America, I would argue that ethnic specificity and vigilance about local contexts are necessary. It is my hope that some of the issues raised in the reimagining of Chinese American subjectivities through diaspora will find appropriate applications to other Asian American and racial minority groups.

54. Hall, "Cultural Identity and Diaspora," 235.

55. Hall, "Cultural Identity and Diaspora," 225.

56. Siu, *Memories of a Future Home*, 5.

57. See, for instance, David Brand, "Asian-American Whiz Kids," *Time Magazine*, Aug. 31, 1987.

58. Radano and Bohlman, *Music and the Racial Imagination*, 1.

59. Frith, *Performing Rites*, 229.

1. *Interlopers in the Realm of High Culture*

1. Robert Lipsyte and Lois B. Morris, "Teenagers Playing Music, Not Tennis," *New York Times*, June 27, 2002.

2. References to the "Asian" (or "Oriental") mother in classical music began appearing in the U.S. mainstream press by the 1980s, when the enrollment of East Asian and Asian American students increased at music schools, particularly on the east and west coasts. See, for instance, Leslie Rubinstein, "Oriental Musicians Come of Age," *New York Times*, Nov. 23, 1980, who observes that the "Oriental" mother has begun to replace the "Jewish" mother in classical music. There is an uncanny similarity in the rhetoric of overzealous parenting used to describe the "Asian" and "Jewish" mother within and beyond the realm of classical music, revealing the degree to which racialized narratives are recycled and flexibly deployed to maintain the existing U.S. racial order. For an astute analysis of the postwar emergence of the stereotypical "Jewish mother" as a figure who emblematized mainstream U.S. anxieties about Jewish American social mobility see Prell, *Fighting to Become Americans*.

3. Throughout this chapter I use the term *Asian* parent—a descriptor used by the parents I interviewed—despite the ways that this generalizing label overlooks ethnic particularity within the Asian American population, refers only to Chinese and Koreans, and downplays the fact that many of the parents I interviewed had lived in the United States for many years and were U.S. citizens. As I discuss later in the chapter, I understand these parents' self-identification as "Asian" as signaling, in part, an awareness of how the U.S. context fails to differentiate between the specificities of their national and ethnic origins.

4. The precise racial demographic of music schools can sometimes be difficult to ascertain, as many music schools, including Juilliard Pre-College, track citizenship status rather than race and ethnicity within their student population. These demographics are drawn from newspaper articles and Juilliard Pre-College yearbooks. See Laura Van Tuyl, "Asian Performers Abound on the American Music Scene," *Christian Science Monitor*, June 18, 1991; Barbara Jepson, "Asian Stars of Classical Music," *Wall Street Journal*, Jan. 2, 1991; Anthony Day, "A Shift in Composition," *Los Angeles Times*, April 3, 1994; Paula Yoo, "Asian Classical Musicians Still Face Stereotyping," *Detroit News*, May 9, 1994; and Cathy Crenshaw Doheny, "Asian Students and Faculty Shine at the Juilliard School," *Asian Fortune News*, July 25, 2010, http://www.asianfortune-news.com/site/article_1010.php?article_id=18 (accessed Oct. 26, 2011). Also see the demographics compiled by Evelyn Shu-Ching Chen in "Major Factors in the Prevalence and Success of Asian and Asian-American Classical Musicians in the United States since World War II," D.M.A. thesis, Juilliard School, 1998.

5. For more on the impact of U.S. immigration legislation for Asian American communities see Hing, *Making and Remaking Asian America through Immigration Policy*.

6. Unless otherwise cited, all quotations attributed to musicians and parents in this chapter and chapter 2 come from oral interviews I conducted with Asian immigrant parents and Asian American musicians living in New York City during 2001–2003 as well as with Asian American classical musicians (students and teachers) attending a music festival during the summer of 2011 in Santa Barbara, California. I held a total of forty-two oral interviews, participated in a range of musical activities, and had countless informal conversations with parents, music professionals, and students. I also conducted less formal interviews with (self-identified) white parents and musicians as well as two music directors of preparatory music schools.

7. Bourdieu, *Distinction*.

8. Charles Ward, "Korean Violinist Has Stellar Debut," *Houston Chronicle*, July 3, 2000; James Oestreich, "The Sound of New Music Is Often Chinese," *New York Times*, April 1, 2001; Robert Lipsyte and Lois B. Morris, "Hated Music, but Hear Him Now," *New York Times*, Oct. 22, 2002; James Oestreich, "Music Works Its (Western) Wiles in China," *New York Times*, May 25, 2003; Robert Maycock, "Is Classical Music Really Headed toward Extinction?," *The Independent*, April 26, 2005; Daniel J. Wakin, "The Keyboard Trade," *New York Times*, Nov. 14, 2005; and Michael Ahn Paarlberg, "Can Asians Save Classical Music?," *Slate*, Feb. 2, 2012, http://www.slate.com/articles/arts/culturebox/2012/02/can_asians_save _classical_music_.html (accessed Sept. 2, 2012).

9. For insightful analyses of Western music in East Asia see Nettl, *Western Impact on World Music*; Kraus, *Pianos and Politics in China*; Eppstein, *Beginnings of Western Music in Meiji Era Japan*; Mittler, *Dangerous Tunes*; Hwang, "Western Art Music in Korea"; Atkins, *Blue Nippon*; Jones, *Yellow Music*; Melvin and Cai, *Rhapsody in Red*; Everett and Lau, *Locating East Asia in Western Art Music*; and Yoshihara, *Musicians from a Different Shore*.

10. Eppstein, *Beginnings of Western Music in Meiji Era Japan*, 5.

11. Atkins, *Blue Nippon*, 49–50.

12. Jones, *Yellow Music*, 24.

13. Kraus, *Pianos and Politics in China*, x.

14. Hwang, "Western Art Music in Korea," 78.

15. Melvin and Cai, *Rhapsody in Red*, 307–313; Kraus, *Piano and Politics in China*, 25.

16. Everett, "Intercultural Synthesis in Postwar Western Art Music," 8. Also see Ong, *Flexible Citizenship*, for an astute analysis of the historical forces and power relations that have maintained Western cultural hegemony in an era of globalization. As Ong notes: "While the 'global cultural economy' of people,

products, and ideas may be characterized by disjunctures, regimes of consumption and credentialization are definitely hierarchized, with Europe and America setting the standards of middle-class style" (89).

17. See Jamie James, "The Rise of a Musical Superpower," *Time*, June 28, 2004; Small, *Musicking*; and Melvin and Cai, *Rhapsody in Red*, 301–302.

18. Chinese (a grouping that includes immigrants from Hong Kong, Taiwan, and China) and Koreans are the two largest Asian groups represented at Juilliard Pre-College specifically and in classical music training in the United States broadly. I see this as reflecting broader post-1965 immigration patterns. Classical music training remains a largely immigrant practice for Asian American families, and in the contemporary period relatively fewer Japanese (in comparison to Chinese and Koreans) immigrate to the United States. My interviewees pointed to the longer history and stronger infrastructure for classical music in Japan and suggested this as another reason why fewer Japanese music students/families migrate to the United States specifically for classical music training. Indeed, as a colonial power, Japan played a large role in the dissemination of Western classical music to China and Korea.

19. See Levine, *Highbrow/Lowbrow*, particularly chapter 2, "The Sacralization of Culture." Also see Horowitz, *Classical Music in America*, for a useful analysis of the highbrow, elitist mentality that pervaded Western classical music in the interwar period.

20. Kraus, *Pianos and Politics in China*, 197.

21. "Piatigorsky Returns from Far East, Urges More U.S. Culture for Asia," *Los Angeles Times*, Oct. 12, 1956. Also see Schuyler Chapin, "China Gets a Lesson from Beverly Sills," *New York Times*, Aug. 23, 1981. It is worth noting that the United States once occupied the position of Asia in relation to Western classical music, viewed in the nineteenth century with suspicion and condescension by Europe as a mechanized land of "steam engines" incapable of producing quality instruments or performers. See, for instance, Kraus, *Piano and Politics in China*, 202–203.

22. See, for instance, Maj. Arthur Loesser, "Western Music in Tokyo," *New York Times*, Aug. 11, 1946; Ely Haimowitz, "Korea Turns to Music of the West," *New York Times*, Sept. 1, 1948; and Richard Korn, "Japanese Musicians Cultivate Western Music," *New York Times*, March 24, 1957.

23. Rolf Jacoby, "Art of West in Korea," *New York Times*, Nov. 27, 1949.

24. Harold C. Schonberg, "In Japan, It's the 3 B's All the Way," *New York Times*, Nov. 11, 1973.

25. Faubion Bowers, "Beethoven's 'Big Nine'—The Japanese Love It," *New York Times*, April 13, 1975. Bowers's observation elides the extent to which the codified set of behaviors established as the appropriate manner of expressing one's enjoyment and appreciation for classical music performance only became ritualized with the stratification and sacralization of high culture in the United States during the late nineteenth century. Moreover, it is worth noting that audience behavior can be attributed to different factors. A New York Philharmonic member I interviewed observed that while on tour with the orchestra in Japan he noticed a marked difference between the quiet and stillness of Japanese audiences compared to those in New York. However, he attributed this distinction to having good manners, observing that "in New York, people are coughing and grunting . . . but maybe [the Japanese] are taught to behave themselves and not let out loose phlegm at every pause there is."

26. Bowers, "Beethoven's 'Big Nine.'"

27. For more on the relationship between musical authenticity, place, nation, and race see Stokes, *Ethnicity, Identity and Music*.

28. Bowers, "Beethoven's 'Big Nine.'" The quoted phrase is from a Japanese music professor lamenting that Japanese musicians lack broader understanding: "In our Western-style musicians where is the *kangeki* (expressiveness or emotion)? Where is the *jidai no nagara* (flow of generations or background)?"

29. The assessment Kraus makes about U.S. media portrayals of Western music in China aptly applies to the specific case of the documentary *From Mao to Mozart: Isaac Stern in China*, directed by Murray Lerner (1980). As Kraus writes: "Our mass media's image of cultural exchange focus on the happiness that *our* music brings to China. Concealed beneath the happy views of instruction in bowing and discussions of tempos is a proselytizing condescension. . . . The world culture system is a system of power, in which China is still weak enough that we accept its art only on our own terms. We welcome landscape paintings and translated poetry which we then put to our own purposes, such as opportunities for speculative investment and the creation of comforting myths about Asian spirituality and communion with nature." Kraus, *Pianos and Politics in China*, 194. In 2004, PBS aired the documentary *Perlman in Shanghai*, which chronicled violinist Itzhak Perlman's three-week trip to the Shanghai Conservatory in the summer of 2002 with his wife and young American musicians from the Perlman Music Program, the summer camp described at the start of this chapter. Filmed more than twenty years after Stern's trip, the documentary presented a similarly "warm and welcoming," if not slightly condescending, picture of Americans (including Asian Americans) teaching the Chinese not just about music, but important life lessons.

30. Many of the young students featured in the film eventually came to study and enjoy careers abroad. In my interview with Wen, a violinist who emigrated from China, she recalled attending Stern's master classes as a young girl, observing: "His visit really influenced a whole generation of violin playing in China, including me, too, I'm sure. You have to understand that he was the first big name American violinist to visit after China opened its doors to the West

in 1976. At the time, the Chinese were so eager to learn, and it made a great impact on teachers and students." For more on the impact of Stern's trip to China, thirty years later, see David Barboza, "Isaac Stern's Great Leap Forward Reverberates," *New York Times*, July 5, 2009.

31. Reflecting on the U.S. culture of classical music in 1991, pianist and music critic Samuel Lipman observed: "Music schools are now drawing an increasing percentage of their students—often, I might add, the best ones—from the Orient. It remains unclear exactly what the motivation for this enormous influx of Asians into our music schools is. What is certain is that, given their limited acquaintance with Western culture, they have special education needs, needs that are now being ignored." Lipman, *Music and More*, 22. I do not mean to single out Lipman but, rather, to highlight the lingering endurance of such views—particularly for an older generation of music professionals—in a field of culture exceedingly steeped in European tradition and reverence for master pedagogues.

32. Kim, *Bitter Fruit*, 46.

33. Palumbo-Liu, *Asian/American*, 201.

34. Morley and Robins, *Spaces of Identity*.

35. Michael Walsh, "'Like a Flower on a Pond': The Classics Flourish in Japan, but How Deep Are Their Roots?," *Time*, Aug. 1, 1983.

36. This should not imply that coverage about the derivative and unthinking nature of the Japanese has not continued unabated. See, for instance, Andrew Clark's description of the state of classical music in Japan in "Music with a Foreign Spirit," *Financial Times*, Feb. 19, 2000. Clark coined the term the "Japan complex" to identify the "acute insecurity" that Japan feels vis-à-vis the West, as people assume that "western branding is automatically better." As evidence for this complex, the reporter points to the NHK symphony, Japan's oldest professional orchestra, which he describes as sounding like a technically proficient machine: "Everyone is playing in tune, at exactly the same pitch, but there's no width to the sound, no breadth to the phrase-ends. It's a bit like a machine. The emphasis is on playing the right notes, not probing behind them. There's a reluctance to let go." The recurring description of the Japanese particularly, and Asians generally, as automatons who play with skill and technical facility leads one to wonder less if the Japanese are *unable* to express feelings and more if they have any feelings to express.

37. See, for instance, Fabian, *Time and the Other*, for an explication of how anthropology institutionalized a construction of non-Western cultural Others as not occupying the same temporality as the West.

38. Joseph Kahn and Daniel J. Wakin, "Classical Music Looks toward China with Hope," *New York Times*, April 3, 2007; Daniel J. Wakin, "Increasingly in the West, the Players Are from the East," *New York Times*, April 4, 2007; and

Daniel J. Wakin, "Pilgrim with an Oboe, Citizen of the World," *New York Times*, April 8, 2007 (parts 1–3 of the series "The Classical Revolution"). For more media reporting on the "explosive" musical and economic growth of China see Jamie James, "The Rise of a Musical Superpower," *Time*, June 28, 2004; Laura Santini, "A Classical Movement in China Gives Pianist Rock-Star Status," *Wall Street Journal*, Sept. 27, 2005; Laura Santini, "Where She's From, Classical Music Is a Growth Industry," *Wall Street Journal*, April 18, 2007; Robert Turnbull, "A Resounding Piano Forte, It's Keyboard as Springboard for Millions of Chinese," *Los Angeles Times*, May 27, 2007; Daniel J. Wakin, "Traveling across Cultures for a Son's Star Turn," *New York Times*, Sept. 21, 2007; Jennifer Lin, "China's 'Piano Fever,'" *Philadelphia Inquirer*, June 8, 2008; and Jeffrey Kluger, "Bernstein in Beijing: China's Classical Music Explosion," *Time*, Nov. 6, 2008.

39. Kahn and Wakin, "Classical Music Looks toward China with Hope."

40. Kahn and Wakin, "Classical Music Looks toward China with Hope."

41. Kahn and Wakin, "Classical Music Looks toward China with Hope."

42. Wakin, "Increasingly in the West, the Players Are from the East."

43. The 2007 *New York Times* series served as part of the impetus for a music school to organize its recruitment trip in 2009 to China, which I discuss in the following chapter.

44. As heralded by "Success Story of One Minority Group in the U.S.," *U.S. News and World Report*, Dec. 26, 1966; and William Peterson, "Success Story: Japanese-American Style," *New York Times Magazine*, Jan. 9, 1966.

45. See, for instance, Osajima, "Asian Americans as the Model Minority"; and Wu, *Yellow*.

46. Song, "Communities of Remembrance," 16.

47. Jun, *Race for Citizenship*, 123–147.

48. Kim, *Bitter Fruit*, 117.

49. Day, "Shift in Composition." There are countless other examples of how mainstream publications reported on the increasing visibility of Asian Americans in classical music training and placed Asian American participation within a model minority framework, emphasizing their culturally distinct traits (while also challenging more blatantly racialized characterization of Asian and Asian American musicians as technical robots or devoid of feeling). See, for instance, Rubinstein, "Oriental Musicians Come of Age"; Van Tuyl, "Asian Performers Abound on the American Music Scene"; Jepson, "Asian Stars of Classical Music"; Yoo, "Asian Classical Musicians Still Face Stereotyping; "Moreover: Asian Strings," *Economist*, Feb. 21, 1998; Hao Huang and Ramona Sohn Allen, "Transcultural Aspects of Music: What Did Confucius Say?," *American Music Teacher*, April/May 2000; and Annie Nakao, "Asians String Together a Classical Profile," *San Francisco Chronicle*, Sept. 19, 2002.

50. Day, "Shift in Composition." Day's description of Asian families is almost identical to that of the violinist and critic Henry Roth, who queries (and then answers): "Why is it that so many violinists of Asian descent, whether born in or outside of the Asian countries, are achieving outstanding prominence and expertise? They come from cultures that have long traditions of reverence for education and the hard-work ethic. Families are closely-knit and children from infancy are taught to respect and obey their elders, and to adopt their elders' values." Roth, *Violin Virtuosos*, 332.

51. Kogan, *Nothing but the Best*, 64–65.

52. Unlike Juilliard's college and graduate divisions, the Pre-College does not offer courses in jazz, dance, musical theater, or drama. The quotation about the Pre-College music curriculum comes from the school's official website, Juilliard Pre-College, www.juilliard.edu/precollege (accessed Sept. 22, 2013).

53. I interviewed only one single mother, who worked at a Chinese beauty salon with her mother. Many parents singled her out to me as having a particularly difficult life. In the other families I interviewed, the father held professional occupations in fields such as business, engineering, and medicine.

54. The patriarchal structure and assumptions followed in these families might account for the reason that boys in particular were discouraged from pursuing music professionally. Many of the Asian American male musicians I interviewed discussed the intense resistance they faced from their parents about their decision to become a musician (although some women faced conflicts as well).

55. Kingsbury, *Music, Talent, and Performance*, 76.

56. Sarah Chang is a prominent Korean American violinist.

57. In light of language limitations (particularly with newer immigrants to the United States) and the relatively structured setting of the oral interview, I did not expect the parents I interviewed to discuss issues of marital strife or discord with me. It is also worth noting that the split-level, transnational family was a traditional one for immigrants in the late nineteenth and early twentieth century, a family structure that persists in the contemporary period. See, for instance, Parreñas, *Children of Global Migration*, for a different class and geographical manifestation of such families.

58. While I did not pursue this topic in my interviews, it would be interesting to examine whether there were further points of division among the Chinese parents I interviewed depending on their country of origin. The Chinese parents I interviewed came from China, Hong Kong, Taiwan, and Vietnam. Although the parents I interviewed did not highlight those differences, referring instead to their shared Chineseness as parents, this should not discount the significance of national differences and cross-straits tensions.

59. Although beyond the scope of this chapter, it would be worth exploring whether discussions of ethnic differences between Koreans and Chinese hint at broader interethnic hostilities between these two groups.

60. As one Korean mother added after her description of the competitiveness of the Chinese: "I mean you are a Chinese girl [*laughs*], but [Chinese girls] behave like they don't have any barriers!" She supported her observation by citing not only her own feelings but also her observations of the behavior of her children's friends and "teachers' comments too."

61. For the assumed correlation between "American" and "white" see, for instance, Lipsitz, *The Possessive Investment in Whiteness*. For an understanding of how normative Americanness and whiteness was forged in both the United States and in their home country see, for instance, Nadia Kim's explication in *Imperial Citizens* of how U.S. imperialism and military intervention and encounters with American-mediated culture impact the racial understandings that Korean immigrants bring with them to the United States.

62. As Kim writes, "Although [Koreans] were fully aware that the world's people could generally be categorized into 'White, Black, and Yellow,' they did not perceive 'Yellow' (or Asian) as their *primary* identity. . . . [Koreans] 'become' Asian due in part to White America's effacing of difference among countless Asian ethnics." Kim, *Imperial Citizens*, 116.

63. The emphasis on the social value and intellectual function of classical music has wide circulation in the United States—from claims that playing Mozart to infants can help stimulate brain activity to the oft-cited statistic (in music circles at least) that music majors have the highest acceptance rates to medical school. Classical music, in this sense, is valorized as a vehicle for educational achievement and social mobility rather than as a desired profession parents have for their children.

64. Stokes, *Ethnicity, Identity and Music*, 19.

65. There is, of course, a complicated historical relationship between cultural hierarchies and class subjectivities in the United States. See, for instance, DiMaggio, "Social Structure, Institutions, and Cultural Goods."

66. A few parents also linked their involvement in classical music to their Christian faith, noting that their first exposure to the music was in church.

67. Some parents, however, did critically challenge the hierarchical separation between classical music and popular forms of music. Despite citing the "prestige" factor associated with classical music, Sookhyun also said, "I don't want to distinguish classical music with other music; whatever people likes to listen, that's what they have to do." Other parents noted that they continued to enjoy listening to classical music and popular music (usually from their country of origin). And finally, a few parents also discussed singing karaoke in their leisure time.

68. The discursive strategy immigrant groups use to position themselves as culturally, if not morally, superior to the white dominant group is a familiar strategy. See, for instance, Espiritu's cogent analysis of how Filipino immigrants use a gendered discourse of morality to contest their racial positioning in the nation and, in the process, decenter whiteness in "'We Don't Sleep Around Like White Girls Do.'"

69. See Ong, *Flexible Citizenship*, for an astute discussion of the limitations that upwardly mobile Chinese transnational subjects encounter in attempting to convert economic capital into high social standing in the United States.

70. Park, *Consuming Citizenship*, 6.

71. See Nadia Kim's discussion of how "language is racialized." As she observes, Korean immigrants connect the sense that whites feel they possess superior language skills over Asian Americans to beliefs about their racial superiority. Kim, *Imperial Citizens*, 176–177.

72. It is worth noting how this narrative of Asian parenting is differently mobilized as evidence that Asian American kids are mentally unstable, suicidal, and/or intellectual robots overwhelmed by parental expectations. See, for instance, Yilu Zhao, "Cultural Divide over Parental Discipline," *New York Times*, May 29, 2002; and the controversy (discussed in greater detail in the epilogue) that ensued after the release of Amy Chua's memoir *Battle Hymn of the Tiger Mother* and her editorial "Why Chinese Moms Are Superior," *Wall Street Journal*, Jan. 8, 2011.

2. "This Is No Monkey Show"

1. Unless otherwise cited, all quotations attributed to musicians and parents in this chapter and chapter 1 come from oral interviews I conducted with Asian immigrant parents and Asian American musicians living in New York City during 2001–2003 as well as with Asian American classical musicians (students and teachers) attending a music festival during the summer of 2011 in Santa Barbara, California. I held a total of forty-two oral interviews, participated in a range of musical activities, and had countless informal conversations on the topic with parents, music professionals, and students. I also conducted less formal interviews with (self-identified) white parents and musicians as well as two music directors of preparatory music schools. And finally, to examine more fully the global circulation of Western classical music, I accompanied a group of music faculty/administrators to China on a recruiting trip during the summer of 2009.

2. For an insightful overview of the reframing of racial inequality through the language of color-blind racism see Bonilla-Silva, *Racism without Racists*.

3. In this chapter I use the category "Asian American" even though I am primarily referring to East Asians. This is due, in large part, to the particular

Asian demographic represented in classical music and the fact that "Asian" stereotypes circulating in this cultural field are specific to East Asians. At the same time, the tendency to align the category Asian American with individuals of East Asian descent applies both to classical music and beyond, an observation also made by a number of the musicians I interviewed. For instance, violinist Midori noted: "What's interesting about the Asian American grouping is that immediately when you think of an Asian American, you think of someone with a Korean face, or a Chinese face, or a Japanese face. You don't usually think of an Indian face, or a Pakistani face. But in Europe, Asian is almost always South Asian—Pakistan and India. I don't think that we [Asian Americans of East Asian descent] think about belonging in the same group with the Indian population, or the Pakistani population or the Sri Lankan population." A South Asian violist I interviewed concurred, noting that although he identifies as both Indian American and Asian American, he is often not perceived as belonging to the latter category; moreover, he felt that his Indian background insulated him from stereotypes about the "Asian musician," which were never placed on him. Given the relatively few musicians of South Asian descent in Western classical music, he felt that Indians/Indian Americans are still viewed as somewhat unique in this cultural field.

4. In both musicology and performance pedagogy music professionals defer to the composer and the primacy of the musical text. As Nicholas Cook writes, the tendency in musicological analysis is to view performance and music as two separate entities—"performance as in essence the reproduction of a text"—rather than "music *as* (not *and*) performance." Cook, "Music as Performance," 204–205.

5. Bach's Chaconne is a movement from a solo violin work and part of the standard violin repertoire.

6. Reasons cited for the declining prestige of high culture arts, particularly in the United States, vary, ranging from the proliferation of media choices to the blurring of the boundaries separating high and popular culture (often from artists working within those fields and audiences). As Paul DiMaggio and Toqir Mukhtar note: "The U.S. public stoutly rejects the proposition that high culture is more valuable than folk or popular culture and the most educated Americans (who should have the greatest stake in cultural hierarchy) are the most united in rejecting it." DiMaggio and Mukhtar, "Arts Participation as Cultural Capital in the United States," 171.

7. The comparison between "museum stuff" and classical music is compelling, especially in light of the increase in attendance that museums have enjoyed in the contemporary period while audiences for other high art forms, such as classical music and ballet, have suffered sharp declines. DiMaggio and Mukhtar attribute this difference to the broader interest in and marketing of

diversity in U.S. culture. While classical music and ballet are firmly rooted in nineteenth-century European culture, art museums have had some success in implementing multicultural programming. DiMaggio and Mukhtar, "Arts Participation as Cultural Capital in the United States," 191. Reflecting on this often-made comparison, musicologist Lawrence Kramer contends that "the museum metaphor is misguided. . . . Museums have become more popular than ever just as classical music has been floundering." He attributes this to the changing rituals of museum etiquette that encourage focused viewing in less "stuffy," ritualized environments: "Unlike the traditional concert hall, the museum has become an animated space by affording opportunities to combine sociability, informality, and the enjoyment of art." Kramer, *Why Classical Music Still Matters*, 12–13.

8. See, for instance, Kramer, *Why Classical Music Still Matters*; and Horowitz, *Classical Music in America*. For newspaper accounts on this topic see Robin Pogrebin, "Opera for $20? New Audiences Hear Siren Song," *New York Times*, Oct. 9, 2006; Bernard Holland, "How to Kill American Orchestras," *New York Times*, June 29, 2003; Michael Kimmelman, "Lamenting the Fade-Out of Classical Radio," *New York Times*, April 17, 2002; Howard Reich, "There's a Crisis in Classical Music," *Chicago Tribune*, Oct. 28, 2001; Gerald Gold, "Classical Music: What Next?," *New York Times*, Jan. 31, 1988. Greg Sandow, a music critic, composer, and educator (some of the courses he has taught at Juilliard focus on marketing and branding in classical music), is a prolific writer on this topic. Much of his writing is collected on his blog, Greg Sandow: The Future of Classical Music, http://www.artsjournal.com/sandow (accessed Sept. 25, 2013). It is worth noting that assessments about the declining state of classical music in the United States contrast sharply with media reports on China, where classical music is portrayed as a booming industry that crackles with the energy of pop music, or Venezuela, which received a great deal of coverage about the role that classical music can play in transforming the lives of disadvantaged youth following the appointment of Gustavo Dudamel as conductor of the Los Angeles Philharmonic in 2009.

9. The article to which Wen referred is Bernard Holland's "A Pathetic Living at the Symphony?," *New York Times*, Nov. 5, 1995. In the article, Holland cites a study conducted by social psychologist Richard Hackman that ranked orchestral players just below federal prison employees in terms of job happiness and satisfaction.

10. It should be noted that the collective nature of orchestral labor refers more to string players, who play in a section and are not heard individually, than to woodwind and brass players. At the same time, orchestra musicians in general are beholden to the musical interpretation of the conductor (and in pit orchestras, also to the singers onstage).

11. Levine, *Highbrow/Lowbrow*.

12. A book cited by a number of my interviewees as evidence of how the intersection between commerce, profit, and classical music marked its death knell is Lebrecht's *Who Killed Classical Music?*, which is a compelling investigation into the business of classical music.

13. Goldin and Rouse, "Orchestrating Impartiality."

14. Cited in Joseph McLellan, "Do Unseen Musicians Get Fairer Hearings?," *Washington Post*, July 13, 1997. Dorothy DeLay was a renowned violin pedagogue whose violin studio included Itzhak Perlman, Cho-Liang Lin, Nadja Salerno-Sonnenberg, Midori, and Sarah Chang, among others; her observations thus carry particular weight in classical music. Also see Chris Pasles, "'Blind' Audition Keeps Politics Out of the Process," *Los Angeles Times*, July 18, 1997.

15. While there are a few programs in place to encourage the participation of underrepresented minorities in classical music—for instance, the Sphinx competition rewards and showcases the talents of African Americans in classical music—they do little to address the socioeconomic and cultural reasons for the low representation of African Americans and Latinos in this cultural field. Indeed, much of the excitement and media frenzy surrounding Dudamel's appointment as music director of the Los Angeles Philharmonic stemmed from hopes of replicating similar programs for disenfranchised communities in Los Angeles and breathing new life into classical music for young kids, particularly those coming from economically depressed, urban neighborhoods. See, for instance, Dudamel's two profiles on the CBS news program 60 *Minutes*, originally aired on February 18, 2008, and May 18, 2010, the latter of which focused on the conductor's instrumental role in creating programs similar to Venezuela's El Sistema in the United States.

16. Cited in Olmstead, *Juilliard*, 282.

17. Michael Ishii and Emma Moon, "On Racism," *Juilliard Journal*, May 1989, 6.

18. Hage, *White Nation*, 37.

19. While outside the scope of this project, it is worth noting that white ethnic immigrants—notably Italian and Jewish immigrants—themselves used classical music as a mode of assimilating into the United States and securing their whiteness.

20. While Asians and Asian Americans are well represented in piano and strings (namely, the violin), reports of their "takeover" are greatly exaggerated both in the mainstream U.S. press and by musicians themselves. Moreover, according to data collected by the American Symphony Orchestra League, while the demographics of top-tier U.S. orchestras (the top twenty-five orchestras based on budget and size) shifted from 1995 to 2000 and 2005, they do not signal a sea change in the demographics of the U.S. culture of classical music. While these numbers and percentages are not definitive, given the inconsistency with which orchestras categorize race and ethnicity (and because not all orchestras

responded to the survey), African American and Latinos represent a tiny percent-age, with a slight trend upward in 2005. Asians constituted about 5 percent of musicians in top orchestras in 1995 and increased to over 9 percent in 2005. While these figures indicate a definite upswing, they do not augur a takeover or inva-sion of Asians. These figures are reprinted in Mark Kanny, "Sounds of Diversity," *Pittsburgh Tribune-Review*, Aug. 12, 2007.

21. For an insightful study of the discourse of white male disenfranchise-ment in the U.S. media landscape see Carroll, *Affirmative Reaction*.

22. For an examination of this discourse see the edited volume by Gilmour et al., *Too Asian?* The volume emerged out of heated debates generated by the article by Stephanie Findlay and Nicholas Köhler, "Too Asian," *Maclean's*, Nov. 10, 2010, about the place of race, Asians, and multiculturalism on Canadian col-lege campuses.

23. See Suein Hwang, "The New White Flight," *Wall Street Journal*, Nov. 19, 2005; and Scott Jaschik, "Too Asian?," *Inside Higher Ed*, Oct. 10, 2006, http://www.insidehighered.com/news/2006/10/10/asian (accessed Sept. 25, 2013).

24. Jaschik, "Too Asian?" A similar "yellow peril" rhetoric has emerged around elite universities being overtaken by Asian students. One representa-tive example of the discourse surrounding alleged Asian overrepresentation in elite universities and the problem it creates for the image and diversity of the school is Timothy Egan's article on UC Berkeley titled "Little Asia on the Hill," *New York Times*, Jan. 7, 2007. In Kent Ono and Vincent Pham's critique of Egan's article, they analyze how the article recycles tired racialized tropes of Asian Americans as foreigners, model minorities, and a "yellow peril" threat, implying that the visible presence of Asians somehow makes UC Berkeley less American: "This kind of article is not directed toward Asian Americans as readers and car-ries the message that Asian Americans are, once again, taking over." Ono and Pham, *Asian Americans and the Media*, 93.

25. The Colburn School is a well-regarded performing arts school in down-town Los Angeles.

26. Joseph Kahn and Daniel J. Wakin, "Classical Music Looks toward China with Hope," *New York Times*, April 3, 2007. The other two articles in the series are Daniel J. Wakin, "Increasingly in the West, the Players Are from the East," *New York Times*, April 4, 2007; and Daniel J. Wakin, "Pilgrim with an Oboe, Citizen of the World," *New York Times*, April 8, 2007.

27. Kraus, *Piano and Politics in China*, 35.

28. See Lang Lang with Ritz, *Journey of a Thousand Miles*, 209. Lang Lang titles this section of his memoir "Citizen of the World," claiming both China and Russia as his "mothers." The gratifying acclaim he receives as a Chinese pianist performing an all-Russian program on Russian soil solidifies the intrinsic ties that the pianist feels to that country.

29. While I have not focused on the gender politics in classical music, this is a rich topic of inquiry (and one that emerged in my interviews) given the masculine and patriarchal traditions embedded in this field of culture. A vivid example of this can be found in the long-standing sexist (and racist) practices of the Vienna Philharmonic, one of the most celebrated orchestras in the world. That orchestra has long defended its right to exclude women and nonwhites on the basis of needing to maintain its "special" Viennese sound. For more on the discriminatory practices of the Vienna Philharmonic see the essays written by composer and cultural critic William Osborne, available on the William Osborne and Abbie Conant website, http://www.osborne-conant.org/index .html (accessed Jan. 11, 2012). For a musicological investigation of gendered discourses embedded in Western classical music see the highly influential work by Susan McClary, *Feminine Endings* (1991). Gender politics are particularly salient for Asian Americans in classical music, given the higher proportion of Asian American women enrolled in classical music training, the perception (and stereotype) that Asian women (particularly those from Korea) view classical music as a mode of enhancing their proper femininity and marriage prospects, and assumptions about the feminization/effeminate nature of high culture and Asian Americans in the U.S. imaginary.

30. Kingsbury, *Music, Talent, Performance*, 106.

31. For more on how beliefs about race and gender impact how music experts hear see Elliott, "Race and Gender as Factors in Judgments of Musical Performance." In Elliott's study, eighty-eight music teachers were shown videotapes of trumpet and flute students and asked to evaluate their performance. As the videotapes were synchronized to identical trumpet and flute performances, the only changing variables were the instrument, gender, and race (white and black) of the performers. The music teachers scored the performance of women lower than men, blacks lower than whites, and female trumpeters lower than female flutists. As this study shows, even among music professionals preconceptions about race and gender—including intersecting gendered and racialized beliefs associated with particular musical instruments—impact evaluations of musical performance.

32. Michael Johnson notes that since 1990, the percentage of Asian players in international piano competitions has increased from 21 percent to 35 percent. Johnson, "The Dark Side of Piano Competitions," *New York Times*, Aug. 8, 2009. It is unclear whether this statistic includes Asian Americans or just Asian nationals. Also see Daniel J. Wakin, "The Keyboard Trade," *New York Times*, Aug. 14, 2005, which describes the "explosion of Chinese talent" and the increasing numbers of Chinese winning (and being selected to take part in) international piano competitions.

33. Also see Kraus, who observes that, for Chinese musicians, "competitions, for all their shortcomings, remain the only way that a non-Western musician can gain respect, by beating Westerners at their own musical games." Kraus, *Piano and Politics in China*, 203.

34. Robin J. Hayes, "Unicorns and Obama" (unpublished manuscript).

35. For instance, European composers from the late Romantic period (which overlaps with the height of European imperialism), such as Maurice Ravel or Claude Debussy, drew on "Oriental" music influences in some of their compositions. See Born and Hesmondhalgh, *Western Music and Its Others*, for an illuminating set of essays that examines the construction of difference and racial othering in Western classical music specifically and Western music more generally.

36. DiMaggio and Mukhta, "Arts Participation as Cultural Capital in the United States," 191.

37. See, for example, the media appearances of Chinese American pianist Marc Yu (born in 1999), who first performed on the *Tonight Show with Jay Leno* at age six and has since appeared on the *Oprah Winfrey Show*, the *Ellen DeGeneres Show*, and in the *National Geographic* documentary called *My Brilliant Brain* (which aired in 2007).

38. For more on alternate concert venues in classical music see David Patrick Stearns, "Classical Music Finding Intimacy and Freedom in Nightclub Venues," *Philadelphia Inquirer*, Sept. 8, 2009; and Anthony Tommasini, "Feeding Those Young and Curious Listeners," *New York Times*, June 16, 2009. Such strategies reveal the porous barriers between high and low culture in the contemporary era. This trend is in keeping with what sociologists note as a shift toward rewarding prestige to consumers who are culturally "omnivorous," that is, fluent in the multiple languages of high, popular, and mass culture. See DiMaggio and Mukhtar, "Arts Participation as Cultural Capital in the United States."

39. See James Oestreich, "The 'Ring' Arrives in Times Square," *New York Times*, Sept. 28, 2010; and Richard Verrier, "Movie Theaters Turn to Live Event Screenings to Fill Seats," *Los Angeles Times*, April 20, 2010.

40. Take, for example, the multicultural programs staged at Carnegie Hall. During the 2009–2010 season it presented "Honor! A Celebration of the African American Cultural Legacy," a festival curated by singer Jessye Norman that highlighted African American musical traditions ranging from jazz, soul, and R&B as well as African American classical performers and composers; and a festival of Chinese culture entitled "Ancient Pasts: Modern Voices," which featured high-profile Chinese musicians performing Chinese traditional music, standard Western classical music repertoire, and contemporary works by Chinese composers. In the following season, Japanese-born conductor Seiji Ozawa

helped orchestrate "Japan: NYC," which explores Japan's long interactions with Western music. While such multicultural programming increasingly abounds, it is worth noting that it has also been cited as a reason for the diminished significance accorded to classical music in the United States. See, for instance, Edward Rothstein, "Orchestras Still Preserve the Myths, but Who Cares Now?," *New York Times*, Feb. 10, 2001.

41. See Alex Hawgood, "Hahn-Bin Straddles Classical Music and Fashion," *New York Times*, Feb. 23, 2011; Fan Zhong, "Les Freaks, C'est Chic," *W Magazine*, July 2011; and the feature on the artist broadcast on the *Today Show* on April 22, 2011.

42. The YouTube Symphony drew its members through audition videos uploaded to the site, encouraged performers of nontraditional symphony orchestra instruments to participate, and capitalized on the interactivity of new media to give viewers the final vote in selecting which musicians would participate in the live concert event. The first concert, which gathered a wide range of classical music luminaries (conductor Michael Tilson Thomas, pianist Lang Lang, violinist Gil Shaham, composer Tan Dun, among others), was held at Carnegie Hall in 2009 and hosted on the YouTube Symphony channel's homepage. For more information see YouTube Symphony Orchestra, http://www.youtube.com/user/symphony (accessed Sept. 25, 2013).

43. For an astute analysis of Yo-Yo Ma's Silk Road Project see Yang, "East Meets West in the Concert Hall." Media coverage of the Silk Road project emphasizes Ma's role as a broker of cultural exchange, though sometimes through vaguely orientalist tropes of ancient trade routes that foster the meeting of West and East. See, for example, Allan Kozinn, "At a Cultural Crossroads, Yo-Yo Ma Becomes a Spice Trader," *New York Times*, May 9, 2002.

44. The "return to roots" discourse is not limited to Asian American musicians. Consider, for example, cellist Matt Haimovitz's CD *Goulash* (Oxingale Records, 2005), which explores his Romanian and Middle Eastern ancestry. The framework for celebrating the diverse cultural heritage of the Americas is evident also in the performance of Latin American composers by Venezuelan conductor Gustavo Dudamel, from the marketing of the Los Angeles Philharmonic's festival "Americas for Americans" to the 2008 recording *FIESTA* with the Simón Bolívar Youth Orchestra, which featured works by Latin American composers.

45. The Ying Quartet was composed of four Chinese American siblings until 2009, when the first violinist was replaced by a nonfamily member.

46. Information about the quartet's biography is available on their official website, Ying Quartet, www.ying4.com (accessed March 1, 2007).

47. Quote from their website, Ying Quartet, www.ying4.com (accessed March 1, 2007). In the performance I attended in Ann Arbor, Michigan, in 2005, the

Ying Quartet introduced their program with a similar narrative. The Ying Quartet's CD *Dim Sum* (Telarc Records, 2008) documents this musical effort.

48. See Stokes, *Ethnicity, Identity and Music*, for the relationship between musical authenticity, place, and race.

49. For more on the difficulties that Asians and Asian Americans face being interpreted (regardless of their intentions) through an orientalist framework by critics and audiences generally, particularly when exploring "Asian" compositions and musical modalities, see Hung, "Performing 'Chineseness' on the Western Concert Stage." Also, Mina Yang astutely observes that given the persistence of stereotypes that circulate in classical music, "Asian musicians are faced with the choice of either erasing their difference and being considered no better than a cultural mimic or, in resisting that model, of foregrounding difference and conforming to existing Orientalist frameworks." Yang, "East Meets West in the Concert Hall," 22.

50. Lang Lang with Ritz, *Journey of a Thousand Miles*.

51. This tension between universalizing and ethnically specific viewpoints by musicians surface in other music forms as well. See, for instance, Monson, *Saying Something*, for a trenchant discussion of the ways that jazz musicians strategically negotiate the contradiction between jazz as an African American and a universal musical form.

52. Hage, *White Nation*, 64.

53. Portamentos refer to the tones between two pitches.

54. Also see Eric Hung's discussion of the implicit hierarchy that pianist Lang Lang created on his *Dragon Songs* CD between works by Chinese composers, frequently framed under the general heading "traditional Chinese music" and not named individually, in contrast to works by European composers, who are always identified by name and piece. This hierarchy extended to the reception of the CD by music critics who were mixed in their reception of the Chinese works: while some viewed these compositions as examples of charming orientalist difference, others charged they were second-rate and derivative at best. Hung, "Performing 'Chineseness' on the Western Stage," 135–136, 142–143.

55. A recent venture is a proposal to open a Chinese campus of Juilliard modeled after the Juilliard Pre-College Division (and thus not offering university degrees). The existence of a Chinese campus would mean that students could audition for the Juilliard School (in New York) in China. See Joyce Lau, "Juilliard to Bring New York–Style Teaching to China," *New York Times*, Jan. 28, 2013.

56. The Sirota quote is from Daniel J. Wakin, "Increasingly in the West, the Players Are from the East," *New York Times*, April 4, 2007.

57. The difficulty was compounded by the ongoing SARS (severe acute respiratory syndrome) epidemic, which put more stringent controls on foreigners entering campus grounds, a situation less strictly enforced for those of East Asian ancestry (i.e., individuals not explicitly marked as "foreign").

58. While they certainly are not representative, when I asked two string faculty members at Beijing's Central Conservatory of Music what led them to leave established careers in London and New York, respectively, both pointed to the high salaries offered by the Chinese government as well as the prospect of an easier life (in contrast to being a racialized migrant abroad).

3. A Love Song to YouTube

1. Number of views as of September 18, 2013.

2. For more on antecedents to YouTube videos, including home movies, personal blogging, webcam culture, and, more broadly, the confessional culture of talk shows and reality television see, for instance, Strangelove, *Watching YouTube*, 41–63; and Matthews, "Confessions to a New Public."

3. All unattributed quotations are from oral interviews I conducted with YouTube musicians in person, on the phone, or on Skype during 2011.

4. Strangelove, *Watching YouTube*, 64. The belief that amateur video and user-generated content represent more authentic or real alternatives to traditional media have led artists to pass themselves off as amateurs on YouTube by creating videos and online personalities that conform to a DIY aesthetic. The controversy that emerged following the discovery that video blogger Lonelygirl15 was a professional actress or that singer-songwriter Marie Digby had industry backing speaks to the capital associated with appearing to be ordinary, homegrown upstarts on YouTube. At the same time, discussions about what it means to be (or to perform being) real online is itself a popular topic of exploration by YouTube video bloggers, underscoring the degree to which users are self-aware of the difference between their public and private selves and self-reflexive about what it means to be authentic and real in a mediated, public landscape. As Jean Burgess and Joshua Green aptly observe, the "possibilities of inauthentic authenticity are now part of the cultural repertoire of YouTube." Burgess and Green, *YouTube*, 29.

5. Grossberg, "Media Economy of Rock Culture," 206.

6. "YouTube Advertisers Now Targeting About-to-Go-Viral Videos" (YouTube press release), *Design News*, May 14, 2008, http://designtaxi.com/news/18862/YouTube-Advertisers-Now-Targeting-About-To-Go-Viral-Videos (accessed Oct. 14, 2012).

7. An online survey I conducted with college students (at UC Davis and UT Austin) generated thirty responses from self-identified Asian American fans of Asian American YouTube artists. Although undergraduates are older than the core fan base for these artists, I used these responses, alongside the vast

amount of user comments and fan videos circulating on YouTube and Facebook, to contextualize my analysis of their appeal to fans.

8. My interviewees described their core fan base as being Asian Americans between the ages of fourteen and seventeen. The youthfulness of this demographic was often made apparent to me both at the concerts I attended and in the comments posted on social media. For example, comments on Facebook asking an artist to open a concert venue to all ages rather than only to those over twenty-one (requests usually granted) or lamenting that a particular performance date was on a school night helped give away the age of many fans.

9. A YouTube channel functions like the artist's homepage and can be customized to show information about the artist, the number of uploaded videos, and the artist's activity (for example, favorite videos and comments on videos).

10. The artist's YouTube channel name is listed in parentheses.

11. Acoustic singing/guitar playing lends itself particularly well to the platform given the ease of singing covers and original songs in front of a webcam, which all of my interviewees did in their early videos.

12. Quoted in Austin Considine, "For Asian-American Stars, Many Web Fans," *New York Times*, July 29, 2011. For more on the traits of the millennial generation see "Millennials: Confident, Connected, Open to Change," Pew Research Center Report, Feb. 24, 2010, www.pewsocialtrends.org/2010/02/24/millennials-confident -connected-open-to-change (accessed Oct. 14, 2012).

13. Burgess and Green, *YouTube*, 105.

14. Jenkins, *Convergence Culture*, 2.

15. Here I draw influence from Maureen Mahon's investigation of black rock musicians who were part of the Black Rock Coalition. As she writes, given their recognition of the ways that blackness limited their participation within the genre of rock and the ways that race mattered in their lives, "a critique of racism was part of their musical and political project." Mahon, *Right to Rock*, 17. While the musicians I interviewed often refrained from making explicit critiques of racism, the framing of their collective presence on YouTube as an "Asian American movement" speaks to their cognizance of the broader significance that race holds in their musical endeavors.

16. *Uploaded: The Asian American Movement*, directed by Kane Diep (2012). See the official website for the film at http://uploadedtaam.com (accessed Sept. 18, 2013).

17. Monson, *Saying Something*, 202.

18. YouTube has continued to enjoy massive audience growth since 2006, when it was already recognized as the "world's fastest growing website." See Pete Cashmore, "YouTube Is World's Fastest Growing Website," *Mashable*, July

22, 2006, http://mashable.com/2006/07/22/youtube-is-worlds-fastest-growing
-website (accessed April 2, 2012). In 2006 YouTube had close to thirteen million
unique users a month, whereas by 2012 YouTube had eight hundred million
unique users a month and more than three billion views a day. See YouTube
Official Blog, "YouTube's Original Channels Go Global," Oct. 7, 2012, http://
youtube-global.blogspot.com/2012/10/youtubes-original-channels-go-global
.html (accessed Oct. 23, 2012).

19. In this chapter, as elsewhere in the book, I draw on the artists' own descriptions of their genre/style of music to guide the categorizations I use.

20. Number as of September 18, 2013.

21. Indeed, it is worth noting that the video garnered both praise and negative (if not outright racist) commentary. Chung herself noted in our interview
that she was not certain if the hip hop website featured the video due to an
admiration of her singing or the fact of her Asianness.

22. This, of course, holds true for all YouTube videos, regardless of race. Lev
Grossman's observation in *Time* magazine is apt: "Some of the comments on
YouTube make you weep for the future of humanity just for the spelling alone,
never mind the obscenity and the naked hatred." Grossman, "You—Yes, You—
Are TIME's Person of the Year," *Time*, Dec. 25, 2006.

23. As Snickars and Vonderau observe in *YouTube Reader*, "according to the
'90-9-1' rule, 90 percent of audiences online neither create content nor comment on videos, 9 percent do so on occasion, and one percent are responsible
for most of the interactions online" (12). Artists can thus "do the math" and
recognize that the haters and trolls that lurk on their YouTube pages constitute
a minority view. At the same time, such knowledge does not necessarily detract
from the sting that personally directed negative comments have on individual
artists.

24. Asian Americans are, as a demographic group, touted to be early
adopters of new technology. See, for example, the Nielsen Report "State of the
Asian-American Consumer Q3 2012," Nov. 15, 2012, http://www.nielsen.com
/us/en/reports/2012/state-of-the-asian-american-consumer-q3-2012.html
(accessed July 11, 2013).

25. At the same time, many YouTube stars, given their public status as
prominent artists on that platform, do speak on the topic of how to achieve
YouTube success. See, for instance, writing on the issue provided by popular
content producer Freddie Wong, "The Secrets of YouTube Success—2012 Edi-
tion," Aug. 29, 2012, http://www.rocketjump.com/blog/the-secrets-of-youtube
-success-updated (accessed Sept. 16, 2013).

26. Admittedly Rafael's comment does not take into account the inequities represented in the early days of YouTube (in terms of having access to a
computer, a webcam, a room, and/or private space from which to record one's

videos as well as general digital literacy and specific knowledge of YouTube culture). Burgess and Green point to this issue, noting that "access to all the layers of participation [on YouTube] is limited to a particular segment of the population—those with the motivations, technological competencies, and site-specific cultural capital to participate at all levels of engagement the network affords. The cultural citizens who have the highest probability of encountering one another are those who engage most deeply with these various layers." Burgess and Green, *YouTube*, 81. In this sense, democratizing discourses aside, individuals have always needed resources to become (or aspire to become) a YouTube star.

27. Snickars and Vonderau, *YouTube Reader*, 11.

28. Strangelove, *Watching YouTube*, 162.

29. "Charlie Bit My Finger—Again!" is one of the most viewed YouTube videos of all time. As of September 16, 2013, it had already garnered over 550 million views. The video, a clip captured by the father, features two little English brothers, one of whom gets bitten (repeatedly) and proclaims "ouch!" after sticking his finger into his baby brother's mouth. HDCYT, "Charlie Bit My Finger—Again," May 22, 2007, http://www.youtube.com/watch?v=_OBlgSz8sSM (accessed Sept. 16, 2013).

30. Burgess and Green, *YouTube*, 6.

31. Here I draw on the definition that media scholar Jean Burgess offers of vernacular creativity as a concept that describes how "everyday creative practices like storytelling, family photographing, scrapbooking, journaling and so on that pre-exist the digital age . . . [are] remediated in digital contexts." In this sense, while the forms of circulation may be new, the creative documentation of ordinary life flourishing online is embedded in a long history. See Henry Jenkins, "'Vernacular Creativity': An Interview with Jean Burgess (Part One)," Oct. 8, 2007, http://henryjenkins.org/2007/10/vernacular_creativity_an_inter .html (accessed Sept. 16, 2013).

32. While YouTube does not release these figures, it is reputed in media articles that the top five hundred YouTube partners earn more than six figures a year. See John Seabrook, "Streaming Dreams: YouTube Turns Pro," *New Yorker*, Jan. 16, 2012. Seabrook's article, as well as Rob Walker, "On YouTube, Amateur Is the New Pro," *New York Times*, June 28, 2012, summarizes well the professionalization of amateur content on YouTube.

33. Brook Barnes, "Disney and YouTube Make a Video Deal," *New York Times*, Nov. 6, 2011.

34. Brian Stelter and Claire Cain Miller, "YouTube Plans to Make Big Bet on New Online Channels," *New York Times*, Oct. 28, 2011. These hundred or so original channels have since been expanded to include sixty global (non-U.S.) channels.

35. Indeed, many of my interview subjects had been devoted Myspace users and thus were cognizant of how quickly trends and allegiances shift in a rapidly changing media landscape.

36. Monterey Park, often dubbed the first "suburban Chinatown," is one of the many Asian ethno-burbs that dot the San Gabriel Valley (SGV). Leland Saito points out that Monterey Park is unique not only for its geographic location but also because of its position as a capital-intensive transnational business hub, its concentration of highly skilled Chinese immigrants, and the political and employment connections Chinese American communities have developed with fellow Latino residents. Saito, *Race and Politics*, 17–21. On the history of Monterey Park see also Li, *Ethnoburb*; and Fong, *First Suburban Chinatown*. Also see Cheng, *The Changs Next Door to the Díazes*, for a nuanced exploration of the lived racial politics of the San Gabriel Valley.

I am basing the estimated age of the crowd on my own decidedly unscientific visual assessment and the large number of hands that were raised when one of the performers asked how many in the audience were under the age of eighteen.

37. JustKiddingFilms is a sketch comedy duo whose YouTube videos often play on and parody the experience of growing up with Asian immigrant parents. Andrew Garcia, best known for making it to the finals of season nine of *American Idol*, is Latino but frequently collaborates with Asian American artists on- and offline.

38. In general, the shows of YouTube artists that I attended emanated a positive and wholesome vibe, with the audience remaining respectful and polite both during the concert and while waiting in line to meet the artists. This may, in part, have to do with the younger age of the audience.

39. Dreamchasers did feature rappers Toestah and J.Reyez, who performed covers by other artists. Korean Canadian rapper J.Reyez was one of the few artists who referenced Asianness in his music; he flipped his cover of Wiz Khalifa's "Black and Yellow" into a swaggered out expression of Asian pride with the revised refrain "cause I'm yellow." This reference to Asianness, however, should not be understood as representing a politicized or historical sense of Asian American identity.

While this chapter does not focus on Asian American hip hop artists on YouTube (in part because many of the popular Asian American YouTube musicians who collaborate tend to work in the pop/singer-songwriter genre), this should not suggest that hip hop artists have not also successfully used YouTube as a platform to gain visibility. Among others, Thai American rapper, comedian, and vlogger Timothy DeLaGhetto (Tim Chantarangsu) and Korean American rapper Dumbfoundead (Jonathan Park) have gained significant followings on YouTube and have collaborated with other Asian American YouTube artists both on- and offline.

40. Balance, "How It Feels to Be Viral Me," 140.

41. As danah boyd notes, what differentiates a "networked public" from unmediated publics located in particular times and places are the following four qualities: persistence, searchability, replicability, and invisible audiences. boyd, "Why Youth (Heart) Social Network Sites," 126.

42. The large Latino population in Monterey Park also helps de-emphasize the black-white binary. According to Saito, in 1990, 57.5 percent of the population was Asian American, 29.6 percent was Latino, and 11.7 percent was white. Saito, *Race and Politics*, 23.

43. It is worth noting that the nature of recorded oral interviews discourages a heavy focus on negative experiences in favor of ideal (or aspirational) perspectives, a point that Ingrid Monson also makes. Speaking specifically about jazz musicians, she observes that the interview is "something of a secondary performance genre for musicians." Monson, *Saying Something*, 20. While the same holds true for Asian American YouTube musicians, who are frequently interviewed for media pieces, I would argue that the constant need to perform a consistent public self is exacerbated by the social networks that these artists work within and depend on to promote themselves and their music.

44. See chapter 2, "All in the Family?," in Tu, *The Beautiful Generation*.

45. Indeed, I was struck by how often the Asian American entertainers featured in the documentary *Uploaded* noted how the lack of mentors (not just role models) made their path in the arts that much more difficult and prompted their desire to fill that role for a younger generation of entertainers. *Uploaded: The Asian American Movement*, directed by Kane Diep (2012). For more information on the film see its official website at http://uploadedtaam.com (accessed Sept. 18, 2013).

46. Quoted in Josh Kun, "Eastern Promise: YouTube Helps Legaci's Breakout," *New York Times*, June 18, 2010.

47. Park, *Consuming Citizenship*, 6.

48. See Considine, "For Asian-American Stars, Many Web Fans"; Kun, "Eastern Promise"; Hayley Tsukayama, "In Online Media, Minorities Find an Audience," *Washington Post*, April 20, 2012; Robert Ito, "Asian Americans Find a Home on YouTube," *Los Angeles Times*, June 22, 2012; and Corey Takahashi, "In a Small Corner of YouTube, a Web Star Is Born," NPR, Jan. 26, 2011, http://www.npr.org/2011/01/26/133218168/in-a-small-corner-of-youtube-a-web-star-is-born (accessed Sept. 17, 2013).

49. Founded in 2000 by Korean American performer/comedian Paul "P. K." Kim, Kollaboration is an arts nonprofit organization that aims to showcase the talents of young Asian American performers through a number of activities, the main one being a talent competition and artist showcase. Many of the artists and judges for the shows are successful YouTube artists, and the talent

competition itself uses YouTube to introduce the contestants before the live show. Since its first show in Los Angeles, the event has grown to fifteen shows in fourteen cities in North America. For more information about the organization see http://www.kollaboration.org (accessed Sept. 17, 2013).

50. For statistics on trends in digital media see the Nielsen Report "New Digital American Family," April 12, 2011, http://www.nielsen.com/us/en/reports/2011/new-digital-american-family.html (accessed Sept. 18, 2013).

51. For more on Asian American participation in a range of popular musical forms see, for instance, Moon, *Yellowface*; Wong, *Speak It Louder*; Wang, "Between the Notes"; Yoshida, *Reminiscing in Swingtime*; Sharma, *Hip Hop Desis*; Tiongson, *Filipinos Represent*; and Zheng, *Claiming Diaspora*.

52. Castro, "Voices in the Minority," 221.

53. Kondo, *About Face*, 189.

54. I would argue that the broader Asian American YouTube community, which includes popular personalities like Ryan Higa, Kevin Wu, and Timothy DeLaGhetto, draw much of their humor from masculinist and heterosexist (if not homophobic) assumptions. Although it is beyond the scope of this chapter, I raise this to contextualize the broader YouTube community in which these musicians participate. For more on the problematic racial, gender, and sexual politics of the Asian American community on YouTube (focusing particularly on Ryan Higa, Wong Fu Productions, and Timothy DeLaGhetto) see Gao, "Virtuosic Virtuality of Asian American YouTube Stars."

55. See Burgess and Green, "Entrepreneurial Vlogger," for an astute analysis of the distinction between YouTube stars and media content providers that do not engage with the participatory dynamics of the website. The difference, as the authors note, is less about being "professional" versus "amateur" or engaging in "market" versus "nonmarket" activity than about being content producers who engage with the participatory and reciprocal nature of YouTube (unlike those who import top-down models of traditional media practices).

56. Given this changed media landscape, Alice Marwick and danah boyd argue for a reconceptualization of celebrity as a continuum, a "*performative practice* rather than a set of intrinsic personal characteristics or external labels. This practice involves ongoing maintenance of a fan base, performed intimacy, authenticity and access, and the construction of a consumable persona." Marwick and boyd, "To See and Be Seen," 140. As the authors note, while the difference between "celebrities" and "micro-celebrities" had previously been one of distance and difference—"a question of popularity, approachability, or mainstream status"—traditional celebrities have begun adopting the practices of micro-celebrities by developing a seeming closeness between themselves and their fans through blogs and microblogs like Twitter (141). At the same time, celebrity is not a democratizing process, and being a celebrity (rather than a

micro-celebrity) still depends on the mutual recognition of an unequal power differential between the celebrity and the celebrity's fans. For more on how "micro-celebrities" draw on the reciprocal dynamics of social media to brand their identity and build their audience base (aka, fans) see Senft, *Camgirls*.

57. Like other digitally savvy members of the millennial generation, these artists are adept at projecting a particular public iteration of self both online and on social networks. As popular and regularly searched for artists on YouTube, my interviewees often commented on working to strike a balance between the openness and accessibility desired, if not required of them, by their fans and the maintenance of privacy (particularly around their romantic life).

58. John Cho and Sandra Oh are perhaps best known for their work in the *Harold and Kumar* films and the television show *Grey's Anatomy*, respectively. Filipino American video blogger/comedian Christine Gambito, also known by her YouTube channel username Happyslip, had an enormously popular YouTube channel from 2006 to 2011. As one of the most viewed YouTube users in 2007, Gambito was part of the first select group of users invited to be a YouTube partner, which allowed her to accrue revenue on her videos through advertisements.

59. If race represents the visual encoding of particular physical features, then this may explain the low representation of South Asians in this particular configuration of the so-called Asian American movement on YouTube.

60. It is worth noting that Chester See, who often collaborates with such popular YouTube stars as David Choi, Ryan Higa, Kevin Wu, and Wong Fu Productions, is not often identified as or perceived to be Asian American. This perception is parodied in the YouTube video "Bananapocalypse," the promotional video introducing the Asian American YouTube channel YOMYOMF, wherein Kevin Wu quizzically asks Chester, "'You're Asian? I thought you were Dutch.'" YOMYOMF, "It Has Begun: Bananapocalypse," June 3, 2012, http://www.youtube.com/watch?v=92z1C-IurE4 (accessed Sept. 18, 2013).

61. Wong, *Speak It Louder*; and Wang, "Rapping and Repping Asian."

62. Pisares, "Do You Mis(recognize) Me."

63. A similar claim could be made about the Poreotics (the Asian American crew that won the fifth season of *America's Best Dance Crew*), who wore sunglasses during their performances. It is worth noting that many of the Asian American hip hop dance crews that gained visibility on *America's Best Dance Crew* collaborate with Asian American YouTube stars on video projects and perform together in Asian American shows.

64. This quote comes from a poster advertising the first ISA show held in 2008 in San Gabriel Valley, California. While in mainstream interviews FM emphasizes their universality and color blindness, their continued support of International Secret Agents, even after their chart-topping success, speaks to their ongoing commitment to Asian American representation.

65. One can find debates about whether FM's sunglasses represent a marketing strategy, a corporate decision, a cool style, or a personal choice online as well. See, for instance, modelminority.com forum, "Subject: Asian Guys Need to Stop Being Ashamed of Their EYES," Feb. 9, 2011, http://modelminority.com /joomla/index.php?option=com_ccboard&view=postlist&forum=8&topic=879 &Itemid=53 (accessed Sept. 18, 2013); or aznheartthrob, "Dear Asian Client, Please Cover Up Those Slanted Eyes. Sincerely, Your Publicist," Bicoastal Bitchin, Sept. 7, 2011, http://bicoastalbitchin.com/tag/fareast-movement (accessed March 26, 2012).

66. Far East Movement got their first big break organizing an Asian American benefit show in L.A.'s Koreatown and continues to support the Asian American community through their involvement with events such as ISA performances. Still, even before achieving mainstream commercial success, FM consciously kept their efforts inside separate from their efforts outside of music as a strategy to broaden their appeal. As KevNish (Kevin Nishimura) of FM observed in 2007: "We make sure we don't talk about [social issues] in our music—because we don't want to be overbearing or preachy—we make the conscious effort to do that outside of our music, through events that we do." Quoted in Christine Chiao, "Name of the Game," *Asia Pacific Arts*, Sept. 7, 2007, http://www.asiaarts.ucla.edu/070907/article.asp?parentID=77400 (accessed March 25, 2012).

67. See, for example, Garofalo, "Culture versus Commerce," which examines shifting historical designations of African American popular music by the mainstream music industry.

68. Roberts, "Michael Jackson's Kingdom," 19.

69. Miller, *Segregating Sound*, 4.

70. Elsewhere in our interview, Vincent pointed to the experience of MC Jin, whose artist management firm, at the time of our interview, represented Vincent as well. Even though he admitted he had not closely followed Jin's early career (he was rather young when the rapper first hit the U.S. music scene), the singer has since collaborated with the rapper on YouTube videos.

71. Brooks, "'This Voice Which Is Not One,'" 40. For more on the cultural legacy of black vocal aesthetics in U.S. musical culture see, for instance, Floyd, *Power of Black Music*; Ramsey, *Race Music*; Neal, *Songs in the Key of Black Life*; and Awkward, *Soul Covers*.

72. Frith, "Pop Music."

73. This echoes Deborah Wong's observations about the Mountain Brothers in *Speak It Louder*. While using the initial C rather than Chung as her stage name may represent a strategy to deflect attention away from her Asianness, Clara denied this was her intention. In our interview she told me, "'C' felt more informal, like 'hey, Clara C.' as opposed to Clara Chung." At the same time, she also noted being "hammered" in interviews by Asian American media outlets trying to "kind of spin it like it's some racial thing." It is worth noting that Filipino American singer Joseph Vincent similarly does not use his more ethnically marked last name, Encarnacion. I did not discuss the reasons behind his stage name in our interview, but in media interviews he has stated that "Vincent" is simply easier to pronounce. See, for instance, Shara Lee, "Joseph Vincent: More Than Just a YouTube Artist," *Converge*, Oct. 12, 2012, http://convergemagazine .com/joseph-vincent-youtube-artist-5831 (accessed Dec. 4, 2012).

74. The conflation of whiteness with the absence of race or, ad hoc, the human race is one of the central premises critiqued in whiteness studies scholarship. See, for instance, Dyer, *White*; and Frankenberg, *White Women, Race Matters*.

75. Nakamura, *Digitizing Race*, 5.

76. Video reposted in Kevin Hsieh, "David Choi commentary on race," Channel APA, June 11, 2009, http://www.channelapa.com/2009/06/david-choi -commentary-on-race.html (accessed March 25, 2012). Views similar to those expressed by Choi in this vlog abound online. See, for instance, the guest blog post by Philip Wang (of Wong Fu Productions) on Angry Asian Man, a blog that covers Asian American topics. As Wang writes, comments made in response to Wong Fu videos such as "'Why Is Everyone Asian?' 'Why's It All Asian?' 'Look at These Asians!'" highlight the "benign" and thus more insidious racism that circulates online. Wang continues: "I highly doubt that when people watch other popular 'white youtubers,' no one's leaving a comment asking, 'Why is everyone White?' This is just on the Internet, too. If seeing a predominantly Asian video online estranges some viewers, how are we ever supposed to be accepted on mainstream media?" http://blog.angryasianman.com/2010/09/guest-post-racism -on-youtube-videos.html (accessed March 25, 2012). Given the friendships and frequent collaborations among Asian American artists on YouTube, it is not surprising to find commonalities in the viewpoints expressed by David Choi and members of Wong Fu Productions.

77. This conundrum, of course, is not limited to Asian American artists but is connected to broader structural and racist impediments that ethnic communities face in marketing and appealing to a larger, more lucrative white market as well as to the segmentation of their own group (which also is marketed to by whites and other ethnic groups). See, for example, what Melvin Oliver and Thomas Shapiro call the "economic detour" in relation to African American business owners in *Black Wealth/White Wealth*.

78. As Jennifer Chung noted in our interview, she commonly encounters assumptions that she sings in another language or is not pursuing music in the United States: "Even today, when I was talking to the cable guy and we were talking and I told him I'm a musician and I post videos on YouTube. And he was like 'Do you sing in English?' I was like 'yeah.' And I know he didn't mean it in

an offensive way at all. . . . It's not his fault, but it's just how our society is. But it's so uncommon [to be an Asian American singer in the United States], I'm sure they just think that it's easier for us if we just sing in Korean or something in our native accent or language." Her observations underscore how the central tenet in Asian American studies of "claiming America" still holds resonance for young Asian Americans.

79. The Other Asians, "Dawen: 'Music is the ultimate media. It can be anything; it can be any mood,'" March 8, 2011, http://theotherasians.com/2011/03/dawen (accessed March 25, 2012).

80. It should be noted that YouTube facilitated Dawen's musical journey to Taiwan. As he recounts on his blog, an influential Taiwanese music producer stumbled upon his creative cover of Bruno Mars's "Just the Way You Are" posted on his YouTube channel and passed it along to Universal Music Taiwan, which the singer signed with in 2012. "From 'American Me' to 'Hello' Taiwan," March 17, 2014, http://www.dawen.us/ (accessed April 2, 2014).

4. Finding Sonic Belonging Abroad

1. Wong Fu Productions, "WF Headed to Taiwan to Direct Music Video for Wang Leehom," Sept. 7, 2011, http://wongfuproductions.com/2011/09/wf -headed-to-taiwan-to-direct-music-video-for-wang-leehom. Wang and Wong Fu Productions later collaborated on a light-hearted comedy skit, uploaded in June 2013, in which the singer plays "Greg," the "long lost" fourth member of Wong Fu Productions, and a narrative short film titled "One" uploaded in January 2014.

2. Wong Fu Productions' comparison of the two pop singers is particu-larly apt from a marketing standpoint as well given that, in 2003, McDonald's replaced Justin Timberlake (who fronted their campaign in Europe and North America) with Wang Leehom for their campaign in Asian markets. See Geoffrey Fowler, "In Asia, It's Nearly Impossible to Tell a Song from an Ad," *Wall Street Journal*, May 31, 2005.

3. The two-part "Behind the Scenes" video that Wong Fu Productions produced documenting the process of making Wang Leehom's music video can be found on their official YouTube channel and website. See Wong Fu Produc-tions, "Wang Lee Hom—'Still in Love with You'—Behind the Scenes 1/2," Nov. 12, 2011, http://www.youtube.com/watch?v=QMWoRSV_7gA, and "Wang Lee Hom—'Still in Love with You'—Behind the Scenes 2/2," Nov. 12, 2011, http:// www.youtube.com/watch?v=lPtwWzodPgs (accessed Sept. 12, 2013).

4. Despite his massive popularity in Asia, it is likely that most Americans have never heard of Wang. While this unfamiliarity can be attributed to a num-ber of factors, it also stems from the fact that Mandopop is marketed primarily

for Chinese-speaking audiences. In this sense, Mandopop differs from Asian popular music industries like Korean popular music (K-pop), which strives to make inroads into secondary English-speaking markets, namely, the United States. For this reason, it is a particular irony that Psy's "Gangnam Style," the massive K-pop hit that gained global popularity through social networks in 2012, was not marketed for crossover success.

5. While Wang is not the only Chinese American pursuing a career in Chinese markets, he is one of the industry's best known. Other Chinese Americans in Mandopop include Vanness Wu, Khalil Fong, Coco Lee, Wilber Pan, David Tao, Evonne Hsu, and Yan Jue, among others. The reverse migration of Asian Americans into Asian markets is prevalent in other popular music industries as well. For instance, Korean Americans have also achieved a great deal of success in K-pop. For more on Korean Americans in K-pop and Korean American fandom of the music see, for instance, Cecilia Kang, "Riding the Seoul Train: Korean American Teens Embrace a Pop Music Hybrid," *Washington Post*, Nov. 26, 2006; and Michelle Woo, "Seoul Idol," *KoreAm*, March 28, 2008, http://iamkoream .com/seoul-idol/ (accessed Sept. 15, 2013).

6. Here I draw from Lok Siu's insightful analysis of diasporic subjectivity as produced through the "triangulation of diasporic communities" that exceeds a dualistic relationship between the homeland and the nation-state of residence. Siu, *Memories of a Future Home*, 13.

7. See Moskowitz, "Mandopop under Siege," for a particularly shrewd analysis of the cultural biases that inform critiques of Mandopop emerging from the United States (including academic scholarship), China, and Taiwan.

8. Harper and Eimer, *Lonely Planet Beijing*, 34.

9. Jimmy Wang, "Nigerian Finds Pop Stardom in Beijing," *New York Times*, March 15, 2011; and James McKinley Jr., "At CMJ, Taiwan Rocks the East Village," *New York Times*, Oct. 20, 2011.

10. On its website, the Oxford Union describes itself as the "world's most prestigious debating society, with an unparalleled reputation for bringing international guests and speakers to Oxford. It has been established for 189 years, aiming to promote debate and discussion not just in Oxford University, but across the globe." See "About the Union," http://www.oxford-union.org/about _us (accessed Sept. 12, 2013). A full video of Wang's talk can be found at Oxford Union, "Wang Leehom, Full Address, Oxford Union," May 10, 2013, http://www .youtube.com/watch?v=p6UDLOXwbNk (accessed Sept. 12, 2013).

11. While Wang presents himself as a lifelong learner who strives to enhance international appreciation of Chinese music—a stance that, as this chapter discusses, is consistent with his public persona—it is worth mentioning that other Taiwanese/Chinese American singers have used social media platforms to deride Chinese pop music as "corny" and "lame." One such instance is Taiwanese

American singer Joanna Wang, whose debut album *Start from Here* (2008) was a success in Chinese markets. She unleashed a blistering assessment of Chinese pop music on the social news and entertainment website Reddit, in which she derided her reputation as the "lame soft 'jazzy' ballad singer in Taiwan/parts of Asia"—aka the "Kenny G of Asia." Lambasting the formulaic ballads that populate Chinese pop, Joanna Wang blamed the tight control yielded by record labels and the unsophisticated musical tastes of Chinese consumers. See newtokyoterror, "I am a Taiwanese Celebrity," Reddit_AMA, 2012, http://www.reddit.com/r/IAmA /comments/k3vbe/i_am_a_taiwanese_celebrity_ama/ (accessed Nov. 1, 2012).

12. It should be stated at the outset that questions about the competing positions that musicians occupy as "local," "inside," or "outside" a musical culture are not limited to Chinese popular music. See, for instance, Jason Stanyek's discussion in "Choro do Norte" of the metaphors of nativity deployed by Brazilian and non-Brazilian performers of choro and Berta Jottar's examination in "The Acoustic Body" of Puerto Rican and Cuban influences in the transnational community of rumba performers in New York City. As this chapter details, the subjectivity that Wang occupies as an ABC in Mandopop provides him with certain privileges (as well as deficits).

13. Chow and de Kloet, *Sonic Multiplicities*, 144. This, too, stands in contrast with longer held historical associations of Taiwan as an outpost for the manufacturing of cheap, shoddily made goods.

14. For more on how the periphery in general—Taiwan, Hong Kong, as well as overseas Chinese—wields critical influence on China and in molding cultural constructions of Chineseness see, for example, Shih, *Visuality and Identity*; Tu, "Cultural China"; Ong and Nonini, *Ungrounded Empires*; Chow and de Kloet, *Sonic Multiplicities*; and Yang, "Mass Media and Transnational Subjectivity in Shanghai." As Yang notes, the example of China forces a reconsideration of center-periphery framework as the "West versus the rest prove inadequate as the outside 'center' that is having the most impact on China today is not the West, but the modernized and commercialized Chinese societies of Taiwan, Hong Kong, and overseas Chinese" (303–304).

15. Moskowitz, *Cries of Joy, Songs of Sorrow*, 2.

16. The enormous success and influence of Taiwan's culture industry in China makes it a particularly appealing model for other foreign entertainment companies trying to break into that market. See, for instance, Susan Butler, "China Breaking Through: Busting Barriers to Big Business on the Mainland—An In-Depth Look," *Billboard*, May 27, 2006, 22–25; and Thibault Worth, "Breaking China, Taiwan-Style," *Billboard*, Jan. 24, 2009, 20.

17. For more on the "apolitical" nature of Taiwan's popular music as a strategy to become part of the mainstream in China see Fung, "Emerging (National) Popular Music Culture in China."

18. For an insightful analysis of the uneven politics of transborder fame across multiple regions and publics see Tsai, "Caught in the Terrains."

19. Wang Hsiao-wen and Chang Yun-ping, "A-Mei Blasted for Not Taking a Stand," *Taipei Times*, Aug. 7, 2004, http://www.taipeitimes.com/News/front /archives/2004/08/07/2003182025, (accessed Dec. 21, 2009). Also see her reflections on the ban on CNN, "Taiwanese Singer Upsets China," May 19, 2011, http://edition.cnn.com/video/#/video/international/2011/05/19/talk.asia .taiwanese.singer.cnn?iref=allsearch (accessed Nov. 13, 2012).

20. Ching, "Asianism in the Age of Late Capitalism."

21. Jung, *Korean Masculinities and Transcultural Consumption*. According to Jung, "trans-pop-consumers" hold three common traits: they are culturally hybrid, pursue a consumer lifestyle geared toward leisure and entertainment, and are technologically sophisticated (76). For the cultural influences on Taiwan's Mandopop (from Japanese music forms to Taiwanese language pop and the Hong Kong music industry) see Moskowitz, *Cries of Joy, Songs of Sorrow*, 30–51.

22. Iwabuchi, *Recentering Globalization*, 16.

23. Quoted in "Leehom: The High-Quality Idol" [in Chinese], Leehom's International Fan Club in Mainland China (original in *MW* magazine), May 22, 2007, http://bbs.leehom-cn.com/thread-103971-1-52.html (accessed July 12, 2010). Unless otherwise noted, English translations of Mandarin-language media materials are by Yi Zhou and song lyrics are by Sylvie Liao.

24. Wong, "Dancing in the Diaspora," 28.

25. It is also worth noting that in those fleeting moments when Wang appears on U.S. screens it is primarily as a Chinese rather than a Chinese American (or American) artist who is speaking/singing in Mandarin. The artist was, for example, one of a medley of Asian pop stars who performed at the closing ceremonies of the Beijing Olympic Games, a supporting actor in Ang Lee's Chinese film *Lust, Caution*, and the "multi-talented Chinese megastar" in the group of celebrities featured in a series of Nike commercials with Kobe Bryant. However, it is possible that this may soon change. As of this writing, Wang has completed shooting a film by Michael Mann (best known for the television series *Miami Vice* and box office hits like *The Last of the Mohicans* and *Heat*) and was announced as the new star of an adaptation of Stan Lee's *Annihilator*, a co-production between Hollywood and Chinese state-run media. See Justin Kroll, "Singing Sensation Wang Leehom to Star in Adaptation of Stan Lee's 'Annihilator,'" *Variety*, July 31, 2013.

26. Thomas Crampton, "In China, Record Companies Find New Ways to Do Business: Pop Stars Learn to Live with Pirates," *New York Times*, Feb. 24, 2003.

27. This is one of the reasons that U.S. celebrities go to Asia to hawk products (though with global technology, it is increasingly difficult for these markets to remain completely separate). See, for instance, Malena Watrous, "How U.S.

Stars Sell Japan to the Japanese," *Salon*, June 29, 2000, http://www.salon.com/2000/06/29/japancelebs (accessed June 21, 2010).

28. For instance, product placements often figure prominently in Mandopop music videos, whereas clips from music videos appear in television advertisements. For more see "'Chaos' of China's Music Industry," *BBC News*, Feb. 21, 2008, http://news.bbc.co.uk/2/hi/asia-pacific/7251211.stm (accessed June 21, 2010); and Geoffrey Fowler, "In Asia, It's Nearly Impossible to Tell a Song from an Ad," *Wall Street Journal*, May 31, 2005.

29. See Shih-lun Chang, "The Future of Taiwanese Pop," *Taiwan Panorama*, January 2007, http://www.taiwan-panorama.com/en/show_issue.php?id=200719601006e.txt&table=2&h1=Art%20and%20Culture&h2=Music (accessed Sept. 15, 2013).

30. Crampton, "In China, Record Companies Find New Ways to Do Business." While issues related to piracy and changing media landscapes are not, of course, limited to Chinese music industries, Crampton suggests that their adeptness at finding alternate sources of revenue (beyond album sales) may make them a model for other music industries to follow. It is also worth emphasizing that even independent U.S.-based singers like David Choi, as noted in the previous chapter, increasingly see their albums as functioning as promotional tools.

31. For more on the impact of karaoke and KTV on Mandopop see, for instance, Moskowitz, *Cries of Joy, Songs of Sorrow*, 10–12; and Ho, "Between Globalisation and Localisation."

32. According to a survey conducted by Sina, a popular Chinese media website, Wang's fans chose love songs as the singer's most suitable style. Of the 5,772 fans who responded to the survey, 53.1 percent selected love songs as their favorite style, followed by R&B (13.9 percent) and hip hop (11.7 percent). See "Save 'Private' Leehom Wang: The Reasons for Saving Leehom Wang" [in Chinese], *Sina Music*, Jan. 7, 2009, http://ent.sina.com.cn/y/2009-01-07/ba2331445.shtml (accessed June 21, 2010).

33. See Catherine Shu, "Mandopop Idol Wang Leehom's DRM-Free Experiment Seeks to Foster Innovation in the Asian Music Industry," TechCrunch, Jan. 20, 2013, http://techcrunch.com/tag/leehom-wang/ (accessed Sept. 12, 2013).

34. Figure current as of September 2013. It is worth noting that as of December 2012 Wang was the most followed person on Weibo, leading Sina to award him the title "Weibo Person of the Year." See "Leehom Is the New King of Weibo," *Straits Times*, Dec. 4, 2012.

35. Eric Lin, "The Boys Are Back in Town," *Taiwan Panorama*, Oct. 10, 2001. The L.A. Boyz were discovered through singing competitions/parties held in several large cities in the United States and sponsored by a Taiwanese record company.

36. Unless otherwise noted, the quoted texts are lyrics (original in English) from the L.A. Boyz song "Jump" ("Tiao").

37. While English is used far less than in the days of the L.A. Boyz (indeed, a song rapped primarily in English, as "Jump" is, would likely not be a commercial hit in the contemporary Chinese music scene), English words and phrases still figure prominently in Mandopop. Although the incorporation of English into the Western-inflected sounds of Mandopop might imply, on the surface, a desire to imitate American forms, such scholars as Marc Moskowitz caution against such uncomplicated interpretations. As he observes: "The prevalence of English words in Mandopop attests to the high status of Western symbols in Asia, but it is important to keep in mind that Western music is incorporated into a specific set of pre-existing local aesthetics. Mandopop often employs English words in ways that would not be appropriate in the West." Moskowitz, *Cries of Joy, Songs of Sorrow*, 45. Wang's albums include some "inappropriate" uses of English as well—as attested by such official English song titles as "The Sun after Washed by Spring Rain."

38. While Mandarin is the official language of Taiwan, imposed on the local population when the Kuomingtang (KMT) government from China took over the island in 1949, Taiwanese remains the native oral dialect and home language for many Taiwanese. The KMT government officially discouraged the use of Taiwanese until martial law was lifted in 1987. See Yip, *Envisioning Taiwan*, 136–137. While the L.A. Boyz were not necessarily versed in the local politics of Taiwan, their emphasis on being Taiwanese, coupled with their selective use of Taiwanese language phrases in their songs, tapped into a larger cultural movement of the 1980s and 1990s that explored a localized Taiwanese identity and culture de-centered from mainland China.

39. Gilroy, *Black Atlantic*, 16.

40. Ashley Dunn, "Rapping to a Bicultural Beat: Dancing Trio from Irvine—the L.A. Boyz—Scores a Hit in Taiwan," *Los Angeles Times*, April 5, 1993.

41. For more on the "authenticity crisis" that Asian American rappers face in hip hop see Oliver Wang, "Rapping and Repping Asian."

42. Wang, "Forum."

43. Eva Tsai, "American Chinese Climb the Taiwan Pop Chart," *Taiwan Panorama*, Aug. 5, 1996.

44. After the group disbanded and went back to the United States, Stanley and Jeffrey Huang later returned to Taiwan's popular music scene. Stanley Huang is a successful solo artist, while Jeffrey Huang founded M.A.C.H.I.—a hip hop collective and entertainment label that draws much of its talent from Chinese Americans and other overseas Chinese.

45. While Chinese Americans may see themselves as more musically authentic in their interpretations of such genres as hip hop or R&B, it is worth questioning whether this emphasis betrays the U.S. perspective they bring to Mandopop and whether the trait of authenticity is even significant to Mandopop fans. Put differently, the question might be reframed as musically authentic to whom? In answering this question, Moskowitz suggests, "Mandopop makes no attempt to pass as 'authentic' for a Western audience and thus, in spite of its heavy Western influences, it can be seen to be self-consciously bound to an East Asian identity." Moskowitz, *Cries of Joy, Songs of Sorrow*, 46. Indeed, given that Mandopop is not marketed to a Western (or English-speaking) audience, artists are not particularly concerned with making music that is palatable or authentic sounding to Western/American ears.

46. Tinna Chang, "American Dreamers: ABC Artists in Taiwan," *Taiwan Review*, July 1, 2002, http://taiwanreview.nat.gov.tw/ct.asp?xItem=743&CtNode=1342 (accessed Sept. 15, 2013).

47. Gupta and Ferguson, "Beyond 'Culture,' " 7.

48. Yasmin Lee Arpon, "Taiwan's ABCs," *Asia News*, Dec. 26, 2008–Jan. 1, 2009, 30–31.

49. As Shu-mei Shih notes, not only do Hollywood films dominate the imagination of Taiwanese youth, but a high percentage of politicians, educators, and bureaucrats also have graduate degrees from the United States. In an extension of racialized discourses that construct Asian Americans as model subjects, Taiwan is now a "model democracy (a.k.a. a model minority)." Shih, *Visuality and Identity*, 170.

50. Shih, *Visuality and Identity*, 167.

51. See, for instance, Tu, "Cultural China," 25.

52. As Sau-ling Wong trenchantly notes, while the concept of an "Asian" diaspora is too inclusive to be politically meaningful (not to mention a political impossibility given the divergent histories, constituencies, and languages within that grouping), an "Asian American" diaspora also is meaningless. Wong, "Denationalization Reconsidered," 17.

53. Wang, "Thinking and Feeling Asian America in Taiwan," 141.

54. The coupling of whiteness with normative Americanness in Taiwan is made manifest in advertisements for English teachers posted by schools that, as part of their qualifications, specify " 'Western-looking applicants,' 'no ABCs [American-Born Chinese] please,' and 'native foreigners only.' " Tracy Jan, "English Teachers Wanted: Must Look Western," *Taipei Times*, June 4, 2000.

55. I found this to be the case during visits to Taipei in 2008 and Beijing and Hong Kong in 2009. Part of the ubiquity of Wang's presence in these spaces stems from the intersecting boundaries separating commerce, promotion, and music in Chinese contexts.

56. Winnie Chung, "Prince of the New Breed," *South China Morning Post*, March 23, 2001.

57. Although *Lust, Caution* failed to reach the same critical and commercial success as Ang Lee's other Chinese-language films—for instance, *Crouching Tiger, Hidden Dragon*—the film's circulation in the United States exposed Wang to American audiences (many of whom may have been unaware of his Asian American background). That Wang enters the U.S. market through Chinese-language media is somewhat paradoxical given that he did not become fluent in Mandarin until he was an adult. At the same time, it suggests that there may be a greater market for Asian rather than Asian American celebrities in the United States. In particular, media coverage discussing Wang's more recent casting in mainstream Hollywood films cite the immense market draw he holds in China. If U.S. racism leads Wang to pursue a career in Chinese-speaking markets, his stardom in Asia (and its rising market power) may now be facilitating his opportunities in the United States.

58. Chinese media and music industry executives have also dubbed Wang a "composer idol" and even a "perfect idol." The "idol" designation both draws relentless media scrutiny to his personal life and makes him a marketable commodity. See "The Future of Taiwanese Pop," *Taiwan Panorama*, June 1, 2007; "Leehom Wang: His Songs and the Shangri-la in His Heart" [in Chinese], *China LanChow*, Sept. 11, 2005, http://www.elanChow.net/ent/yywx/200511 /20051126173008.shtml (accessed June 20, 2010); and "Wang Lee-hom: No Disguising Talent," *China Daily*, July 24, 2010, http://news.xinhuanet.com /english2010/entertainment/2010-07/24/c_13412904.htm (accessed Aug. 4, 2010). Wang is famously tight-lipped about his romantic life, although he did post an announcement on Facebook confirming marriage to his girlfriend in November 2014. However, the artist's reluctance to discuss aspects of his romantic life over the course of his career has not stopped rumors from circulating about his romantic entanglements with various female stars and rumblings about his potential homosexuality.

59. This is a standardized biography culled from Wang's official website, English and Chinese media coverage, online fansites, and blogs. To the extent that many of these same details are replicated (and reposted) in many different forums, these particular facts about Wang's background and image (some of which may be exaggerations, like his perfect SAT scores) have become standardized and concretized as the accepted standard narrative about his background.

60. In a 2009 interview on the CNN program *Talk Asia*, during which Wang was followed backstage as he prepared to conduct the Hong Kong Philharmonic for a series of sold-out concerts (in which he also performed the violin and sang some of his hit songs), he discussed his U.S. upbringing and pressures he felt to fit an "Asian American" narrative of success by pursuing a career path such as medicine. For a full video of the three-part interview see http://edition.cnn.com /2009/SHOWBIZ/01/09/ta.wangleehom/index.html (accessed Sept. 15, 2013).

61. "Hom Run!," *Teens*, June 2006; archived on the fansite Hom Sweet Home, http://homsweethome.com/?page_id=51 (accessed Aug. 12, 2010).

62. This comes from an investigation of two mainland Chinese fansites (Wang's Baidu forum at http://tieba.baidu.com/f?kw=%CD%F5%C1%A6%BA%EA; and Leehom's international fan club, "OurHome China," at http://bbs.leehom-cn.com) as well as a Taiwanese fansite (http://www.leehomwang.net/phpBB2).

63. Chow and de Kloet, "Production of Locality in Global Pop."

64. This should not discount the ways that Asian political leaders and intellectuals also draw on orientalist discourses of neo-Confucianism to tout their own values as superior to those of the West. Yet, as Leigh Jenco suggests, the discourse of "Asian values" may well represent more than just political instrumentalism or chauvinist pronouncements of "Asian" cultural exceptionalism; it might also be about making claims about the future: to assert and situate Asia "as a site of future modernity, rather than a repository of 'tradition' or an epigone of the West." Jenco, "Revisiting Asian Values," 255. However, given that Mandopop is not a music form marketed to, nor in wide circulation in, the United States, Wang does not have to contend with the specific ideological function that model minority stereotypes play as a disciplining mechanism in the United States.

65. Quoted in "Tanya Chua, Leehom Wang Win Top Music Awards," *China Post*, June 11, 2006, http://www.chinapost.com.tw/i_latestdetail.asp?id=38890 (accessed Sept. 15, 2013).

66. This acceptance speech was, for a time, posted on Wang's website, http://www.wangleehom.com/press/byleehom/view?id=274 (accessed July 15, 2010). Although his official website has since been updated, this speech can still be found reposted on numerous online fansites and blogs for the singer.

67. Ong, "Experiments with Freedom," 238.

68. Also see Jun, *Race for Citizenship*, 123–147, for the overlap between model minority and neoliberal discourses.

69. Fung, "Western Style, Chinese Pop," 71.

70. See Flora Wang, "Education Ministry Launches Character-Building Plan," *Taipei Times*, June 18, 2009; and "Pop Singer Named Goodwill Ambassador for Shanghai Expo Taipei Pavilion," *Taiwan Today News*, Dec. 22, 2009. The songs of Mandopop star Jay Chou are similarly used as part of the educational material approved for use in schools in China and Taiwan. The singer notes the sense of responsibility he feels as a role model to young people, particularly since his songs are part of the approved educational materials used to teach students. See, for instance, "Jay Chou: Asia's Reluctant Superstar," CNN *Talk Asia*, Sept. 8, 2008, http://edition.cnn.com/2008/WORLD/asiapcf/09/03/ta.jaychou/index.html?iref=newssearch(accessed Sept. 13, 2013).

71. Here I draw on Anthony Fung's insightful analysis in "Western Style, Chinese Pop" of how singer Jay Chou achieved massive popularity in China through an adroit ability to secure corporate and state support by refashioning Chineseness into a stamp of cool and creating a hip hop/R&B vibe that draws on American culture but also evokes the national culture of China.

72. Ang, *On Not Speaking Chinese*, 78.

73. "Patriot Games," *South China Morning Post*, Sept. 27, 2007.

74. While "Descendants of the Dragon" has a complicated history of use in China, Hong Kong, and Taiwan, Wang sidesteps these questions in his relatively straightforward, patriotic interpretation of the song. The songwriter Hou wrote the song out of frustration with the decision of the United States to sever diplomatic ties with Taiwan and establish formal relations with the PRC. The song subsequently gained popularity as a patriotic expression of Chinese pride. For an astute analysis of the complex deployment of nationalistic songs like "Descendants of the Dragon" in China, Taiwan, and Hong Kong see Chow, "Me and the Dragon." Chow's examination of how nationalistic songs like "Descendants of the Dragon" were used to shore up feelings of Chinese unity in Hong Kong during the years leading up to (and following) reunification with China reveals how, despite the original intentions of the songwriter, popular songs can be appropriated to promote particular dominant ideologies.

75. For more on the overlapping U.S. and Chinese discourses that constitute diaspora see Andrea Louie, "When You Are Related to the 'Other.'" As Louie writes, "While Chinese Americans may be generations removed from China, they are still viewed by others (and therefore view themselves) as needing to have some sort of relationship with China. These ideas are reinforced both by a U.S. racial politics that views Chinese Americans as perpetual foreigners and by a mainland Chinese politics that emphasizes their racial and cultural ties to Chinese soil. Chinese Americans' images of China involve often conflicting ideas of China as a paradise, as a proud and ancient civilization, and as an evil Communist empire" (743).

76. Appadurai, *Modernity at Large*, 172.

77. Chow, "Me and the Dragon," 550. See Tu's "Cultural China" for a well-known elaboration on the concept of cultural China, a concept analyzed and critiqued by such scholars as Shu-mei Shih (*Visuality and Identity*), Ien Ang (*On Not Speaking Chinese*), and Allen Chun ("Fuck Chineseness"), among others.

78. The belief that the twenty-first century belongs to China is, of course, popularly propagated in U.S. media, though often through the lens of suspicion and unease. See, for instance, *Time*'s cover story by Michael Elliott, "China Takes on the World," Jan. 11, 2007; and *Newsweek*'s special report "China's Century," May 9, 2005. It is worth noting that China's ascent symbolizes a threat not only to U.S. global hegemony but also to certain factions in Taiwan, those who fear becoming subsumed into/by China.

79. All quotes attributed to Wang in this section, unless otherwise cited, are from the series of journal entries that originally appeared in the Taiwan newspaper *Xin Bao* and on the website of Sony Music (Asia Department) to promote the albums *Forever's First Day* (2000) and *The One and Only* (2001). They also, for a time, were posted on Wang's website, http://www.wangleehom.com/works /journal/view?id=871 (accessed Aug. 20, 2010), and can be found reposted on countless fansites and blogs. The singer is famously tight-lipped about his personal life, but his reticence has done little to keep widespread speculation about his love life from circulating in Chinese media and on blogs and fansites.

80. Here I draw insight from Chih-ming Wang's analysis of Yao Ming's bigness as a "metonymical instantiation of China's global becoming." Wang, "Capitalizing the Big Man," 265.

81. For more on how these questions have been explored, particularly in East Asian popular music cultures, see, for example, Atkins, *Blue Nippon*; Sterling, *Babylon East*; Condry, *Hip-Hop Japan*; and Jones, *Yellow Music*.

82. Other Taiwan-based singers associated with "Chinese Wind" and largely responsible for its widespread popularity include Jay Chou and David Tao. Like Wang, their popular music draws on Chinese traditional instruments and sounds as well as classical Chinese arts and poetry. For an astute gendered analysis of "Chinese Wind" songs by singers from Hong Kong see chapter 3, "Blowing in the China Wind," in Chow and de Kloet, *Sonic Multiplicities*.

83. See Brian Hu for an astute commentary on the controversies that emerged around Wang's use of the phrase "chinked out" within Chinese American communities and around Taiwanese aboriginal singer A-Mei's use of the term "Chinese girl" within local Taiwanese communities. The heated debates variously waged online by Chinese Americans about Wang did not, as Hu notes, properly contextualize the international dimension of Wang's music and audience and the singer's desire to explore the nuances of Chinese American identity within a global Chinese context located outside the United States. Hu, "Pop Goes the C-Words," *Asia Pacific Arts*, http://www.asiaarts.ucla.edu/070608 /article.asp?parentid=42893 (accessed Aug. 20, 2010).

84. "Leehom: I Want to Use Music to Resist Discrimination" [in Chinese], *Beijing Entertainment-Information*, Jan. 31, 2005, http://www.huaxia.com/yl/yltk /442916.html (accessed July 15, 2010).

85. Based on posts on Wang's Baidu fan page, it is fair to say that some of his Chinese fans recognize the racial discrimination that exists against Chinese Americans in the United States and cite this as a reason why Wang is pursuing a music career in Asia. This is, however, a contested topic. Some fans note that Wang loves Chinese culture, and it is therefore only natural that he sings

Chinese music. Others argue that his music is not as good as other American artists' and that is why he cannot pursue a career in the United States. Still others assert that given the rising status of China and the large population of Chinese around the world, it is simply not necessary to release an album in the United States in order to achieve global success.

86. Kuan-Hsing Chen argues in *Asia as Method* (257–268) that the collective study of decolonization and deimperialization in East Asia must include a cogent analysis of the exclusions embedded in the category "Chinese" and the expression and naturalization of Han Chinese racism.

87. Wong, *Speak It Louder*, 215.

88. Shih, *Visuality and Identity*, 83. At the same time, long-standing debates, for example, about whether China's Fifth Generation Filmmakers, such as Zhang Yimou and Chen Kaige, or contemporary composer Tan Dun commodify visions and soundscapes of China to appeal to Western markets and audiences, may well be beside the point given the slippery boundaries demarcating orientalist and anti-orientalist gestures. As Yiu-Wai Chu suggests, the real question may be how orientalism circulates within a global cultural economy and what/whose visions of Chineseness become privileged. Chu, "Importance of Being Chinese."

89. Music scholar W. Anthony Sheppard, for instance, interprets Wang's "chinked out" music as an orientalist gesture. See Sheppard, "Global Exoticism and Modernity: The Case of 'Chinked Out' Music," paper delivered at a conference organized around Asian popular music held at Princeton University in March 2011.

90. See Tu, *The Beautiful Generation*, especially chapter 5.

91. As Sau-ling Wong observes in "Dancing in the Diaspora" (27–28), this celebration of multiculturalism—not that dissimilar to congratulatory displays of multiculturalism in the United States—is part of how China markets its image to itself and to the international community.

92. "Leehom: I Want to Use Music to Resist Discrimination."

93. Karen Sum, "Perfect 10," *Teens*, May 2005, http://wangleehom.com/press /leehom/view?id=138 (accessed Aug. 1, 2010).

94. Baranovitch, *China's New Voices*, 21.

95. The search for a "usable past," a concept introduced in the U.S. context by Van Wyck Brooks in 1915, is not, of course, particular to Chinese communities. See Brooks, *America's Coming of Age*.

96. See "Leaves in America, Roots Are Here" [in Chinese], Leehom's International Fan Club in Mainland China (original in *Beijing News*), July 21, 2007, http://bbs.leehom-cn.com/thread-121232-1-44.html (accessed July 5, 2010). In the article, Wang is grouped with other ABC singers whose obsessive desire to find roots and assert pride in their Chinese identity is viewed, on the one hand,

as a compensatory measure for their ABC status and, on the other hand, as nationalist evidence that "descendants of the dragon" will always be drawn back to their origins and love of Chinese culture.

97. While Kunqu holds cultural capital as one of China's most treasured high art forms, its popularity, along with the number of performers trained in this ancient art, has greatly declined. Against this backdrop, the Chinese state has begun investing money to encourage students to pursue Kunqu, and contemporary artists like Jun Zhang, director of Shanghai's Kunqu Opera Theater, have started incorporating modern pop sensibilities into their presentations of Kunqu performances. While Wang has received criticism in the Chinese press for drawing on Kunqu superficially as a marketing tool, artists like Zhang (whom Wang has invited to perform with him onstage) argue that the singer approaches the Chinese traditional arts with true passion in his heart and that popular music/singers cannot be expected to truly absorb the full complexity of Kunqu. See Jodi Xu, "The Opera House Rules," *Time*, Oct. 25, 2007; David Barboza, "Reviving 'The Peony Pavilion' with Modern Shading," *New York Times*, Aug. 17, 2010; and "'Prince of Kun Opera' Jun Zhang Responded to the Critique," Aug. 24, 2006, Leehom's International Fan Club in Mainland China (original at Sina Entertainment), http://bbs.leehom-cn.com/thread-85092-1-68 .html (accessed July 14, 2010).

98. "Leehom Wang Sings the Song for the Real TV" [in Chinese], Xinhua Net, April 11, 2007, http://www.taizhou.com.cn/a/20070411/content_18746.html (accessed July 11, 2010).

99. It should be noted that as a Chinese American, Wang's understanding of China and Chinese culture is the product of multiple mediations. In fact, the singer notes that his first introduction to Chinese music and his inspiration for drawing on the traditional arts of Beijing opera and Kunqu came from the film *Farewell My Concubine* (1993), a transnational media text that circulated primarily outside of China, which he reports viewing multiple times as a teenager in the United States. See "Wang Lee-hom 'Singing Hip-Hop, Chinese Style,'" *Shenzhen Daily*, Feb. 28, 2006.

100. "Hom Run!"

101. In interviews Wang references drawing inspiration from the strong self-esteem evoked by rappers, a stance he finds mirrored in ancient leaders like Emperor Qian Long. See, for instance, "Leehom Wang Talks about His New Album with Sina: A Concert Will Be Held in Mainland China Soon" [in Chinese], Sina.com, Feb. 22, 2006, http://ent.sina.com.cn/y/2006-02-22/2203994403.html (accessed June 22, 2010).

102. "Leehom Wang Talks about His New Album with Sina."

103. The trajectory of MC Jin's career, while outside the scope of this chapter, is worthy of its own discussion. For an excellent discussion of Jin's career

in the United States (prior to his move to Hong Kong) see Wang, "These Are the Breaks." While Jin did gain some visibility in Hong Kong as an actor and rapper, he failed to reach a broad Chinese audience. The complexity of his raps in Cantonese notwithstanding, that he spoke Cantonese rather than Mandarin limited the reach of his potential market. Moreover, Jin's subsequent thematic turn to his born-again Christian faith was not particularly aimed toward a mass audience. In 2012, following the birth of his son, Jin returned to live in the United States. For more on Jin's career in Hong Kong see Ling Woo Liu, "Home Boy," *Time Asia*, Sept. 24, 2008; and Miguel Gonzalez Jr., "Chinese-American Rapper MC Jin Discovers God, Cantonese," *Wall Street Journal*, Sept. 1, 2010; as well as the rapper's own writings collected on his blog MC Jin: Brand New Me; for example, the post "Farewell Old Me," May 29, 2012, http://mcjin.com/blog /farewell-old-me/#more (accessed Oct. 12, 2012).

104. Condry, *Hip-Hop Japan*, 30.

105. Ralph Frammolino, "You Can't Get a Bad Rap Here," *New York Times*, Nov. 12, 2004.

106. Jimmy Wang, "Now Hip-Hop, Too, Is Made in China," *New York Times*, Jan. 23, 2009.

107. Wang, "Now Hip-Hop, Too, Is Made in China."

108. For more on assumptions of racial inauthenticity that Asian American rappers face in the U.S. context see, for example, Wang, "Rapping and Repping Asian"; Sharma, *Hip Hop Desis*; and Wong, *Speak It Louder*.

109. While spatial limitations prevent a full exploration here, African American hip hop artists also have incorporated Asian iconography into their image and sound. See, for instance, Ongiri, "'He Wanted to Be Just Like Bruce Lee.'"

110. For instance, China's largest online and film-downloading site, www .verycd.com, describes the album *Shangri-la* as a hybrid sound from heaven that fuses Western music with Chinese traditional beauty and *Heroes of Earth* as a special union between modern American styles and Chinese classical poetry.

111. See "The 'Chinese Wind' Swept the Music Field" [in Chinese], Leehom's International Fan Club in Mainland China (original in *Dongnan*), July 19, 2007, http://bbs.leehom-cn.com/thread-120882-1-44.html (accessed July 11, 2010); and "Popular Music House: The Whole City Is Swept by the 'Chinese Wind'" [in Chinese], Leehom's International Fan Club in Mainland China (original at i7Hitoradio.com), March 8, 2007, http://bbs.leehom-cn.com/thread-102985-1-54 .html (accessed July 12, 2010).

112. See Brian Hu, "Leehom's Roots Music," *Asia Pacific Arts*, Sept. 7, 2007, http://www.asiaarts.ucla.edu/article.asp?parentid=77393 (accessed Sept. 15, 2013), for an insightful analysis on the multifaceted nature of roots in Wang's album *Change Me*.

113. There is significant overlap in the reasons fans cite for loving the singer—his appearance, his musical passion, his nice disposition, his work ethic, his versatile talents, and his inspiring music. While it is not possible to tell ethnicity from their usernames, many Chinese American (and Chinese Canadian) fans self-identify as such in their posts (as do white fans).

114. These comments appear in the forum section of the fan club Hom Sweet Home—Leehom Wang's U.S. and Canada Fan Club under the heading "Leehom chit chat" and the question "Leehom making a difference in your life?" http://s9 .zetaboards.com/HOM_SWEET_HOME_Forum/topic/7038988/1 (accessed Dec. 3, 2012).

115. Personal e-mail communication, July 20, 2011.

116. Jenkins, *Fans, Bloggers, and Gamers*, 152–172.

117. De Kloet, "Sonic Imaginations," 25.

118. Louie, *Chineseness across Borders*, 30.

119. For an insightful analysis of how the heterogeneity of accents in *Crouching Tiger, Hidden Dragon* makes audible the vibrancy of Sinophone communities located outside of China see Shih, *Visuality and Identity*, 1–39. As Shih perceptively observes, a key feature of Lee's directorial style is allowing actors to speak in their "natural" voices and not enforcing or authenticating the Beijing accent as the most correct way to speak Chinese.

120. "Leehom Wang Came to Beijing to Promote His New Album: He Was Touched by the Journey in Voice" [in Chinese], Longnan Window (originally from *Beijing News*), Sept. 6, 2007, http://www.longnan.cc/html/musicg/2007-9 /8/124236494.html (accessed June 23, 2010).

121. "Save 'Private' Leehom Wang." On his online fansites Chinese fans also debate whether Wang should employ a permanent lyric writer—much like his oft-mentioned rival Jay Chou does—or whether, given his constantly changing style, he would have to change lyricists too often and that only he can express what is truly in his heart.

122. "Leehom's 'Change Me': ABC's Chinese Heart" [in Chinese], Leehom's International Fan Club in Mainland China (original at Sina Entertainment), July 21, 2007, http://bbs.leehom-cn.com/thread-121185-1-43.html (accessed July 5, 2010). Such criticisms, while focused on Wang's identity as an ABC, should also be contextualized more broadly within nationalistic PRC critiques that musicians from Hong Kong and Taiwan—leaders of the musical style "Chinese Wind"—cannot fully understand traditional Chinese culture with the same complexity and depth as those from China.

123. Ang, *On Not Speaking Chinese*, 35.

124. On his mainland Chinese fansite on Baidu, Wang's fans have compiled a list of the "mistakes" and jokes with language he has made and call it "ABC logic." Thus while the singer may make occasional gaffes or not comprehend

local slang, his fans also defend him by noting how he can play with language in ways that native Chinese speakers cannot.

125. Cited in "Talk Asia Meets Wang Leehom," CNN *Talk Asia*, Jan. 14, 2009, http://www.cnn.com/2009/SHOWBIZ/01/09/ta.wangleehom/#cnnSTCText (accessed Sept. 13, 2013). A video of the three-part interview is available at http://edition.cnn.com/2009/SHOWBIZ/01/09/ta.wangleehom/index.html (accessed Sept. 13, 2013).

126. Quoted in Mark Small, "West Meets East," *Berklee Today*, Oct. 22, 2009, http://www.berklee.edu/bt/212/coverstory.html (accessed Sept. 13, 2013).

Epilogue

1. Amy Chua, "Why Chinese Mothers Are Superior," *Wall Street Journal*, Jan. 8, 2011.

2. Chua, *Battle Hymn of the Tiger Mother*, 22. Page references to this book hereafter appear parenthetically in the text.

Ang, Ien. *On Not Speaking Chinese: Living between Asia and the West*. London: Routledge, 2001.

Appadurai, Arjun. *Modernity at Large: Cultural Dimensions of Globalization*. Minneapolis: University of Minnesota Press, 1996.

Atkins, E. Taylor. *Blue Nippon: Authenticating Jazz in Japan*. Durham, NC: Duke University Press, 2001.

Awkward, Michael. *Soul Covers: Rhythm and Blues Remakes and the Struggle for Artistic Identity*. Durham, NC: Duke University Press, 2007.

Balance, Christine. "How It Feels to Be Viral Me: Affective Labor and Asian American Performance." *Women's Studies Quarterly* 40, nos. 1–2 (spring/summer 2012): 138–152.

Banet-Weiser, Sarah. "Branding the Post-feminist Self: Girls' Video Production and YouTube." In *Mediated Girlhoods: New Explorations of Girls' Media Culture*, edited by Mary Celeste Kearney, 277–294. New York: Peter Lang, 2011.

Baranovitch, Nimrod. *China's New Voices: Popular Music, Ethnicity, Gender, and Politics, 1978–1997*. Berkeley: University of California Press, 2003.

Bonilla-Silva, Eduardo. *Racism without Racists: Color-Blind Racism and Racial Inequality in Contemporary America*. Lanham, MD: Rowman and Littlefield, 2006.

Born, Georgina, and David Hesmondhalgh, eds. *Western Music and Its Others: Difference, Representation, and Appropriation in Music*. Berkeley: University of California Press, 2000.

Bourdieu, Pierre. *Distinction: A Social Critique of the Judgement of Taste*. Translated by Richard Nice. Cambridge, MA: Harvard University Press, 2002 [1979].

boyd, danah. "Why Youth (Heart) Social Network Sites: The Role of Networked Publics in Teenage Social Life." In *MacArthur Foundation Series on Digital Learning—Youth, Identity, and Digital Media Volume*, edited by David Buckingham, 119–142. Cambridge, MA: MIT Press, 2007.

Brooks, Daphne, "'This Voice Which Is Not One': Amy Winehouse Sings the Ballad of Sonic Blue(s)face Culture." *Women and Performance: A Journal of Feminist Theory* 20, no. 1 (2010): 37–60.

Brooks, Van Wyck. *America's Coming of Age*. New York: B. W. Huebsch, 1915.

Burgess, Jean, and Joshua Green. "The Entrepeneurial Vlogger: Participatory Culture beyond the Professional-Amateur Divide." In *The YouTube Reader*, edited by Pelle Snickar and Patrick Vonderau, 89–107. Stockholm: National Library of Sweden, 2009.

———. *YouTube: Online Video and Participatory Culture*. Cambridge, UK: Polity, 2009.

Carroll, Hamilton. *Affirmative Reaction: New Formations of White Masculinity*. Durham, NC: Duke University Press, 2011.

Castro, Christi-Ann. "Voices in the Minority: Race, Gender, Sexuality, and the Asian American in Popular Music." *Journal of Popular Music Studies* 19, no. 3 (2007): 221–238.

Chang, Lan Samantha. *Hunger: A Novella and Stories*. New York: W. W. Norton, 1998.

Chen, Kuan-Hsing. *Asia as Method: Toward Deimperialization*. Durham, NC: Duke University Press, 2010.

Cheng, Wendy. *The Changs Next Door to the Díazes: Remapping Race in Suburban California*. Minneapolis: University of Minnesota Press, 2013.

Chiang, Mark. *Cultural Capital of Asian American Studies: Autonomy and Representation in the University*. New York: New York University Press, 2009.

Ching, Leo. "Asianism in the Age of Late Capitalism." *Public Culture* 12, no. 1 (2000): 233–257.

Chow, Yiu Fai. "Me and the Dragon: A Lyrical Engagement with the Politics of Chineseness." *Inter-Asia Cultural Studies* 10, no. 4 (2009): 544–564.

Chow, Yiu Fai, and Jeroen de Kloet. "The Production of Locality in Global Pop—A Comparative Study of Pop in the Netherlands and Hong Kong." *Participations* 5, no. 2 (2008).

———. *Sonic Multiplicities: Hong Kong Pop and the Global Circulation of Sound and Image*. Chicago: University of Chicago Press, 2013.

Chu, Yiu-Wai. "The Importance of Being Chinese: Orientalism Reconfigured in the Age of Global Modernity." *boundary 2* 35, no. 2 (2008): 183–206.

Chua, Amy. *Battle Hymn of the Tiger Mother*. New York: Penguin, 2011.

Chun, Allen. "Fuck Chineseness: On the Ambiguities of Ethnicity as Culture as Identity." *boundary 2* 23, no. 2 (1996): 111–138.

Condry, Ian. *Hip-Hop Japan: Rap and the Paths of Cultural Globalization*. Durham, NC: Duke University Press, 2006.

Cook, Nicholas. "Music as Performance." In *The Cultural Study of Music*, edited by Martin Clayton, Trevor Herbert, and Richard Middleton, 204–214. New York: Routledge, 2003.

de Kloet, Jeroen. "Sonic Imaginations: Notes on the Opaque Seduction of (Canto)pop." *IIAS Newsletter* 32 (November 2003). http://www.iias.nl /iiasn/32/RR_sonic_imaginations.

DiMaggio, Paul. "Social Structure, Institutions, and Cultural Goods: The Case of the United States." In *The Politics of Culture: Policy Perspectives or Individuals, Institutions, and Communities*, edited by Gigi Bradford, Michael Gary, and Glenn Wallach, 133–155. New York: New Press, 2000.

DiMaggio, Paul, and Toqir Mukhtar. "Arts Participation as Cultural Capital in the United States, 1982–2002: Signs of Decline?" *Poetics* 32 (2004): 169–194.

Dirlik, Arif. "Chinese History and the Question of Orientalism." *History and Theory* 35, no. 4 (1996): 96–118.

———. "Race Talk, Race, and Contemporary Racism." *PMLA* 123, no. 5 (2008): 1363–1379.

Dyer, Richard. *White: Essays on Race and Culture*. New York: Routledge, 1997.

Elliott, Charles A. "Race and Gender as Factors in Judgments of Musical Performance." *Bulletin of the Council for Research in Music Education*, no. 127 (winter 1995/1996): 50–56.

Eppstein, Ury. *The Beginnings of Western Music in Meiji Era Japan*. Lewiston, NY: Edwin Mellen Press, 1994.

Espiritu, Yen Le. "'We Don't Sleep Around Like White Girls Do': Family, Culture, and Gender in Filipina American Lives." *Signs* 26, no. 2 (2001): 415–440.

Everett, Yayoi Uno. "Intercultural Synthesis in Postwar Western Art Music." In *Locating East Asia in Western Art Music*, edited by Yayoi Uno Everett and Frederick Lau, 1–21. Middletown, CT: Wesleyan University Press, 2004.

Everett, Yayoi Uno, and Frederick Lau, eds. *Locating East Asia in Western Art Music*. Middletown, CT: Wesleyan University Press, 2004.

Fabian, Johannes. *Time and the Other: How Anthropology Makes Its Object*. New York: Columbia University Press, 1983.

Feld, Steven. "Communication, Music, and Speech about Music." In *Music Grooves*, edited by Steven Feld and Charles Keil, 77–95. Chicago: University of Chicago Press, 1994.

Fellezs, Kevin. "Silenced but Not Silent: Asian Americans and Jazz." In *Alien Encounters: Popular Culture in Asian America*, edited by Mimi Thi Nguyen and Thuy Linh Nguyen Tu, 69–110. Durham, NC: Duke University Press, 2007.

Floyd, Sam, Jr. *The Power of Black Music: Interpreting Its History from Africa to the United States*. New York: Oxford University Press, 1995.

Fong, Timothy. *The First Suburban Chinatown: The Remaking of Monterey Park, California*. Philadelphia: Temple University Press, 1994.

Fong-Torres, Ben. *The Rice Room: Growing Up Chinese American from Number Two Son to Rock 'n' Roll*. New York: Penguin, 1994.

Frankenberg, Ruth. *White Women, Race Matters: The Social Construction of Whiteness*. Minneapolis: University of Minnesota Press, 1993.

Frith, Simon. "Towards an Aesthetic of Popular Music." In *Music and Society: The Politics of Composition, Performance and Reception*, edited by Richard Leppert and Susan McClary, 133–150. Cambridge: Cambridge University Press, 1987.

———. *Performing Rites: On the Value of Popular Music*. Cambridge, MA: Harvard University Press, 1998.

———. "Pop Music." In *The Cambridge Companion to Pop and Rock*, edited by Simon Frith, Will Straw, and John Street, 93–108. Cambridge: Cambridge University Press, 2001.

Fung, Anthony. "The Emerging (National) Popular Music Culture in China." *Inter-Asia Cultural Studies* 8, no. 3 (2007): 425–437.

———. "Western Style, Chinese Pop: Jay Chou's Rap and Hip-Hop in China." *Asian Music* 39, no. 1 (2008): 69–80.

Gao, Cindy. "The Virtuosic Virtuality of Asian American YouTube Stars." *Feminist Media Theory: Iterations of Social Difference* 10, no. 3 (2012). http://sfonline.barnard.edu/feminist-media-theory/the-virtuosic-virtuality-of-asian-american-youtube-stars (accessed Sept. 27, 2013).

Garofalo, Reebee. "Culture versus Commerce: The Marketing of Black Popular Music." *Public Culture* 7, no. 1 (1994): 275–287.

Gilmour, R. J., Davina Bhandar, Jeet Heer, and Michael C. K. Ma. *Too Asian? Racism, Privilege, and Post-secondary Education*. Toronto: Between the Lines, 2012.

Gilroy, Paul. *Black Atlantic: Modernity and Double-Consciousness*. Cambridge, MA: Harvard University Press, 1993.

Gold, Thomas. "Go with Your Feelings: Hong Kong and Taiwan Popular Culture in Greater China." *China Quarterly* 136 (December 1993): 907–925.

Goldin, Claudia, and Cecilia Rouse. "Orchestrating Impartiality: The Impact of 'Blind' Auditions on Female Musicians." *American Economic Review* 90, no. 4 (2000): 715–741.

Gorbman, Claudia. "Scoring the Indian: Music in the Liberal Western." In *Western Music and Its Others: Difference, Representation, and Appropria-*

tion in Music, edited by Georgina Born and David Hesmondhalgh, 234–253. Berkeley: University of California Press, 2000.

Grossberg, Lawrence. "The Media Economy of Rock Culture: Cinema, Post Modernity and Authenticity." In Sound and Vision: The Music Video Reader, edited by Simon Frith, Andrew Goodwin, and Lawrence Grossberg, 185–209. London: Routledge, 1993.

Guo, Lei, and Lorin Lee. "The Critique of YouTube-Based Vernacular Discourse: A Case Study of YouTube's Asian Community." Critical Studies in Media Communication 30, no. 1 (2013): 1–16.

Gupta, Akhil, and James Ferguson. "Beyond 'Culture': Space, Identity, and the Politics of Difference." Cultural Anthropology 7, no. 1 (1992): 6–23.

Hage, Ghassan. White Nation: Fantasies of White Supremacy in a Multicultural Society. New York: Routledge, 2000.

Hall, Stuart. "Cultural Identity and Diaspora." In Identity: Community, Culture, Difference, edited by Jonathan Rutherford, 222–237. London: Lawrence and Wishart, 1998.

Harper, Damian, and David Eimer. Lonely Planet Beijing (City Travel Guide). Hawthorn, Australia: Lonely Planet Publications, 2010.

Hing, Bill Ong. Making and Remaking Asian America through Immigration Policy. Stanford: Stanford University Press, 1993.

Ho, Wai-chung. "Between Globalisation and Localisation: A Study of Hong Kong Popular Music." Popular Music 22, no. 2 (2003): 143–157.

———. "Music and Cultural Politics in Taiwan." International Journal of Cultural Studies 10, no. 4 (2007): 463–483.

Horowitz, Joseph. Classical Music in America: A History of Its Rise and Fall. New York: W. W. Norton, 2005.

Hung, Eric. "Performing 'Chineseness' on the Western Concert Stage: The Case of Lang Lang." Asian Music 40, no. 1 (2009): 131–148.

Hwang, Okon. "Western Art Music in Korea." PhD dissertation, Wesleyan University, 2001.

Iwabuchi, Koichi. Recentering Globalization: Popular Culture and Japanese Transnationalism. Durham, NC: Duke University Press, 2002.

Jenco, Leigh. "Revisiting Asian Values." Journal of the History of Ideas 74, no. 2 (2013): 237–258.

Jenkins, Henry. Convergence Culture: Where Old and New Media Collide. New York: New York University Press, 2006.

———. Fans, Bloggers, and Gamers: Exploring Participatory Culture. New York: New York University Press, 2006.

Jones, Andrew. Yellow Music: Media Culture and Colonial Modernity in the Chinese Jazz Age. Durham, NC: Duke University Press, 2001.

Jottar, Berta. "The Acoustic Body: *Rumba Guarapachanguera* and Abakuá Sociality in Central Park." *Latin American Music Review* 30, no. 1 (2009): 1–24.

Jun, Helen. *Race for Citizenship: Black Orientalism and Asian Uplift from Pre-emancipation to Neoliberal America*. New York: New York University Press, 2011.

Jung, Sun. *Korean Masculinities and Transcultural Consumption: Yonsama, Rain, Oldboy, K-Pop Idols*. Hong Kong: Hong Kong University Press, 2011.

Kim, Claire Jean. *Bitter Fruit: the Politics of Black-Korean Conflict in New York City*. New Haven, CT: Yale University Press, 2000.

Kim, Nadia. *Imperial Citizens: Koreans and Race from Seoul to LA*. Stanford: Stanford University Press, 2008.

Kingsbury, Henry. *Music, Talent, and Performance: A Conservatory Cultural System*. Philadelphia: Temple University Press, 1988.

Kogan, Judith. *Nothing but the Best: The Struggle for Perfection at the Juilliard School*. New York: Random House, 1987.

Kondo, Dorinne. *About Face: Performing Race in Fashion and Theater*. New York: Routledge, 1997.

Koshy, Susan. "Morphing Race into Ethnicity: Asian Americans and Critical Transformations of Whiteness." *boundary 2* 28, no. 1 (2001): 151–191.

Kramer, Lawrence. *Why Classical Music Still Matters*. Berkeley: University of California Press, 2007.

Kraus, Richard. *Pianos and Politics in China: Middle-Class Ambitions and the Struggle over Western Music*. New York: Oxford University Press, 1989.

Kun, Josh. *Audiotopia: Music, Race, and America*. Berkeley: University of California Press, 2005.

Lam, Joseph Sui Ching. "Embracing 'Asian American Music' as an Heuristic Device." *Journal of Asian American Studies* 2, no. 1 (1999): 29–60.

Lang Lang, with David Ritz. *Journey of a Thousand Miles: My Story*. New York: Random House, 2009.

Lebrecht, Norman. *Who Killed Classical Music? Maestros, Managers, and Corporate Politics*. Secaucus, NJ: Carol Publishing Group, 1997.

Lee, Robert. *Orientals: Asian Americans in Popular Culture*. Philadelphia: Temple University Press, 1999.

Levine, Lawrence. *Highbrow/Lowbrow: The Emergence of Cultural Hierarchy in America*. Cambridge, MA: Harvard University Press, 1988.

Li, Wei. *Ethnoburb: The New Ethnic Community in Urban America*. Honolulu: University of Hawai'i Press, 2009.

Lieu, Nhi. *The American Dream in Vietnamese*. Minneapolis: University of Minnesota Press, 2011.

Lim, Shirley Geok-lin. "Assaying the Gold: Or, Contesting the Ground of Asian American Literature." *New Literary History* 24, no. 1 (1993): 147–196.

Lin, Sylvia Li-Chun. "Toward a New Identity: Nativism and Popular Music in Taiwan." *China Information* 17, no. 2 (2003): 83–107.

Lipman, Samuel. *Music and More, Essays, 1975–1991*. Evanston, IL: Northwestern University Press, 1992.

Lipsitz, George. *Dangerous Crossroads: Popular Music, Postmodernism and the Poetics of Place*. London: Verso, 1994.

———. *The Possessive Investment of Whiteness*. Philadelphia: Temple University Press, 1998.

———. *Footsteps in the Dark: The Hidden Histories of Popular Music*. Minneapolis: University of Minnesota Press, 2007.

Louie, Andrea. "When You Are Related to the 'Other': (Re)locating the Chinese Homeland in Asian American Politics through Cultural Tourism." *positions* 11, no. 3 (2003): 735–763.

———. *Chineseness across Borders: Renegotiating Chinese Identities in China and the United States*. Durham, NC: Duke University Press, 2004.

Lowe, Lisa. *Immigrant Acts: On Asian American Cultural Politics*. Durham, NC: Duke University Press, 1996.

Lye, Colleen. *America's Asia: Racial Form and American Literature, 1893–1945*. Princeton, NJ: Princeton University Press, 2005.

Mahon, Maureen. *Right to Rock: The Black Rock Coalition and the Cultural Politics of Race*. Durham, NC: Duke University Press, 2004.

Maira, Sunaina. *Desis in the House: Indian American Youth Culture in New York City*. Philadelphia: Temple University Press, 2002.

Marwick, Alice, and danah boyd. "To See and Be Seen: Celebrity Practice on Twitter." *Convergence* 17, no. 2 (2011): 139–158.

Matthews, Nicole. "Confessions to a New Public: Video Nation Short." *Media, Culture, and Society* 29, no. 3 (2007): 435–448.

McClary, Susan. *Feminine Endings: Music, Gender, and Sexuality*. Minneapolis: University of Minnesota Press, 1991.

Melamed, Jodi. "The Spirit of Neoliberalism: From Racial Liberalism to Neoliberal Multiculturalism." *Social Text* 24, no. 4 (2006): 1–24.

———. *Represent and Destroy: Rationalizing Violence in the New Racial Capitalism*. Minneapolis: University of Minnesota Press, 2011.

Melvin, Sheila, and Jindong Cai. *Rhapsody in Red: How Western Classical Music Became Chinese*. New York: Algora, 2004.

Miller, Karl. *Segregating Sound: Inventing Folk and Pop Music in the Age of Jim Crow*. Durham, NC: Duke University Press, 2010.

Mittler, Barbara. *Dangerous Tunes: The Politics of Chinese Music in Hong Kong, Taiwan, and the People's Republic of China since 1949*. Wiesbaden, Germany: Harrassowitz Verlag, 1997.

Monson, Ingrid. *Saying Something: Jazz Improvisation and Interaction*. Chicago: University of Chicago Press, 1996.

Moon, Krystyn. *Yellowface: Creating the Chinese in American Popular Music*. New Brunswick, NJ: Rutgers University Press, 2004.

Moore, MacDonald Smith. *Yankee Blues: Musical Culture and American Identity*. Bloomington: Indiana University Press, 1985.

Morley, David, and Kevin Robins. *Spaces of Identity: Global Media, Electronic Landscapes and Cultural Boundaries*. London: Routledge, 1995.

Moskowitz, Marc. "Mandopop under Siege: Culturally Bound Criticisms of Taiwan's Pop Music." *Popular Music* 28, no. 1 (2009): 69–83.

———. *Cries of Joy, Songs of Sorrow: Chinese Pop Music and Its Cultural Connotations*. Honolulu: University of Hawai'i Press, 2010.

Nakamura, Lisa. *Digitizing Race: Visual Cultures of the Internet*. Minneapolis: University of Minnesota Press, 2008.

Nakamura, Lisa, and Peter A. Chow-White, eds. *Race after the Internet*. New York: Routledge, 2012.

Neal, Mark Anthony. *Songs in the Key of Black Life: A Rhythm and Blues Nation*. New York: Routledge, 2003.

Nettl, Bruno. *The Western Impact on World Music: Change, Adaptation, and Survival*. New York: Schirmer, 1985.

Ng, Jennifer, Sharon S. Lee, and Yoon K. Pak. "Contesting the Model Minority and Perpetual Foreigner Stereotypes: A Critical Review of Literature on Asian Americans in Education." *Review of Research in Education* 31, no. 1 (2007): 95–130.

Nguyen, Viet. *Race and Resistance: Literature and Politics in Asian America*. New York: Oxford University Press, 2002.

Ninh, erin Khuê. *Ingratitude: The Debt-Bound Daughter in Asian American Literature*. New York: New York University Press, 2011.

Okihiro, Gary. *Margins and Mainstreams: Asians in American History and Culture*. Seattle: University of Washington Press, 1994.

Oliver, Melvin L., and Thomas M. Shapiro. *Black Wealth/White Wealth: A New Perspective on Racial Inequality*. New York: Routledge, 1997.

Olmstead, Andrea. *Juilliard: A History*. Urbana: University of Illinois Press, 1999.

Omi, Michael, and Howard Winant. *Racial Formation in the United States: From the 1960s to the 1990s*. New York: Routledge, 1994.

Ong, Aihwa. *Flexible Citizenship: The Cultural Logics of Transnationality*. Durham, NC: Duke University Press, 1999.

———. "Experiments with Freedom: Milieus of the Human." *American Literary History* 18, no. 2 (2006): 229–244.

Ong, Aihwa, and Donald Nonini, eds. *Ungrounded Empires: The Cultural Politics of Modern Chinese Transnationalism*. New York: Routledge, 1997.

Ongiri, Amy Abugo. "'He Wanted to Be Just Like Bruce Lee': African Americans, Kung Fu Theater and Cultural Exchange at the Margins." *Journal of Asian American Studies* 5, no. 1 (2002): 31–40.

Ono, Kent, and Vincent Pham. *Asian Americans and the Media*. Cambridge, UK: Polity, 2009.

Osajima, Keith. "Asian Americans as the Model Minority: An Analysis of the Popular Press Image in the 1960s and 1980s." In *Reflections on Shattered Windows: Promises and Prospects for Asian American Studies*, edited by Gary Okihiro, Shirley Hune, Arthur Hansen, and John Liu, 165–174. Pullman: Washington State University Press, 1988.

Palumbo-Liu, David. *Asian/American: Historical Crossings of a Racial Frontier*. Stanford: Stanford University Press, 1999.

Park, Edward, and John Park. *Probationary Americans: Contemporary Immigration Policies and the Shaping of Asian American Communities*. New York: Routledge, 2005.

Park, Lisa. *Consuming Citizenship: Children of Asian Immigrant Entrepreneurs*. Stanford: Stanford University Press, 2005.

Parreñas, Rhacel S. *Children of Global Migration: Transnational Families and Gendered Woes*. Stanford: Stanford University Press, 2005.

Peterson, Richard A., and Roger M. Kern. "Changing Highbrow Taste: From Snob to Omnivore." *American Sociological Review* 61, no. 5 (1996): 900–907.

Pisares, Elizabeth H. "Do You Mis(recognize) Me: Filipina Americans in Popular Music and the Problem of Invisibility." In *Positively No Filipinos Allowed: Building Communities and Discourse*, edited by Antonio T. Tiongson Jr., Edgardo V. Gutierrez, and Ricardo V. Gutierrez, 172–198. Philadelphia: Temple University Press, 2006.

Powers, Richard. *The Time of Our Singing*. New York: Picador, 2003.

Prell, Riv-Ellen. *Fighting to Become Americans: Jews, Gender, and the Anxiety of Assimilation*. Boston: Beacon, 1999.

Radano, Ronald, and Philip V. Bohlman, eds. *Music and the Racial Imagination*. Chicago: University of Chicago Press, 2000.

Ramsey, Guthrie. *Race Music: Black Cultures from Be-Bop to Hip Hop*. Berkeley: University of California Press, 2004.

Roberts, Tamara. "Michael Jackson's Kingdom: Music, Race, and the Sound of the Mainstream." *Journal of Popular Music Studies* 23, no. 1 (2011): 19–39.

Ross, Alex. *Listen to This*. New York: Farrar, Straus and Giroux, 2010.

Roth, Henry. *Violin Virtuosos: From Paganini to the 21st Century*. Los Angeles: California Classic Books, 1997.

Saito, Leland T. *Race and Politics: Asian Americans, Latinos, and Whites in a Los Angeles Suburb*. Urbana: University of Illinois Press, 1998.

Salvato, Nick. "Out of Hand: YouTube Amateurs and Professionals." *TDR: The Drama Review* 53, no. 3 (2009): 67–83.

Senft, Theresa. *Camgirls: Celebrity and Community in the Age of Social Networks*. New York: Peter Lang, 2008.

Sharma, Nitasha. *Hip Hop Desis: South Asian Americans, Blackness, and a Global Race Consciousness*. Durham, NC: Duke University Press, 2010.

Shih, Shu-mei. *Visuality and Identity: Sinophone Articulations across the Pacific*. Berkeley: University of California Press, 2007.

Shin, Hyunjoon. "Have You Ever Seen the Rain? And Who'll Stop the Rain? The Globalizing Project of Korean Pop (K-pop)." *Inter-Asia Cultural Studies* 10, no. 4 (2009): 507–523.

———. "Reconsidering Transnational Cultural Flows of Popular Music in East Asia: Transbordering Musicians in Japan and Korea Searching for 'Asia.'" *Korean Studies* 33 (2009): 101–123.

Shukla, Sandhya. *India Abroad: Diasporic Cultures of America and England*. Princeton, NJ: Princeton University Press, 2003.

Siu, Lok. *Memories of a Future Home: Diasporic Citizenship of Chinese in Panama*. Stanford: Stanford University Press, 2005.

Small, Christopher. *Musicking: The Meanings of Performing and Listening*. Middletown, CT: Wesleyan University Press, 1998.

Snickars, Pelle, and Patrick Vonderau. "Introduction." In *The YouTube Reader*, edited by Pelle Snickars and Patrick Vonderau, 9–21. Stockholm: National Library of Sweden, 2009.

So, Christine. *Economic Citizens: A Narrative of Asian American Visibility*. Philadelphia: Temple University Press, 2009.

Song, Min Hyoung. "Communities of Remembrance: Reflections on the Virginia Tech Shootings and Race." *Journal of Asian American Studies* 11, no. 1 (2008): 1–26.

Stanyek, Jason. "Choro do Norte: Improvising the Transregional Roda in the United States." *Luso-Brazilian Review* 48, no. 1 (2011): 100–129.

Steele, Claude. *Whistling Vivaldi: And Other Clues to How Stereotypes Affect Us*. New York: W. W. Norton, 2010.

Sterling, Marvin. *Babylon East: Performing Dancehall, Roots Reggae, and Rastafari in Japan*. Durham, NC: Duke University Press, 2010.

Stern, Isaac, with Chaim Potok. *My First 79 Years: Isaac Stern*. New York: Knopf, 1999.

Stokes, Martin, ed. *Ethnicity, Identity and Music: The Musical Construction of Place*. New York: Berg, 1994.

Strangelove, Michael. *Watching YouTube: Extraordinary Videos by Ordinary People*. Toronto: University of Toronto Press, 2010.

Tiongson, Antonio T., Jr. *Filipinos Represent: DJs, Authenticity, and the Hip Hop Nation*. Mineapolis: University Minnesota Press, 2013.

Tsai, Eva. "Caught in the Terrains: An Inter-referential Inquiry of Transborder Stardom and Fame." In *The Inter-Asia Cultural Studies Reader*, edited by Kuan-Hsing Chen and Chua Beng Huat, 323–344. New York: Routledge, 2007.

Tu, Thuy Linh Nguyen. *The Beautiful Generation: Asian Americans and the Cultural Economy of Fashion*. Durham, NC: Duke University Press, 2011.

Tu, Wei-ming. "Cultural China: The Periphery as the Center." In *The Living Tree: The Changing Meaning of Being Chinese Today*, edited by Wei-ming Tu, 1–34. Stanford: Stanford University Press, 1994.

———, ed. *The Living Tree: The Changing Meaning of Being Chinese Today*. Stanford: Stanford University Press, 1994.

Vanweelden, Kimberly, and Isaiah R. McGee. "The Influence of Music Style and Conductor Race on Perceptions of Ensemble and Conductor Performance." *International Journal of Music Education* 25, no. 1 (2007): 7–17.

Wang, Chih-ming. "Capitalizing the Big Man: Yao Ming, Asian America, and the China Global." *Inter-Asia Cultural Studies* 5, no. 2 (2004): 263–278.

———. "Thinking and Feeling Asian America in Taiwan." *American Quarterly* 59, no. 1 (2007): 135–155.

———. "Forum: On Teaching Asian American Literature Outside the U.S." *Asian American Literary Review*, Sept. 3, 2012, http://aalrmag.org/outside usforum (accessed Sept. 27, 2013).

Wang, Oliver. "Between the Notes: Finding Asian America in Popular Music." *American Music* 19, no. 4 (2001): 439–465.

———. "These Are the Breaks: Hip-Hop and AfroAsian Cultural (Dis)-Connections." In *AfroAsian Encounters: Culture, History, Politics*, edited by Heike Raphael-Hernandez and Shannon Steen, 146–166. New York: New York University Press, 2006.

———. "Rapping and Repping Asian: Race, Authenticity, and the Asian American MC." In *Alien Encounters: Popular Culture in Asian America*, edited by Mimi Thi Nguyen and Thuy Linh Nguyen Tu, 35–68. Durham, NC: Duke University Press, 2007.

Wong, Deborah. *Speak It Louder: Asian Americans Making Music*. New York: Routledge, 2004.

Wong, Sau-ling C. "Denationalization Reconsidered: Asian American Cultural Criticism at a Theoretical Crossroads." *Amerasia Journal* 21, nos. 1–2 (1995): 1–27.

———. "When Asian American Literature Leaves 'Home': On Internationalizing Asian American Literary Studies." In *Crossing Oceans: Reconfiguring American Literary Studies in the Pacific Rim*, edited by Noelle Brada-Williams and Karen Chow, 29–40. Hong Kong: Hong Kong University Press, 2004.

———. "Dancing in the Diaspora: Cultural Long-Distance Nationalism and the Staging of Chineseness by San Francisco's Chinese Folk Dance Association." *Journal of Transnational American Studies* 2, no. 1 (2010): 1–35, http://escholarship.org/uc/item/50k6k78p (accessed Sept. 27, 2013).

Wu, Frank. *Yellow: Race in America beyond Black and White.* New York: Basic Books, 2003.

Yang, Mayfair. "Mass Media and Transnational Subjectivity in Shanghai: Notes on (Re)Cosmopolitanism in a Chinese Metropolis." In *Ungrounded Empires: The Cultural Politics of Modern Chinese Transnationalism*, edited by Aihwa Ong and Donald Nonini, 287–322. New York: Routledge, 1997.

Yang, Mina. "East Meets West in the Concert Hall: Asians and Classical Music in the Century of Imperialism, Post-colonialism, and Multiculturalism." *Asian Music* 38, no. 1 (2007): 1–30.

Yip, June. *Envisioning Taiwan: Fiction, Cinema, and the Nation in the Cultural Imaginary.* Durham, NC: Duke University Press, 2004.

Yoshida, George. *Reminiscing in Swingtime: Japanese Americans in American Popular Music: 1925–1960.* San Francisco: National Japanese American Historical Society, 1997.

Yoshihara, Mari. *Musicians from a Different Shore: Asians and Asian Americans in Classical Music.* Philadelphia: Temple University Press, 2007.

Yoshino, Kenji. *Covering: The Hidden Assault on Our Civil Rights.* New York: Random House, 2006.

Zheng, Su. *Claiming Diaspora: Music, Transnationalism, and Cultural Politics in Asian/Chinese America.* New York: Oxford University Press, 2010.

Note: Page numbers followed by *f* indicate figures.

Bartók, Béla, 69

Battle Hymn of the Tiger Mother (Chua), 186, 187; Asian stereotypes in, 188; marketing of, 190; whiteness in, 189. *See also* Chua, Amy; parenting, Asian; "tiger mothers"

blackness: and Far East Movement, 18; and hip hop, 132; and Mandopop, 5, 153–154, 170, 176–178; and media, 117; and rock and roll, 219n15

Bohlman, Philip, 11, 27

Bourdieu, Pierre, 2, 93

boyd, danah, 223n41, 224n56

Brooks, Daphne, 133

Burgess, Jean, 107, 218n4, 221n26; on vernacular creativity, 221n31

Butterfly Lovers Concerto, 95

Cantopop, 147, 181. *See also* Mandopop

Carnegie Hall, 215n40

Castro, Christi-Ann, 121

celebrity: in Asia, 158; and marketing, 231n27; as practice, 224n56; in U.S., 161

Chan, Wesley, 106, 144. *See also* Wong Fu Productions

Chang, Lan Samantha, 1

Chang, Sarah, 47, 48, 49

Chen, Jason, 106, 111, 137

Chen, Kuan-Hsing, 239n86

Chen Kaige, 239n88

Chin, Frank, 170

China: diaspora of, 167–168; and globalization, 20–21, 146, 149–150, 168, 180, 182; multiculturalism in, 172, 239n91; music schools in, 39, 97–98, 218n58; periphery, relationship with, 230n14; Taiwan, relationship with, 23, 149; Western classical music in, 32–33, 39–40. *See also* Mandopop; Taiwan

Chinese Americans: ABC (American-born Chinese) identity of, 144, 152, 155–158, 170, 171, 173, 180, 239n96; as diasporic, 23, 145, 176, 200n53, 237n74; racism against, 170–171, 238n85; stereotyping of, 208n60; as transna-

tional musicians, 155. *See also* Asian Americans

Chineseness: and authenticity, 165; as diasporic, 150, 157, 166–167, 182; and globalization, 146, 150, 168, 179; and music marketing, 92–93

Chinese opera, 173–174, 240n97, 240n99

"Chinese Wind" (*Zhongguo feng*), 169, 238n82

Cho, John, 126, 225n58

Choi, David, 101–103, 103f, 105–106, 127, 225n60; on audience, 137; on Far East Movement, 128–129; as grandfather of YouTube, 104, 109–110; on production values, 113; on race, 135–136, 227n76; on visibility, 108; "YouTube (A Love Song)," 101–103, 140–141

Chou, Jay, 137, 236n70, 237n71, 238n82, 242n121

Chow, Yiu Fai, 161, 166, 237n74

Chow-White, Peter, 18

Chu, Yiu-Wai, 239n88

Chua, Amy, 9, 186–191. See also *Battle Hymn of the Tiger Mother* (Chua); parenting, Asian; "tiger mothers"

Chun, Allen, 237n77

Chung, Jennifer, 106, 110–111, 111f, 112, 115, 227n78; on Asian American market, 120; on Asianness, 133, 220n21

Chung, Kyung-wha, 59

Clara C. (Clara Chung), 21, 104–105; on Asian pop music, 137; on community, 122; on pop culture, Asians in, 124–125; on production value, 114; and whiteness, 133–134, 226n73; on YouTube community, 118; on YouTube fans, 123

classical music (Western), 3; African Americans in, 73, 212n15, 213n20; Asian Americans in, 8, 29, 41–42, 104–105, 206n49, 207n54; Asians in, 29, 39–40, 41–42; Asian "takeover" of, 24, 65, 93, 99, 191; and assimilation, 212n19; blind auditions in, 16, 73; child prodigies in,

music competitions, 84–85, 214n32,
215n33
musicians, Asian American: in Asian
markets, 144–145; and Asian music,
171; differentiability of, 77–78; and
gender politics, 214n29; marketing of,
107; and orientalism, 217n49; sexualization of, 89; "sounding Asian,"
80–81, 82–83, 86; stereotyping of, 65,
67, 73–75, 80, 83–84, 98; and traditional Asian music, 91–92; visibility
of, 77–78, 107, 108. See also classical
music (Western); Wang, Leehom;
YouTube artists
"music moms," 28–29, 43–63; as Asian,
29, 201n2; class status of, 45; parenting
style of, 49–53, 56, 59–60; racialization
of, 29; and work ethic, 189. See also
Chua, Amy; classical music (Western);
Juilliard School; music schools
musicology, 210n4
music schools: Asian Americans in, 37;
Asians in, 37, 205n31; in China, 39,
97–98, 218n58; Chinese students
in, 40; demographics of, 29, 201n4;
immigrants in, 48–49; in Korea, 33;
transnational families in, 44, 47–48.
See also classical music (Western); Juilliard School; "music moms"
Myspace, 222n35

Nakamura, Lisa, 18, 134
neoliberalism: and identity, 17–18;
and marketing, 120; and model mi-
nority discourse, 21; and modernity,
21; and parenting, 186; and self-
improvement, 162–163
New York Philharmonic, 71, 211n9
Ng, Jennifer, 195n9
Ngo, Tom, 117, 124; on Asian American
musicians, 136
Nguyen, Viet, 6
NHK Symphony Orchestra, 205n36
Nielsen Company, 121
Ninh, erin Khûe, 6

Norman, Jessye, 215n40
Nothing but the Best (Kogan), 43

Oh, Sandra, 126, 225n58
Omi, Michael, 19
Ong, Aihwa, 162, 202n16
Ono, Kent, 213n24
orchestras: demographics of, 212n20;
labor in, 71, 87, 211n10
orientalism, 35, 36; and globalization,
239n88; in music, 171; techno-
orientalism, 37–38, 39, 205n36,
206n49
Ozawa, Seiji, 215n40

Pak, Yoon K., 195n9
Palumbo-Liu, David, 7, 37
parenting, Asian, 49–53, 59–60, 62, 77,
186–188, 189, 209n72; and discipline,
56, 65–66; work ethic in, 57, 65–66. See
also *Battle Hymn of the Tiger Mother*
(Chua); Chua, Amy; "music moms";
"tiger mothers"
Park, Jay, 21, 199n47
Park, Lisa, 58, 120
Perlman, Itzhak, 28, 204n29
Perlman in Shanghai, 204n29
Perlman Music Program, 28, 204n29
Pham, Vincent, 213n24
Pisares, Elizabeth, 128
pop music, 3; and Asian Americans, 13;
and Asian American subjectivity, 25;
in China, 168; and race, 131–132, 133,
226n67
Poreotics, 225n63
Prohgress (James Roh), 17. See also Far
East Movement (FM)
Psy, 229n4

race: black-white binary, 117–118, 131,
223n42; and classical music, 1–12, 13–14,
34, 35–36, 61, 66–67, 68, 73–77, 79–80,
85–87, 87–88, 93, 214n31; and digital
technology, 18, 199n38; and genre,
131; and rock and roll, 10–11, 196n16,